ONCE UPON A TIME IN
West Hollywood

ONCE UPON A TIME IN
West Hollywood

L.A. THROUGH THE LENS OF A TEENAGER IN THE '70S

A PHOTOGRAPHIC JOURNAL

JEFF KATZ

Copyrighted Material

Once Upon a Time in West Hollywood: L.A. Through the Lens of a Teenager in the '70s

Copyright © 2019 by Jeff Katz.
All Rights Reserved.

No part of this publication may be reproduced, stored in a retrieval system or transmitted, in any form or by any means—electronic, mechanical, photocopying, recording or otherwise—without prior written permission from the publisher, except for the inclusion of brief quotations in a review.

For information about this title or to order other books and/or electronic media, contact the publisher:

Jeff Katz
jeff@ladetroit59.com

ISBNs:
978-1-7339742-0-2 (print)
978-1-7339742-1-9 (eBook)

Printed in the United States of America

Cover and Interior design: 1106 Design

Photo on page 12 courtesy of Sheri Katz

INSPIRATION AND THANKS

**Family is the
greatest kind of love**

**La famiglia è il più
grande tipo di amore**

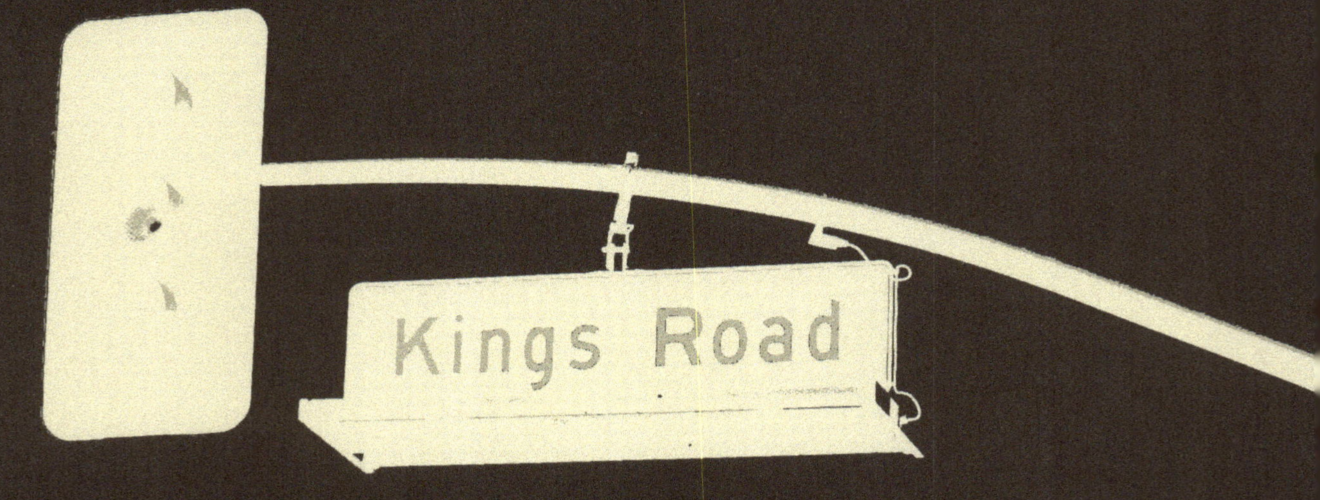
Kings Road

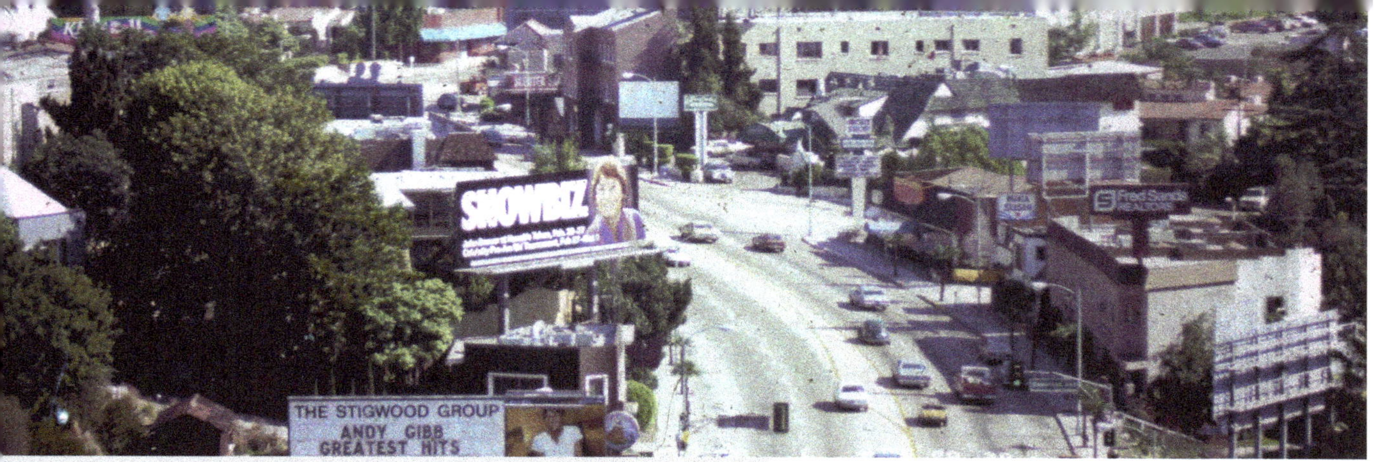

MY PHOTOGRAPHIC JOURNAL
1970-1984

Growing up in the Shadow of the Sunset Strip: In 1966, I was seven when our California journey began. Dad drove the Oldsmobile the entire 2400-mile journey (Mom didn't drive) on old Route 66 from the tree-lined suburbs to a new life of high-density apartment living. Our first Hollywood home was at 1045 N. Edinburgh, one block north of Laurel Elementary School, where I would soon begin first grade. Our apartment was literally across the street from the famous Pink Pussycat Burlesque club. I remember as a seven-year-old thinking we didn't see pink buildings in Huntington Woods, Michigan.

A year later we moved to a newer apartment building at the end of the block, called Romaine Towers, 8011 Romaine Avenue, where we lived for seven years. We rented a 2-bedroom apartment on the ground floor right next to the trash chute. It was during this time I started to play with cameras, more specifically a Kodak Instamatic 126 cartridge film camera with 12 exposures. My earliest photos in this book were taken at Dodger Stadium on June 14, 1970, Fan Appreciation Day, when I was 10 years old.

Later, I attended Bancroft Junior High School, in the heart of Hollywood, located in an industrial area. Like most schools in the Los Angeles Unified School District, Bancroft was a tough, concrete-jungle school. "Play" and "ground" are the characteristics of an inner-city school. The photos I took during my time there, mostly from 1972 to 1973, make that point.

In January 1974, age 14, I purchased my first 35mm camera, a used Asahi Pentax from Elliot Salter's Pawn Shop on Santa Monica Boulevard in West Hollywood. It was $85, a lot of money for a 14-year-old kid used to having forty cents in my pocket. The person who owned the camera before me was a Vietnam Veteran who pawned the camera. I still have the camera, and the pawn shop is still in business!

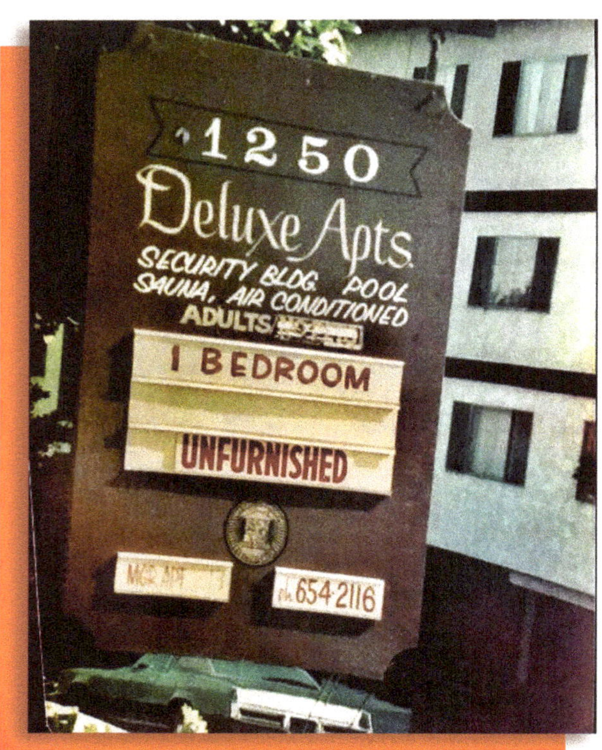

In June 1974, we moved to 1250 N. Kings Road, a block and a half south of the Strip. Hanging out at the Hyatt House and Tower Records, if you were lucky, you might run into John Lennon or Elton John! Sunset Strip in the '70s was at its rock n' roll peak just like the bands. I spent that summer on the rooftop pool at the legendary Hyatt House, too cool a hangout for a 14-year-old, and my last summer without a job.

I'm fortunate I took the photos when I did. Who could have imagined social media? All the photos in this book are original photos taken by me (and a few taken of me) from the age of ten, up through the 1984 Olympics, when

Left: 1250 N. Kings Road, West Hollywood. Adults, no pets? Kids grudgingly allowed. Somehow they let us in. The building was apartments that rented for $200-$300 a month; now they're condos selling for $600,000-$700,000. 1975. **Below:** Olympic torch run. Pride and Jubilation in the throngs of the thousands of people in Fullerton, Orange County, 30 miles from L.A., who watched the torch edge closer to Los Angeles four days before the opening ceremonies. Will this excitement be duplicated in 2028? You bet!

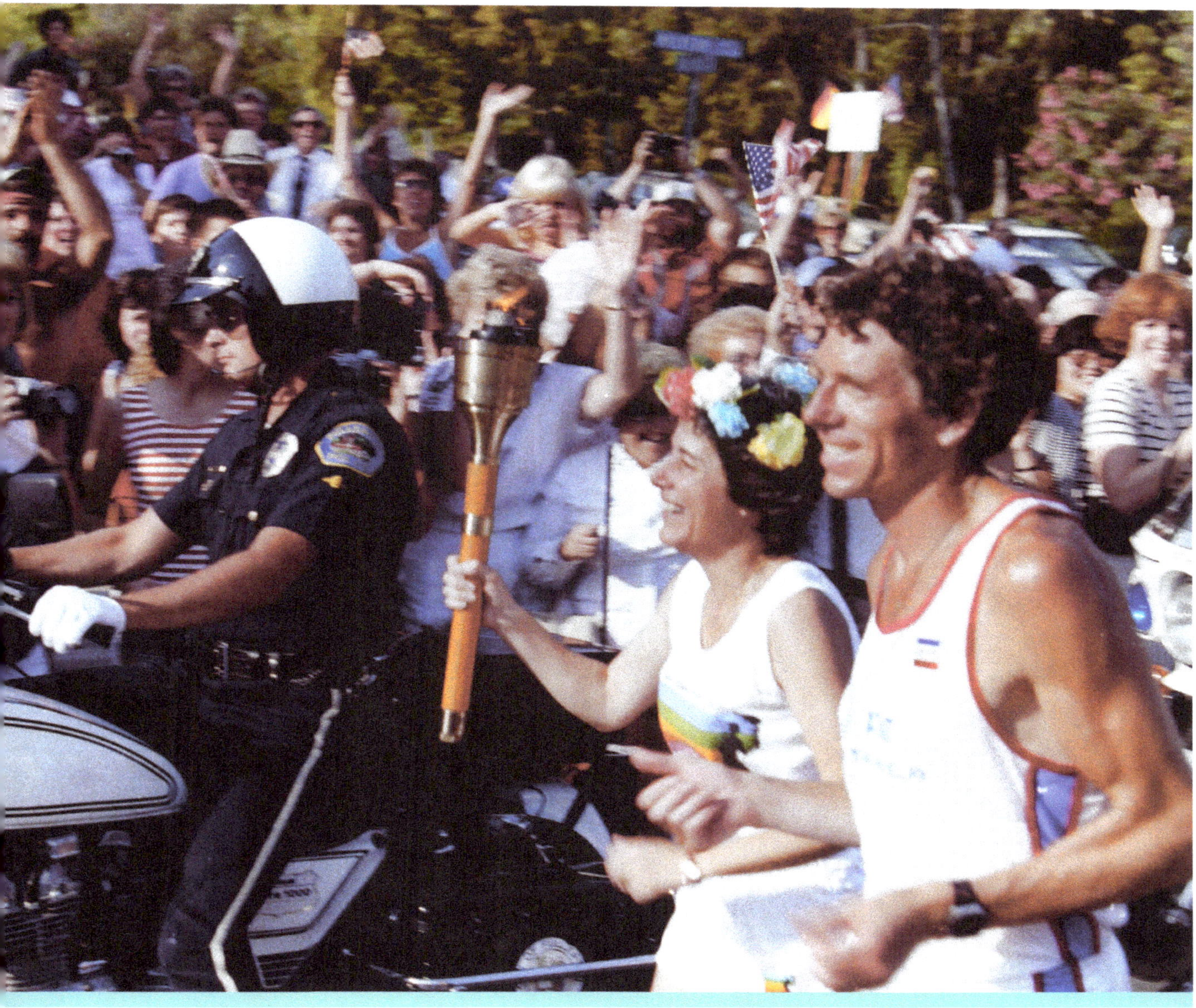

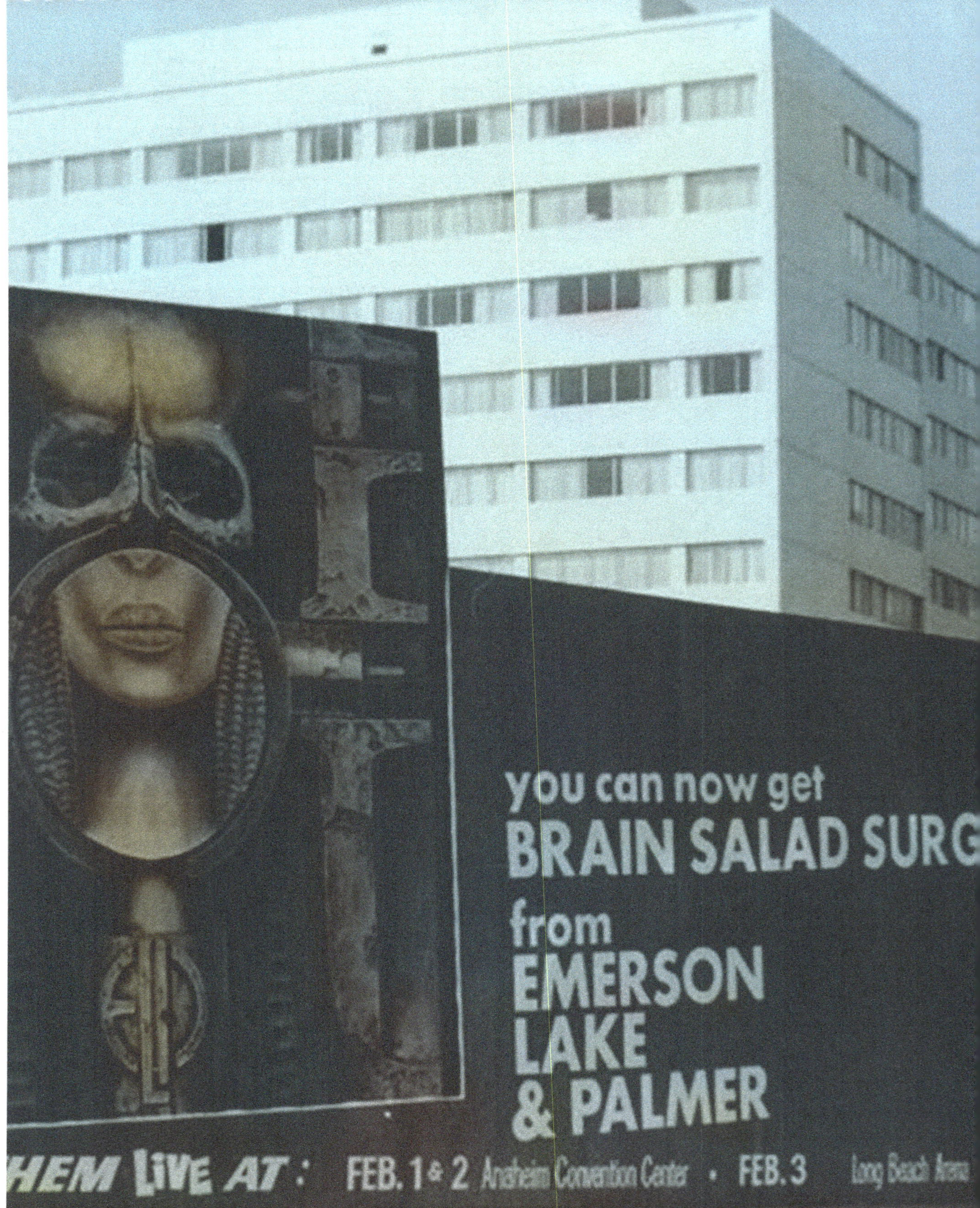
you can now get
BRAIN SALAD SURG
from
EMERSON
LAKE
& PALMER
HEM LiVE AT : FEB. 1 & 2 Anaheim Convention Center • FEB. 3 Long Beach Arena

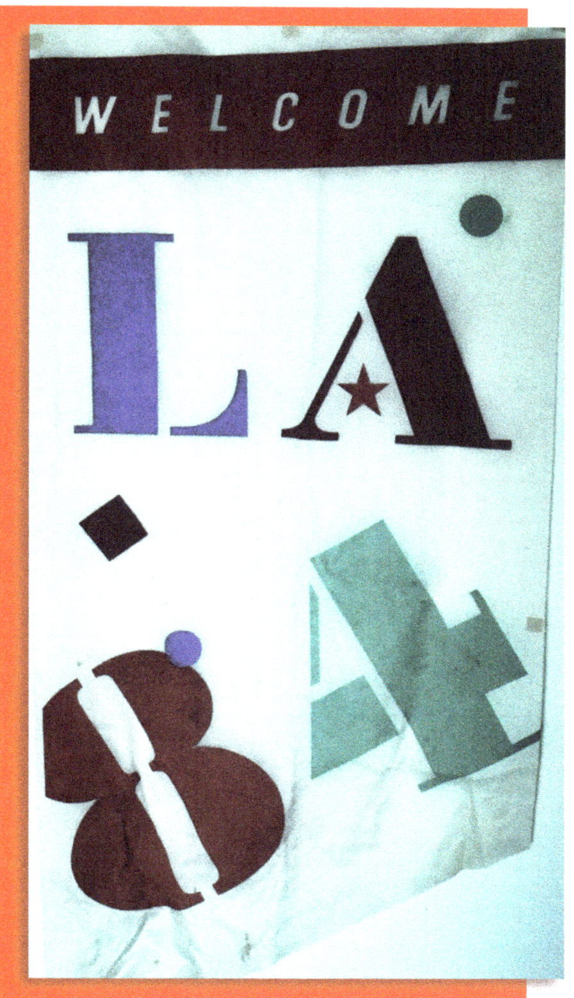

I was 25. I photographed baseball, family outings, Junior High, the Sunset Strip. The photos sat in a drawer for decades. Looking back, I wish I had taken more photos. Thanks to social media, I have found an outlet for these old photos and got the inspiration to write this book, a personal journey based on chapters of my life growing up in Los Angeles, which will hopefully provoke memories for the reader.

The photographs captured moments in time through the eyes of a very young kid without any formal training in photography. It's fun to look back at the cars of the day and the Sunset Strip, when hand-painted billboards didn't get lost in the shadow of tall buildings and construction cranes. Los Angeles was a low-rise city, not yet grown up, long before the term "gentrification" existed. The Internet was still a generation away.

Left: Sunset Strip Billboard, Kings Road. I love this album cover. Progressive Rock was in fashion for a few years. A live TRIPLE album was made of the advertised Anaheim show. Beyond the billboard: Apartments renting for $250-$350 a month, now the Mondrian Hotel at $400 a night. 1974. **Above:** Olympic Colors. The "new wave" '80s colors on thousands of street flags like this one I absconded with welcomed the world to Los Angeles for two glorious weeks and created the fresh, dynamic atmosphere.

Right: West Hollywood in the '70s was a low-rise city. Clear days were few and far between. The cluster of buildings in the distance is the Park La Brea apartments and Miracle Mile Wilshire Blvd. The Pan Pacific Auditorium, which burned down in 1989, is also in the photo, along with Fairfax High and CBS Studios, which just sold the 40-acre property in 2018 for $750 million. 1975.

CONTENTS

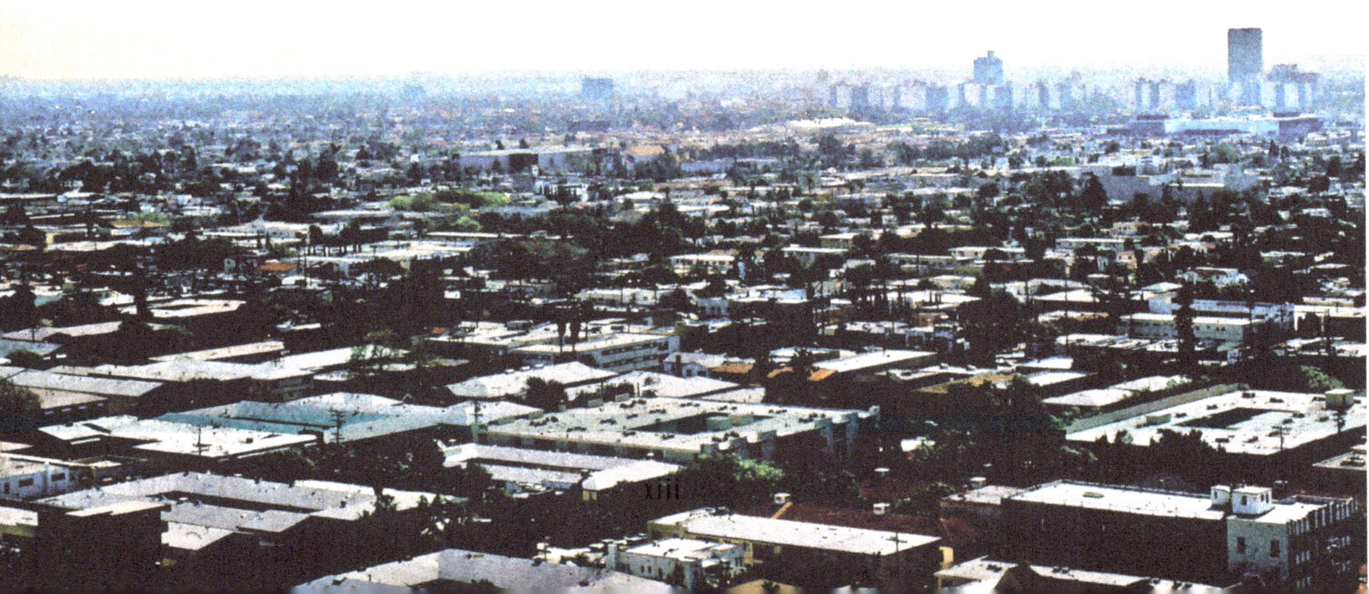

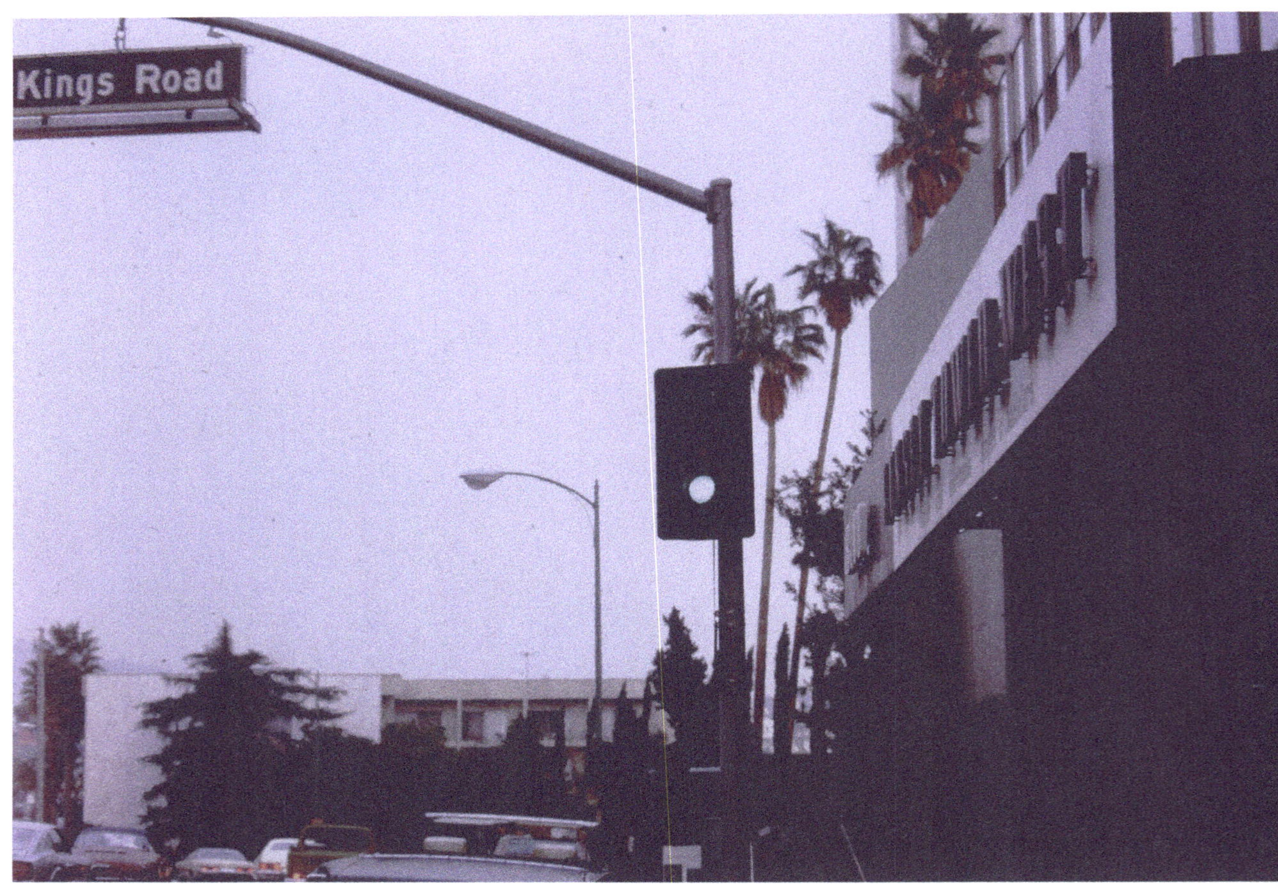

Above: Sunset Tower West 8400 Sunset Boulevard at Kings Road, where apartments were renting for $250 a month when I took this photo, and is now a hotel. 1974.

Right: Billboard Sunset Blvd. & Marmont Lane. I loved disco. I loved Saturday Night Fever. Tony Manero (Travolta) worked in a hardware store during the day, just like me. But I couldn't dance. 1977.

WEST HOLLYWOOD
THROUGH THE LENS OF A TEENAGER

grew up in West Hollywood, California. I was between 14 and 17 years old when I took most of the photos in this chapter, a kid growing up in the city and getting my education in the street.

Many people look back on the '70s as the Glory Days of the Sunset Strip, and it was a fun place for an adventurous teenager to hang out. Some images were family photos, and others were just random cars or other street scenes. Los

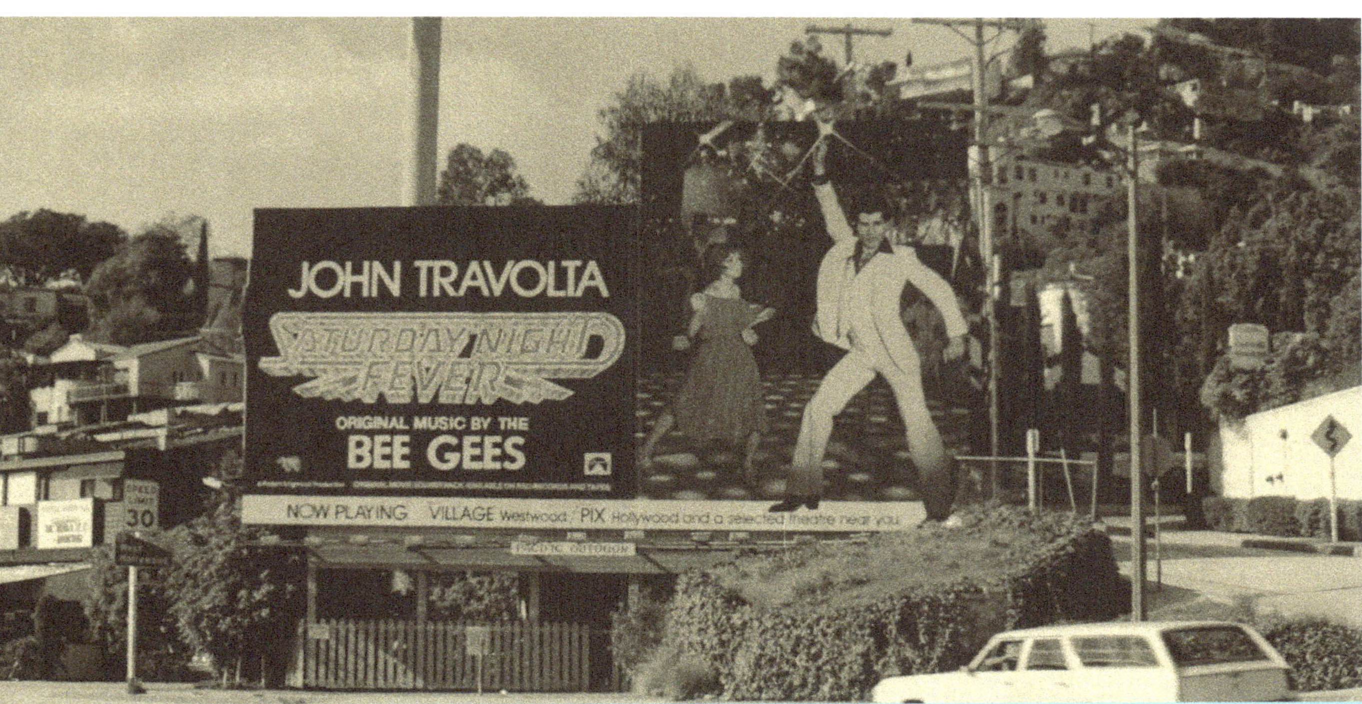

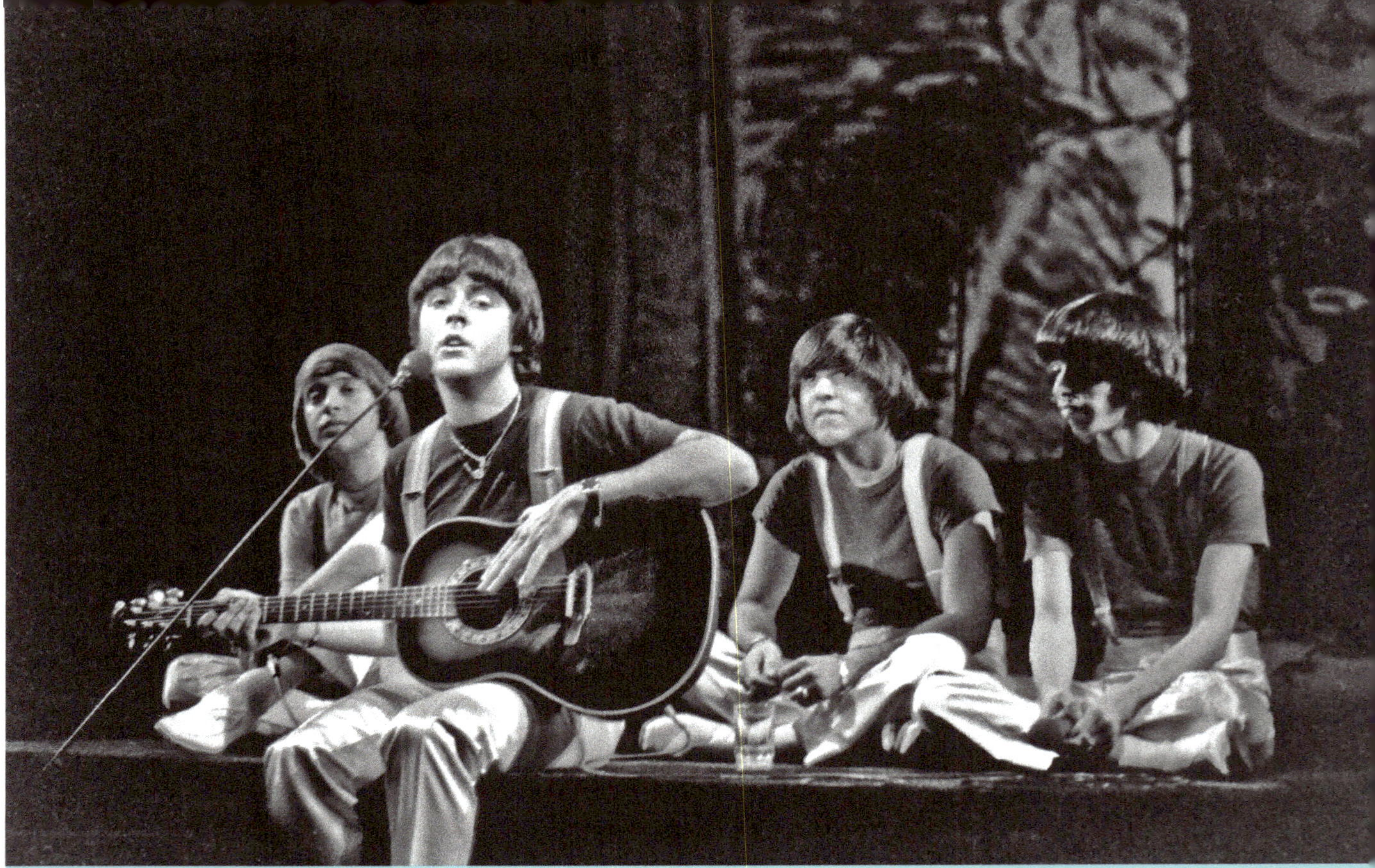

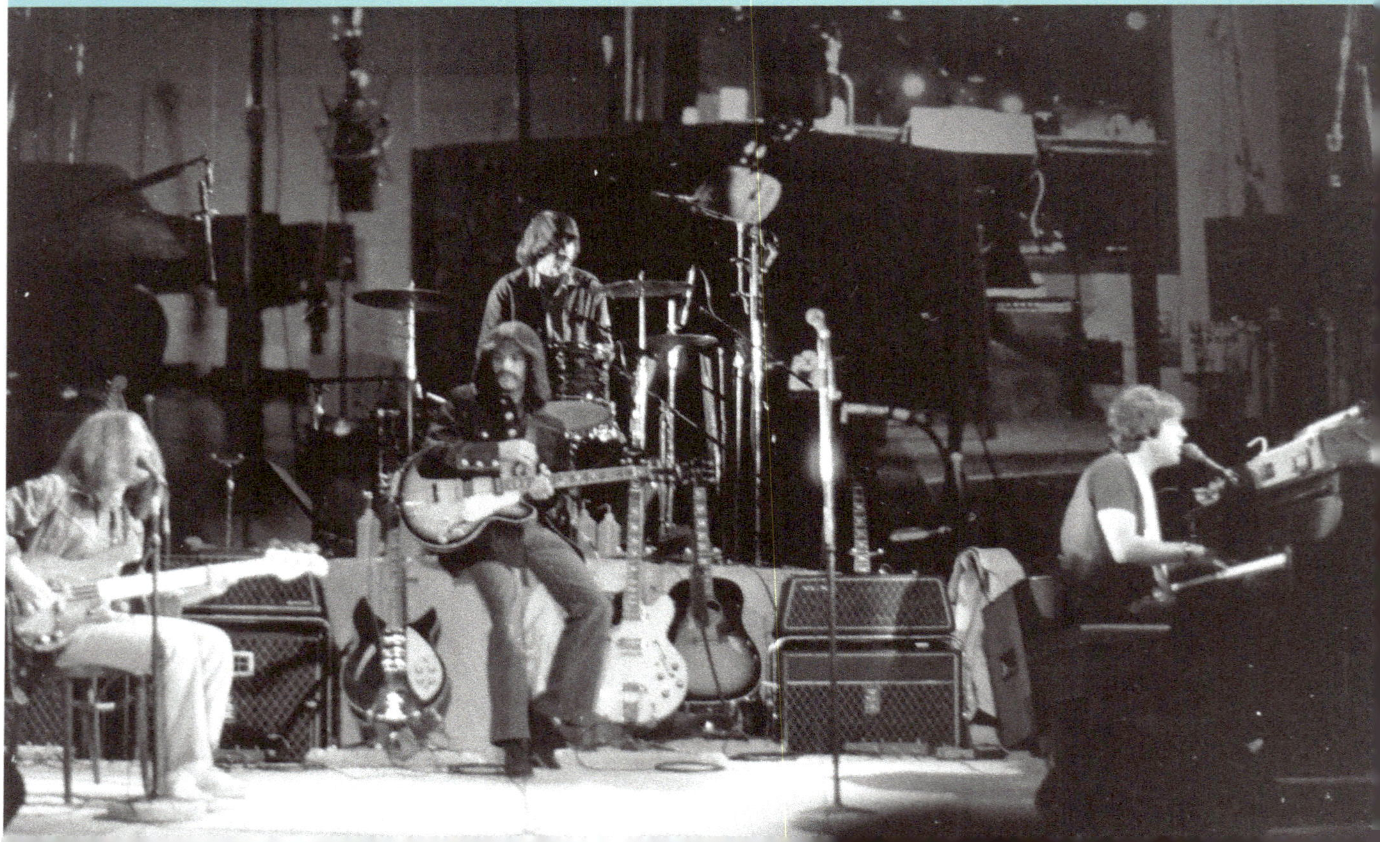

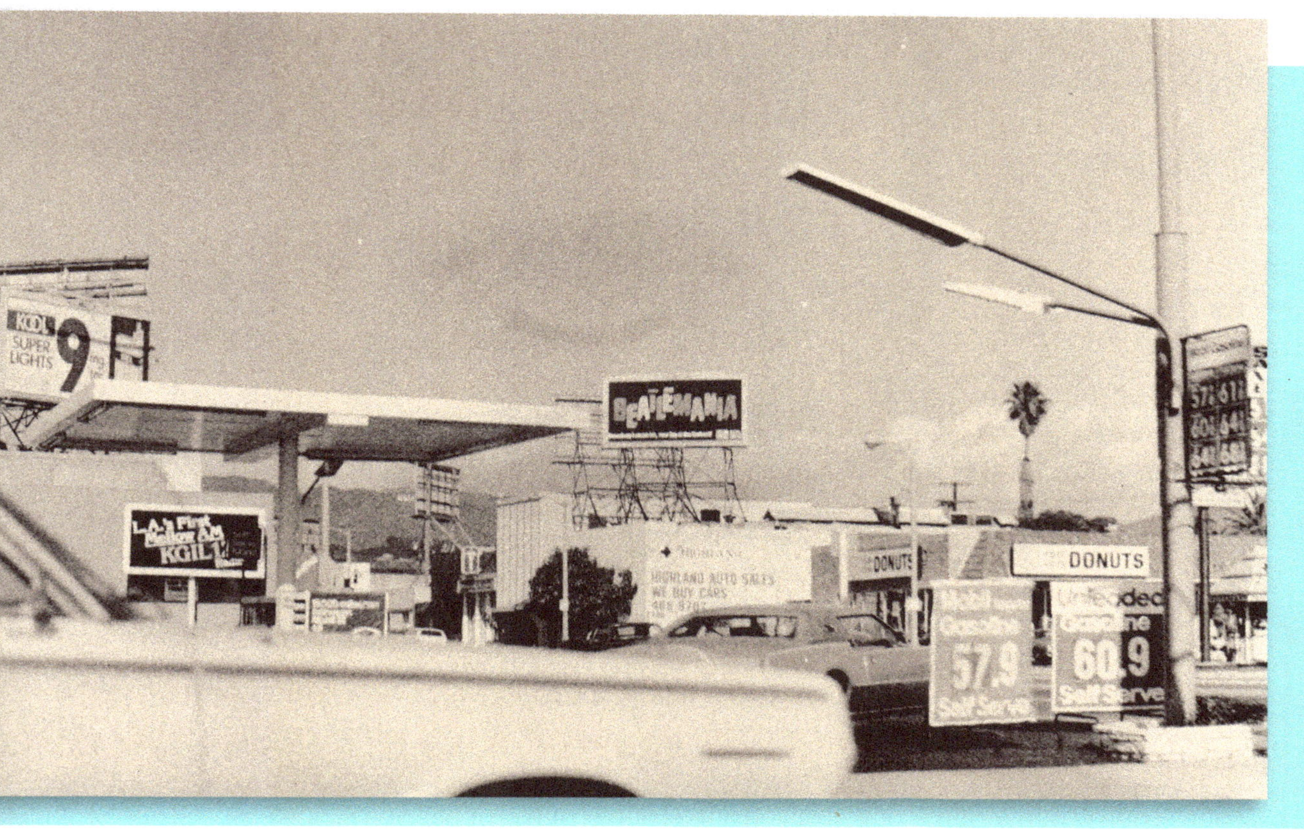

Angeles in the 1970s was a low-rise city. Walking east on the Sunset Strip to Crescent Heights and then hiking up Laurel Canyon to Mt. Olympus felt like the country, a lifestyle I desired, a contrast to the high-density apartment life I lived. The sounds of Joni Mitchell, Steely Dan, and The Eagles were in my head and in those Hills of Hollywood during the summer of '74.

Top Left: Beatlemania was alive and well at the Shubert Theater, Century City. Faux Paul sings "Yesterday." 1978. **Bottom Left:** Longhaired Beatles as portrayed before their breakup eight years earlier. 1978. **Above:** Billboard for Beatlemania. I believe that is the corner of Highland & Melrose. Dig those gas prices. I was driving my 1968 Lincoln Cougar that ran on premium. 1978.

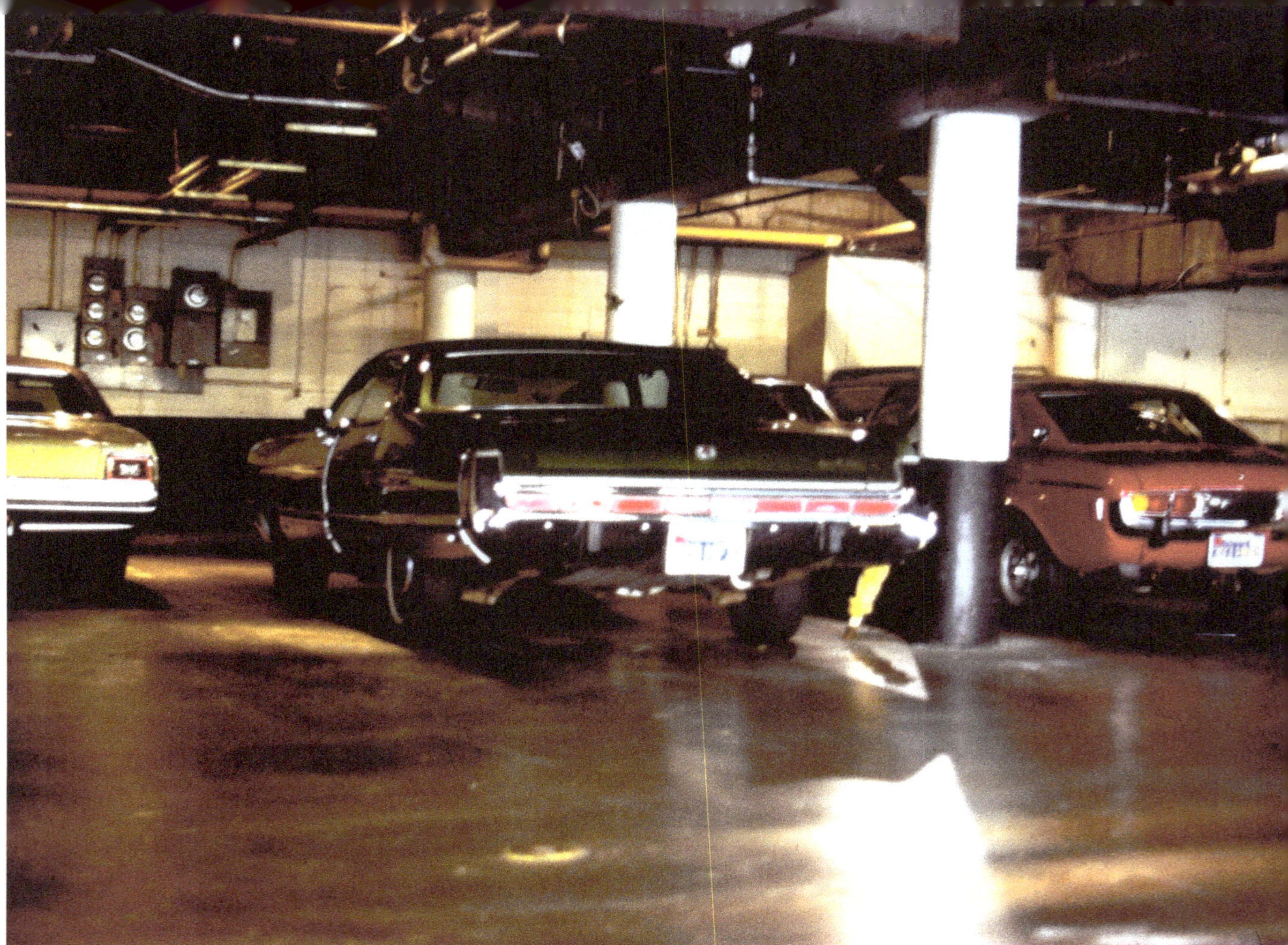

Top Left: 1250 N. Kings Road garage, parking was tight for my Dad's big Buick. 1974. **Top Right:** Bar Mitzvah. The day I became a Man: Culmination of five years of Hebrew School three days a week, and I end up with a powder blue tux. Hollywood Temple Beth El, Crescent Heights & Fountain, West Hollywood. 1972. **Bottom Right:** Rabbi Michael Menitoff, Harvard Graduate, called the "Hippie Rabbi" by the "establishment" congregants. Rabbi Menitoff had a radio show on KABC 790 in Los Angeles in the '70s called "Religion on the Line." 1972.

I spent the entire summer of 1974 hanging out at the rooftop pool at the legendary Hyatt House, and, being only 14, I was not old enough to appreciate the Scene in front of me. *Almost Famous* I wasn't, but that has always been one of my favorite movies because I could relate to the main character, the young writer exposed to the Scene at a young age.

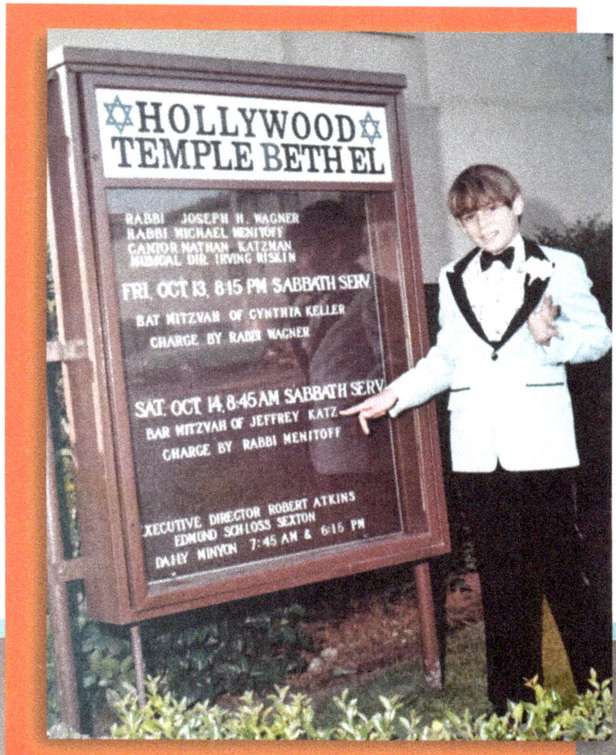

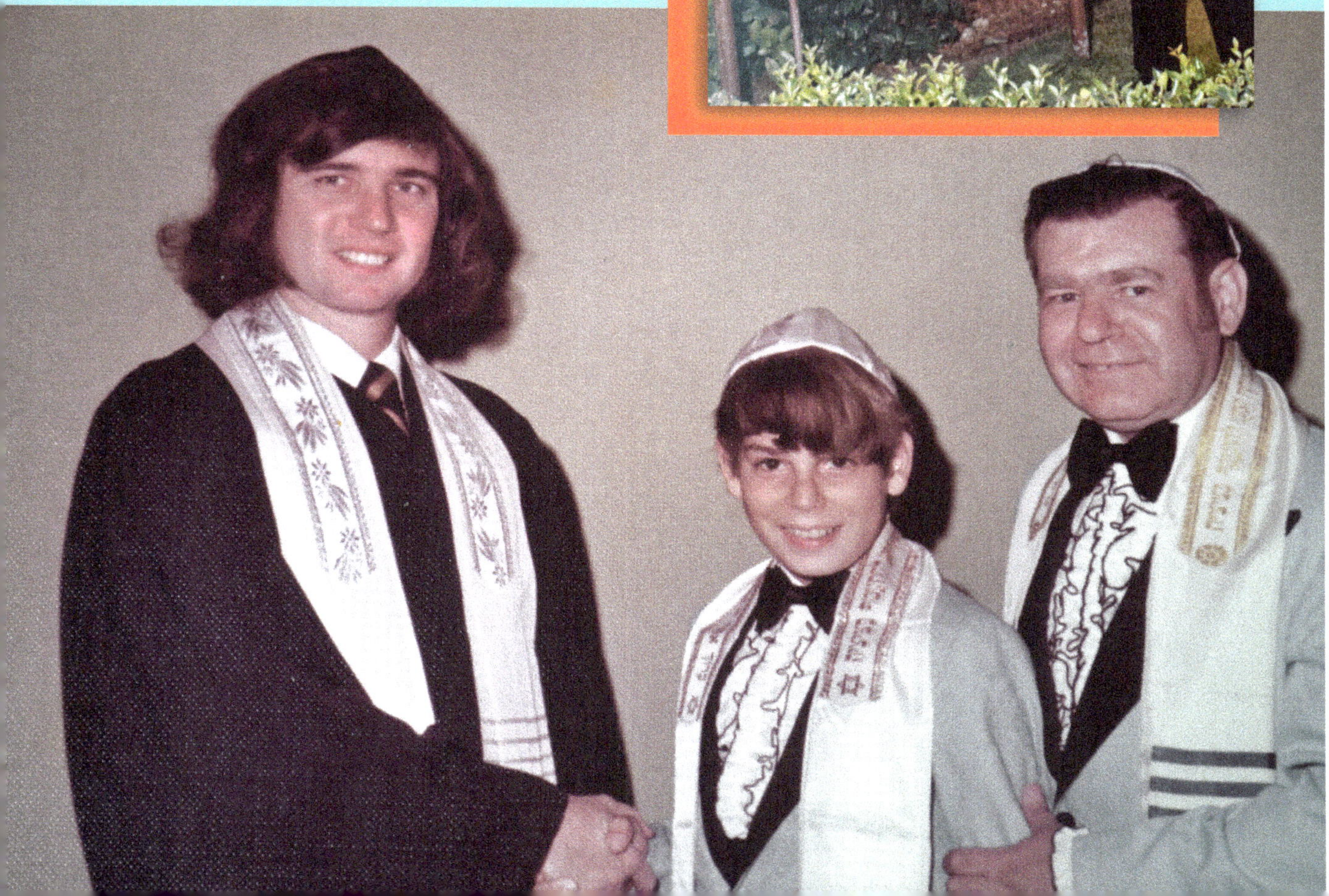

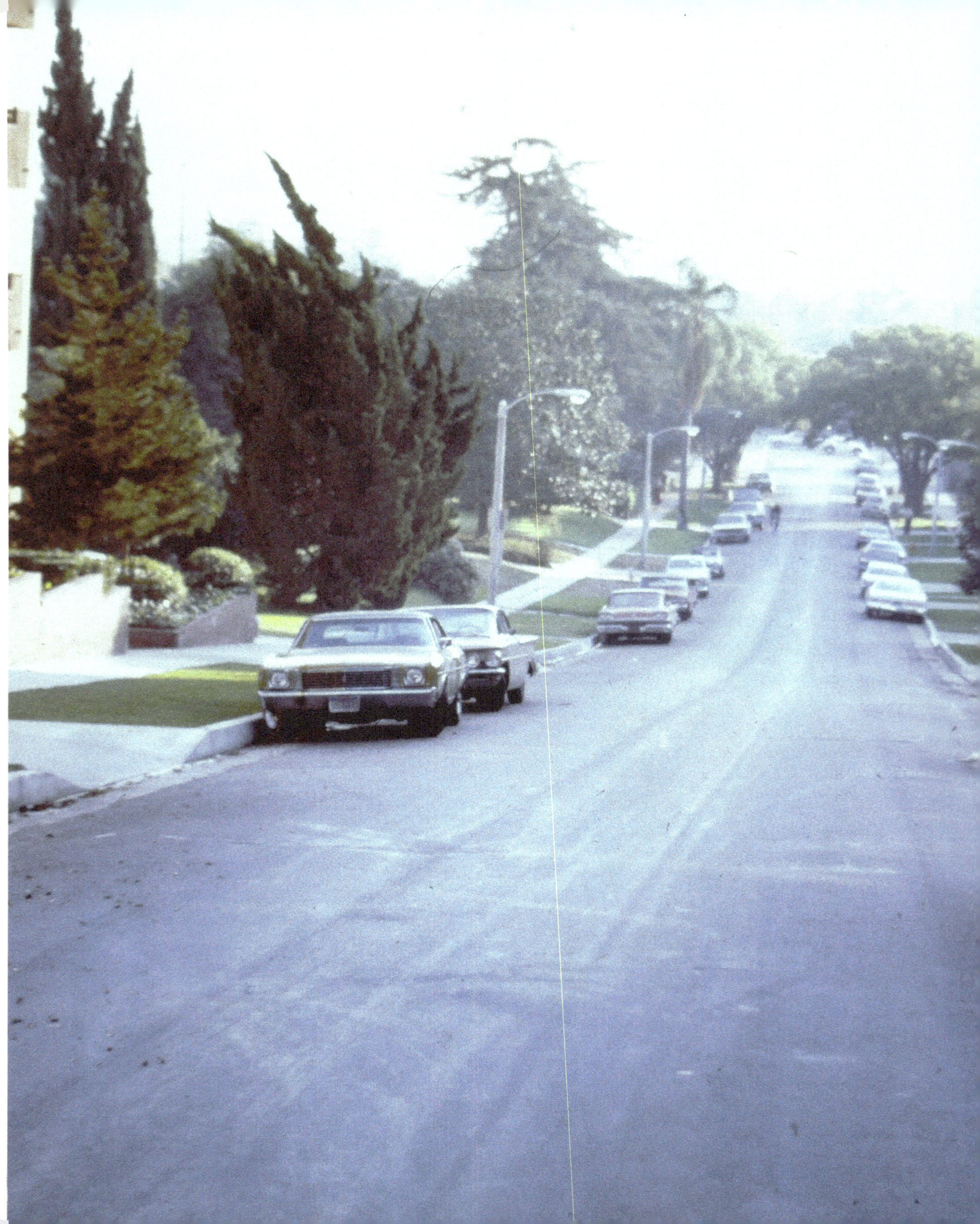

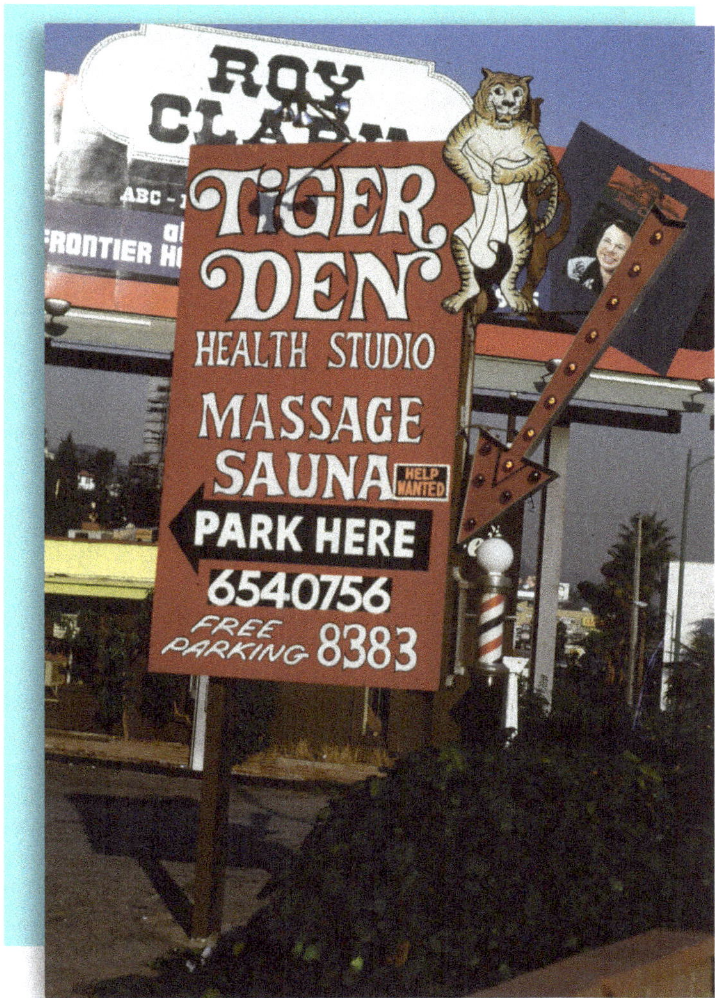

Far Left: Looking south toward Santa Monica Boulevard and the smoggy air in the distance, there were still single-family homes on Kings Road, replaced by high-density condos and apartments. 1975. **Left:** The Tiger Den massage parlor was advertised as "A great place to relax" and was open from 10am to 4am. It was located at 8383 Sunset Blvd. at Kings Road across the street from the Hyatt House. Massage parlors were very popular in West Hollywood in those pre-AIDS days. RIP 2018 Roy Clark. 1974.

Growing up in West Hollywood in the 1970s gave me a lifetime of interesting stories. Taking the way-back machine back four decades gives me an appreciation of growing up during a period of time that I took for granted. I hope these photos take the reader back to a fun place and time!

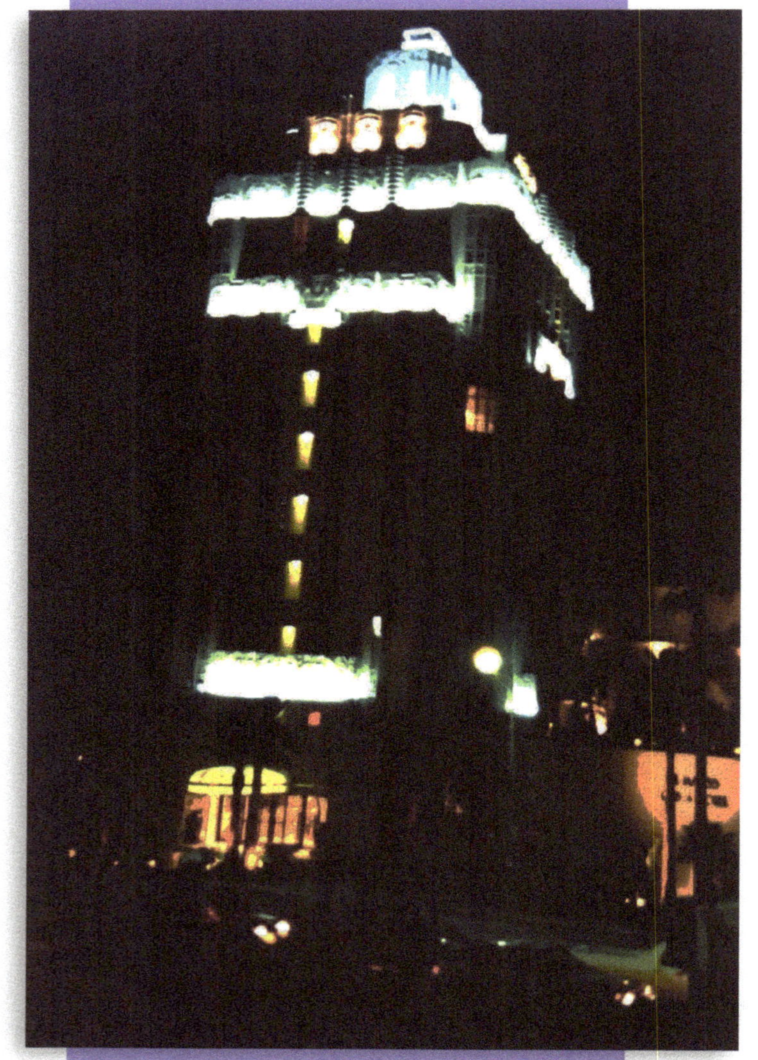

Left: Legendary Sunset Tower Hotel, 8358 Sunset Blvd. When I grew up in West Hollywood in the 1970s, this historic building was a rundown apartment. Taken from a moving car, even a blurry image portrays a beautiful Art Deco masterpiece. 1980. **Below:** Sunset Strip billboard. Tom Scott & the LA Express. Great jazz/fusion band. Killer original lineup included Larry Carlton, Max Bennett, Joe Sample, Hank Guerin, and the great Tom Scott on the horns. They had played on Joni Mitchell's all-time classic "Court & Spark" album. 1974.

Top Right: Aretha. Legend. Sunset Strip billboard. Sunset Strip billboards in the '70s were hand painted and created in 5–10 days and rented for $1500–$3000 a month, less than a 2-bedroom apartment today. 1974. **Bottom Right:** Beverly Center under construction: West Hollywood looking southwest. Bekins Van & Storage, now the Emser Tile Building on Santa Monica Boulevard, in the foreground. The Pacific Design Center (Blue Whale) on the right stands out. 1980.

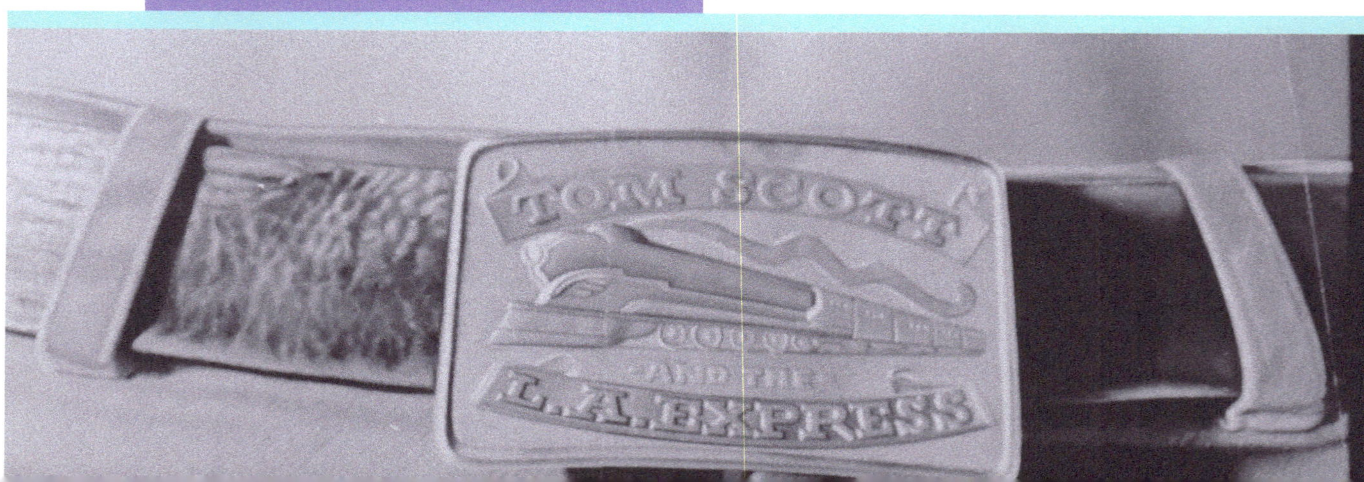

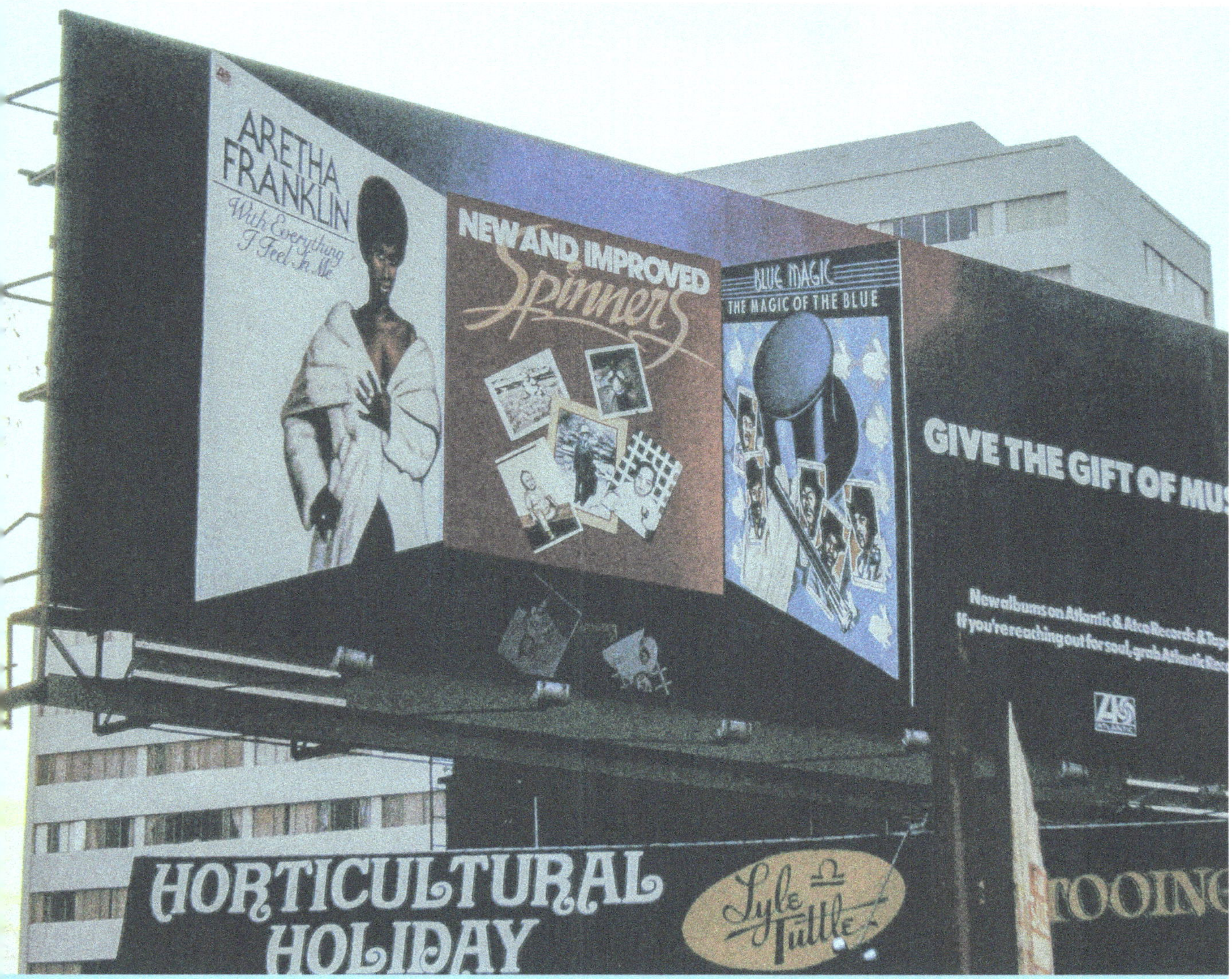

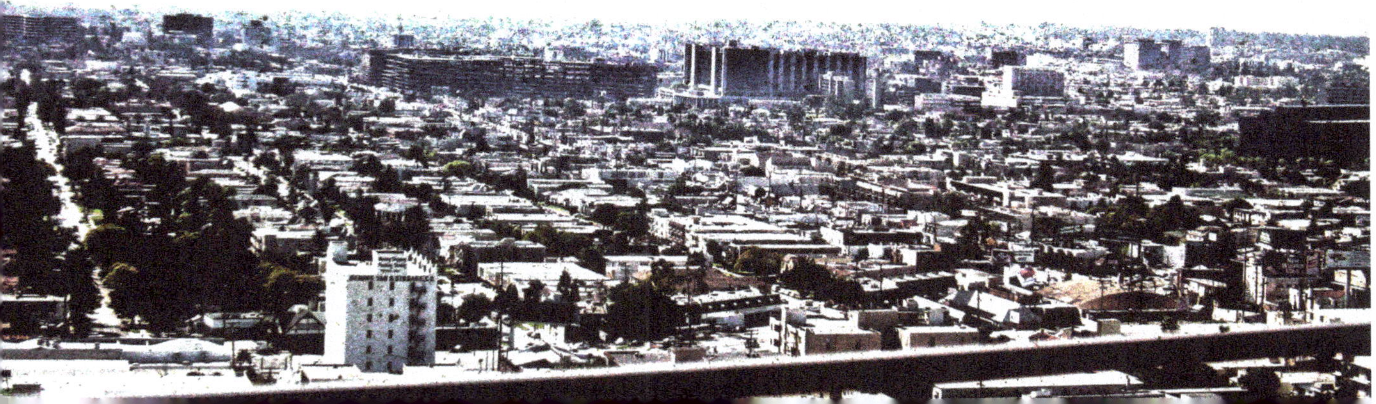
ARETHA FRANKLIN
With Everything I Feel 'n Me
NEW AND IMPROVED
Spinners
BLUE MAGIC
THE MAGIC OF THE BLUE
GIVE THE GIFT OF MUS
New albums on Atlantic & Atco Records & Tape
If you're reaching out for soul, grab Atlantic Reco
HORTICULTURAL HOLIDAY
Lyle Tuttle
TOOIN

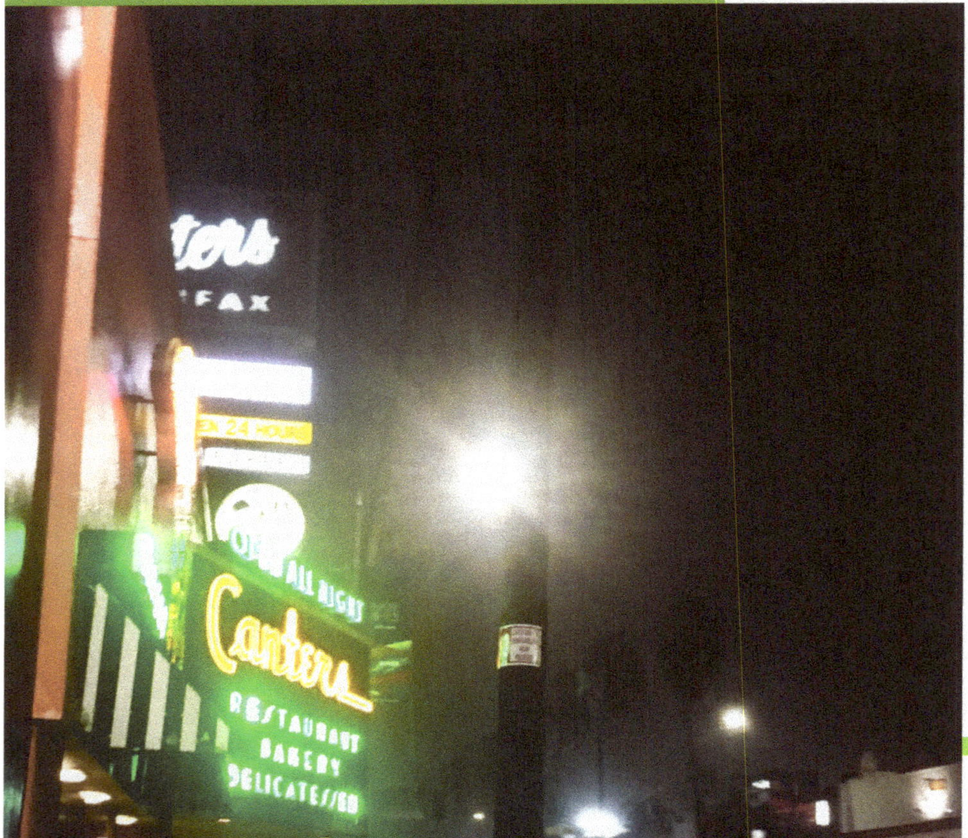

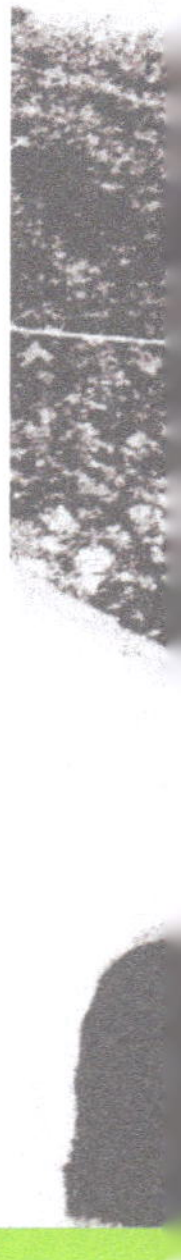

Left: I've been going to Canters since 1966. Fairfax Avenue West Hollywood. Recent photo. 2018. **Top Right:** Close Encounters. Look around. We Are Not Alone. Sunset Strip billboard. 1977. **Bottom Right:** *Serpico* was released in 1973 between *The Godfather* I & II. Throw in **Dog Day Afternoon**, released in 1975, and you have the Grand Slam of greatest '70s films by one actor. 1974.

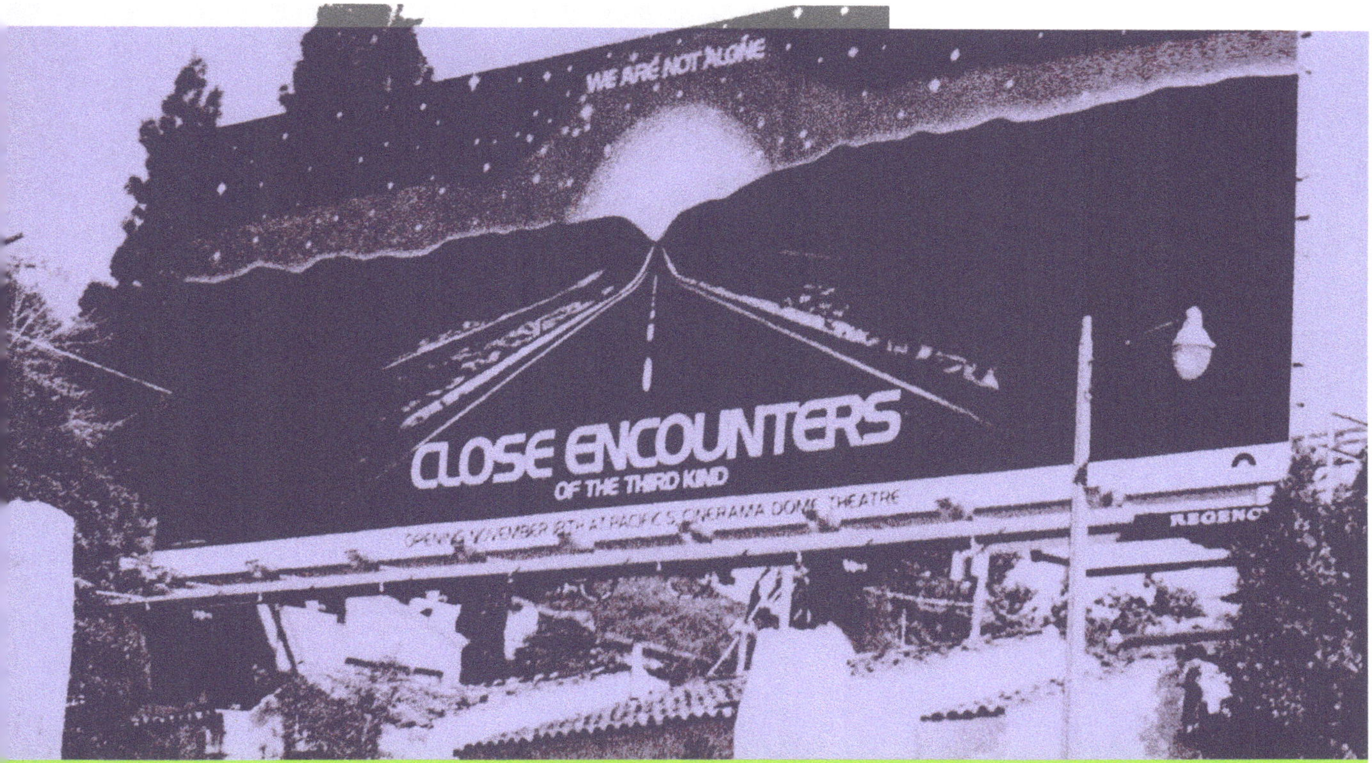

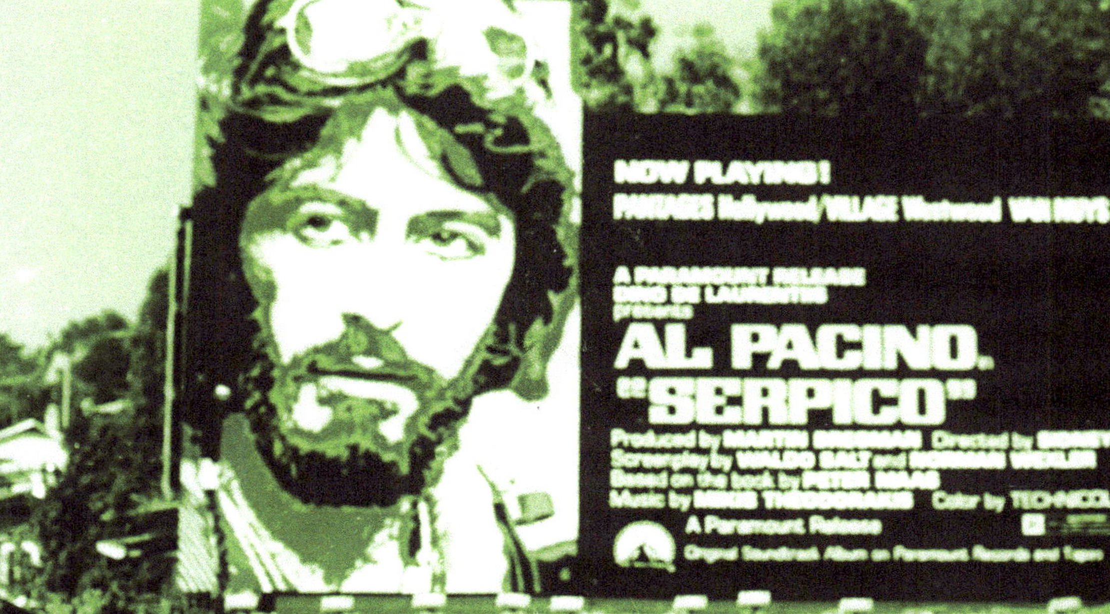
WE ARE NOT ALONE
CLOSE ENCOUNTERS
OF THE THIRD KIND 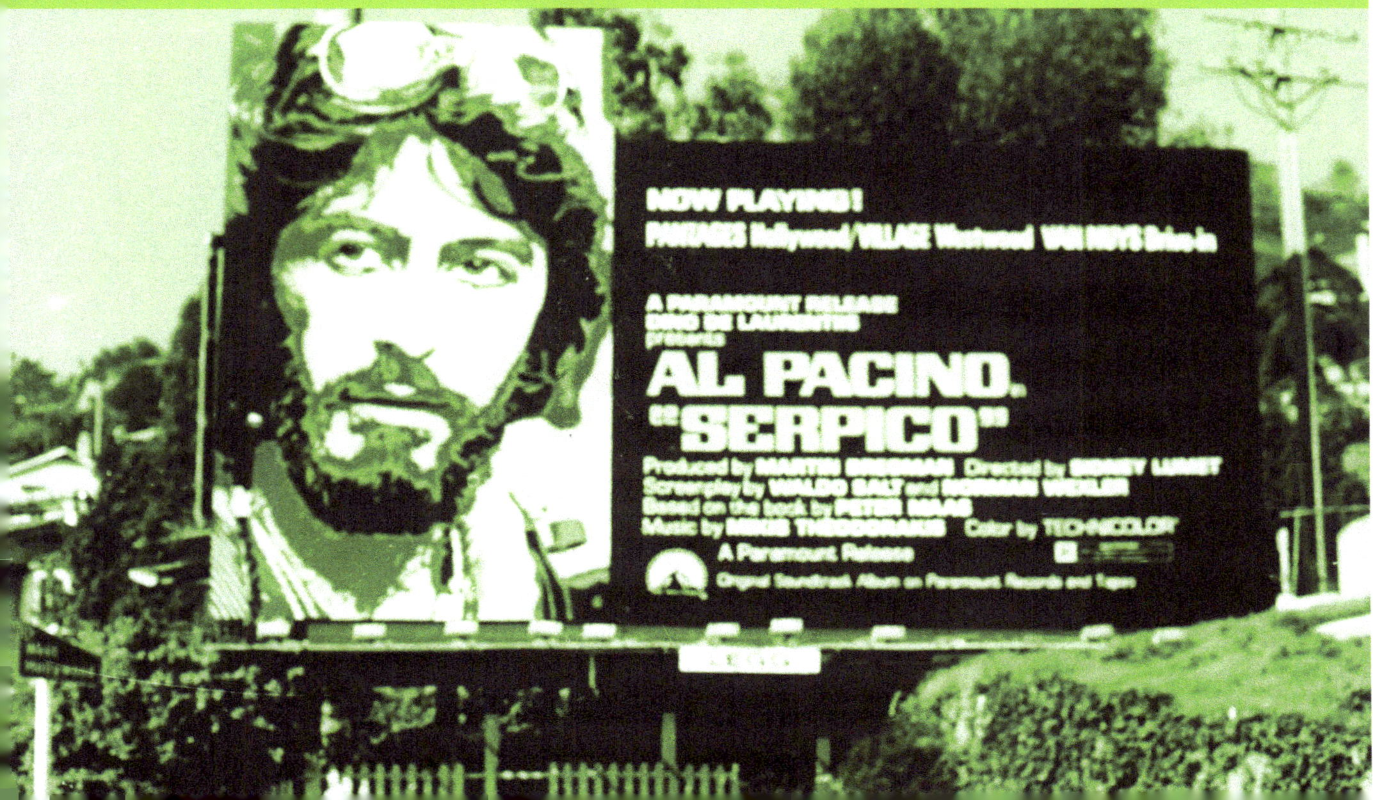
OPENING NOVEMBER 8TH AT PACIFIC'S CINERAMA DOME THEATRE
REGENC
NOW PLAYING!
PANTAGES Hollywood/VILLAGE Westwood VAN NUYS Drive-In
A PARAMOUNT RELEASE
DINO DE LAURENTIIS presents
AL PACINO.
"SERPICO"
Produced by MARTIN BREGMAN Directed by SIDNEY LUMET
Screenplay by WALDO SALT and NORMAN WEXLER
Based on the book by PETER MAAS
Music by MIKIS THEODORAKIS Color by TECHNICOLOR
A Paramount Release
Original Soundtrack Album on Paramount Records and Tapes

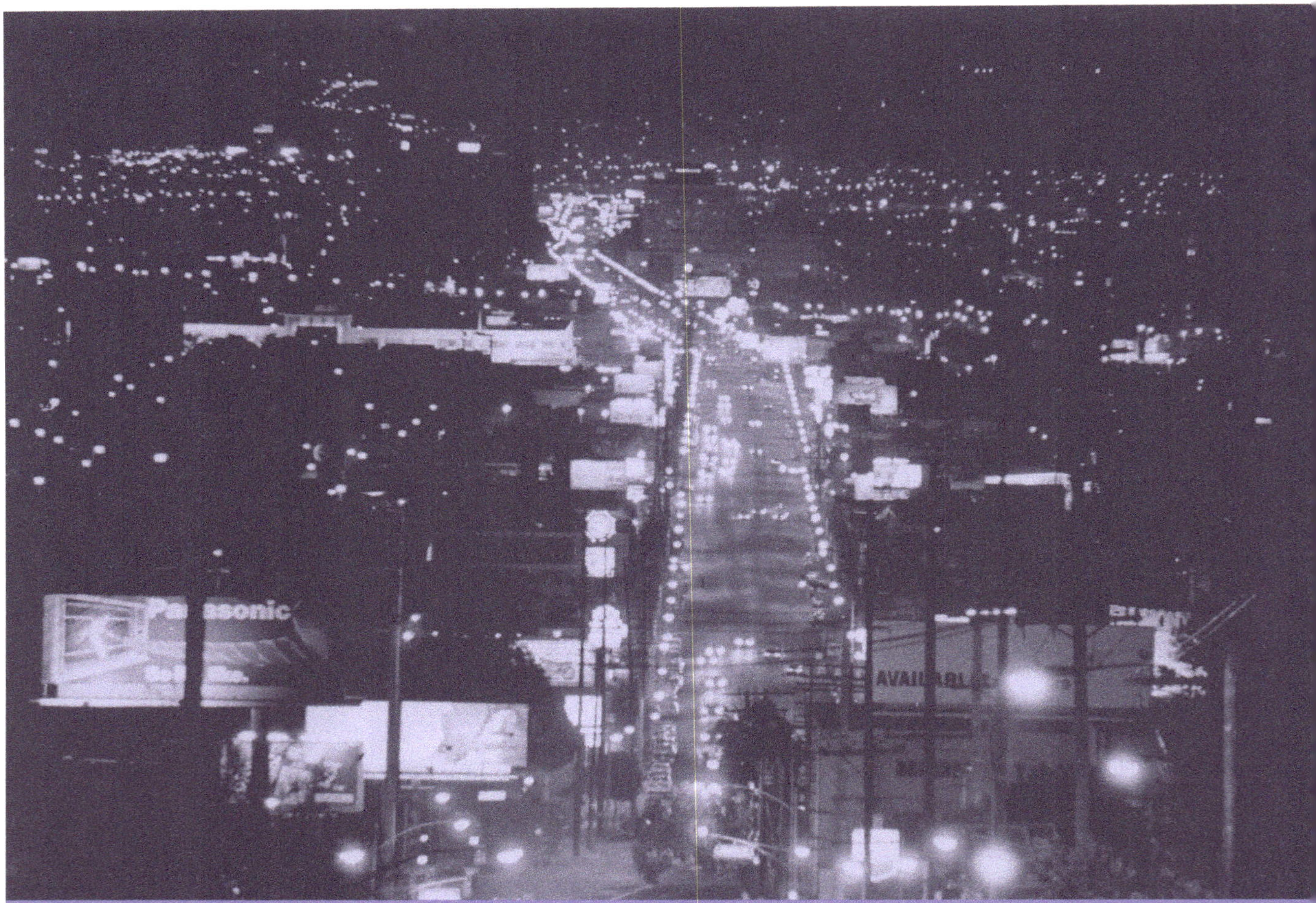

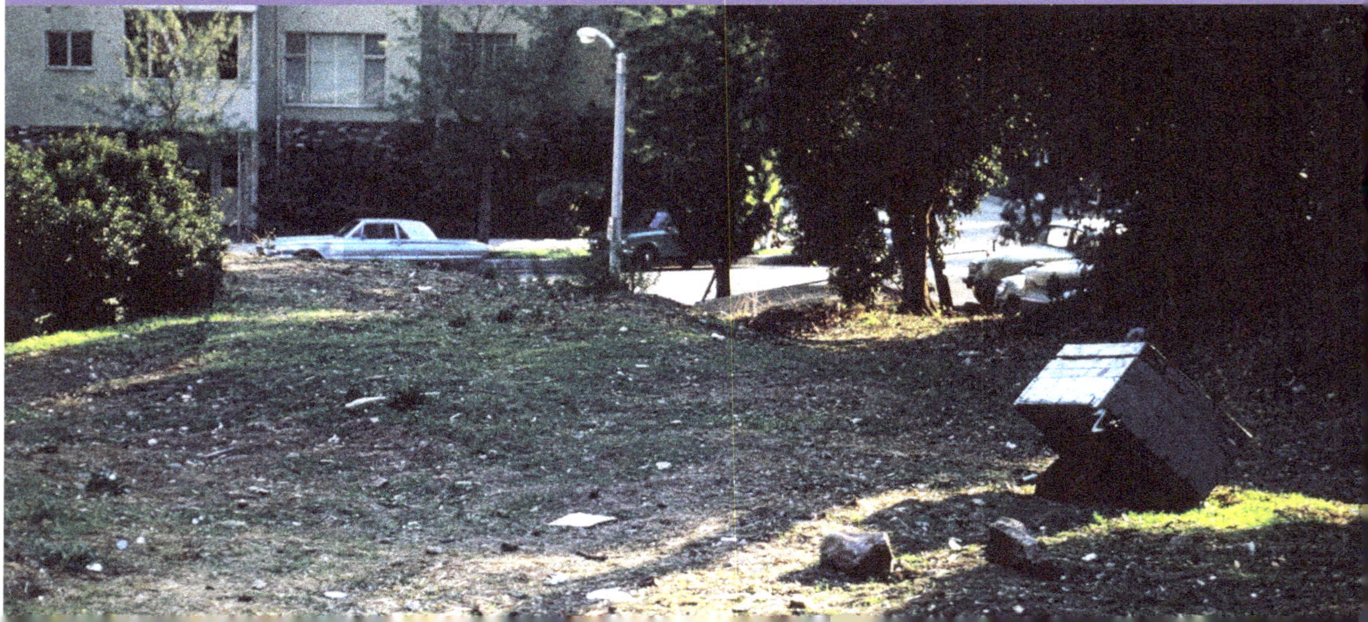

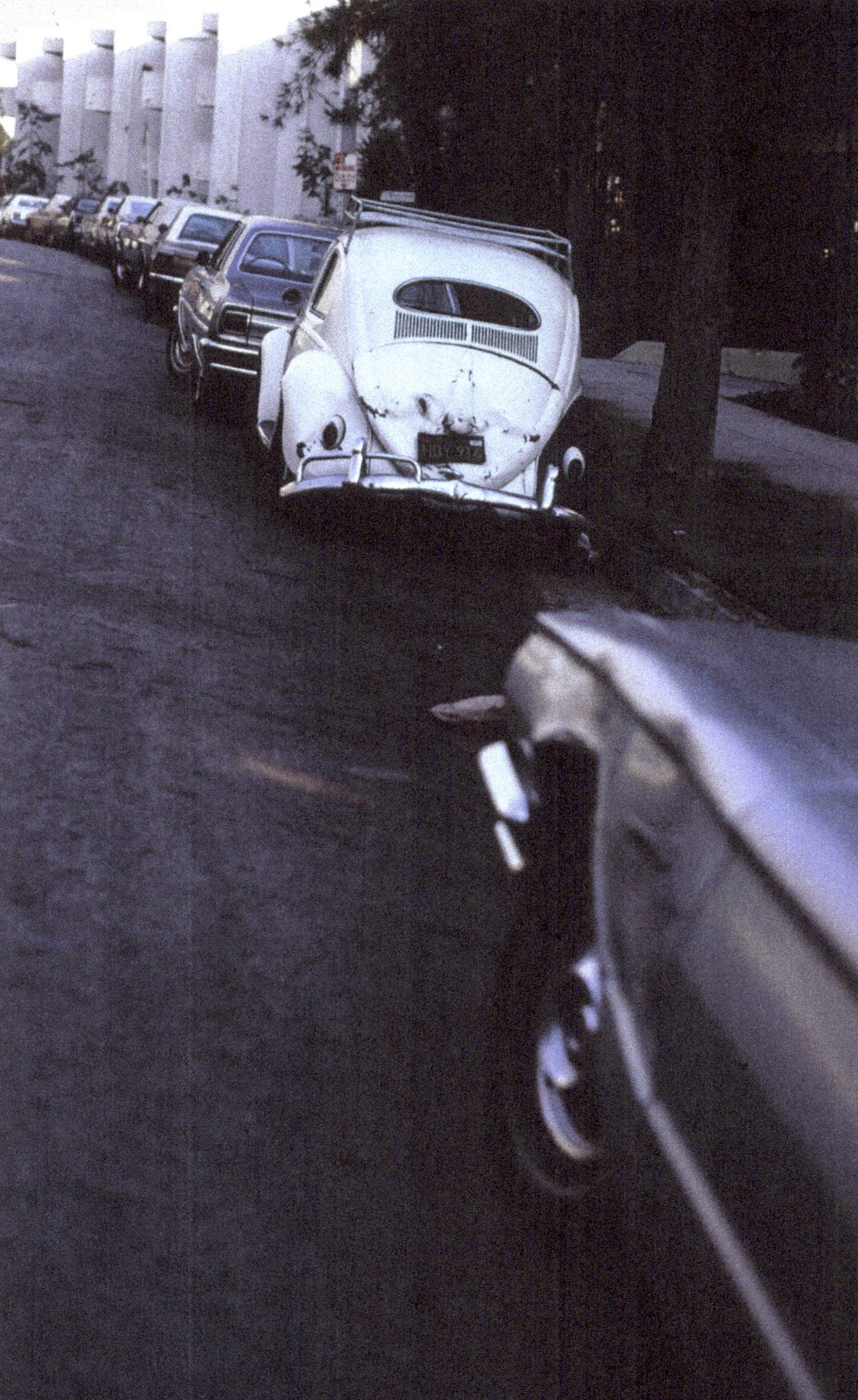

Top Left: City of Lights: Sunset & La Cieniega. Beautiful image of West Hollywood looking south on La Cieniega Blvd. 1977. **Bottom Left:** You don't find many empty lots in West Hollywood. As a 15-year-old when I took this, I could not have predicted years later I'd be selling lots like this as a realtor. Cool car in the background. 1975. **Right:** Ordinary photos look interesting decades later. Fender bender, unknown street, West Hollywood. 1974.

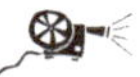

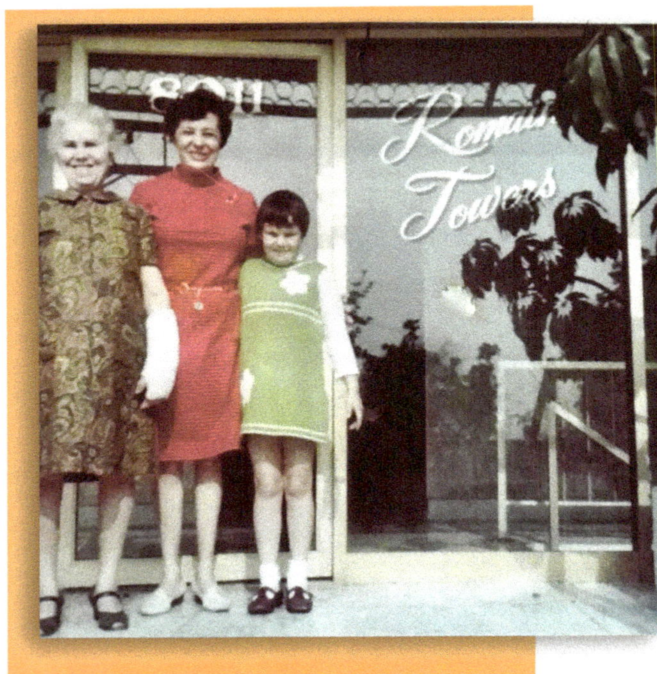

Left: Family photo! Grandma, Mom, and my sister, Sharon. Grandma should have not been climbing chairs, and I could see where I got my skinny runner's legs from. In front of our apartment Romaine Towers 8011 Romaine Avenue, West Hollywood. 1973. **Bottom:** McDonald's on La Brea: The highlight of my week were 2 plain hamburgers, fries, Coke on Saturday night. Hey, I was only 14! Somehow, McDonald's tasted better when I was a kid. At this point in time, they had served more than 14 billion burgers. In 2010 McDonald's stopped counting at 99 billion. 1974.

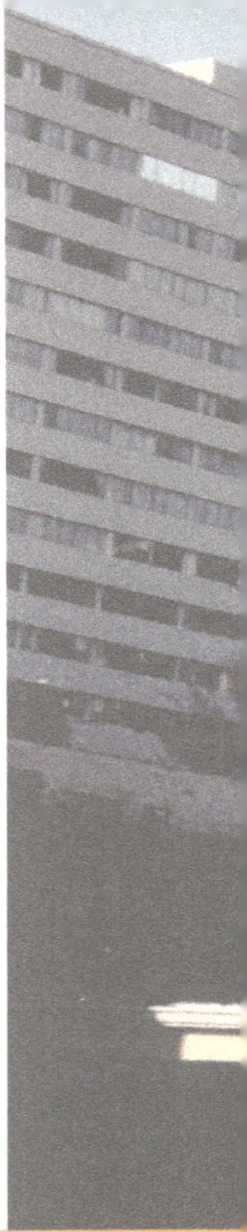

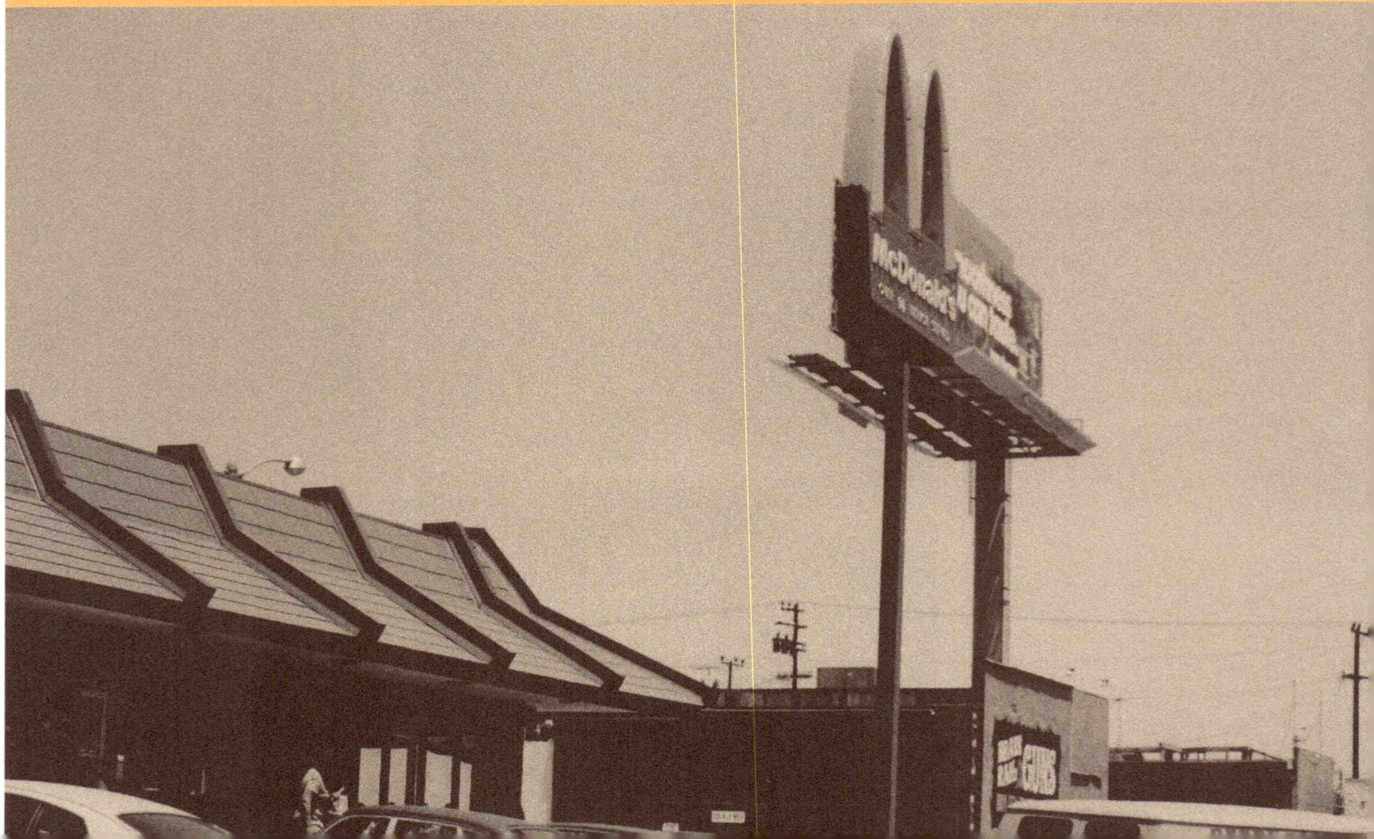

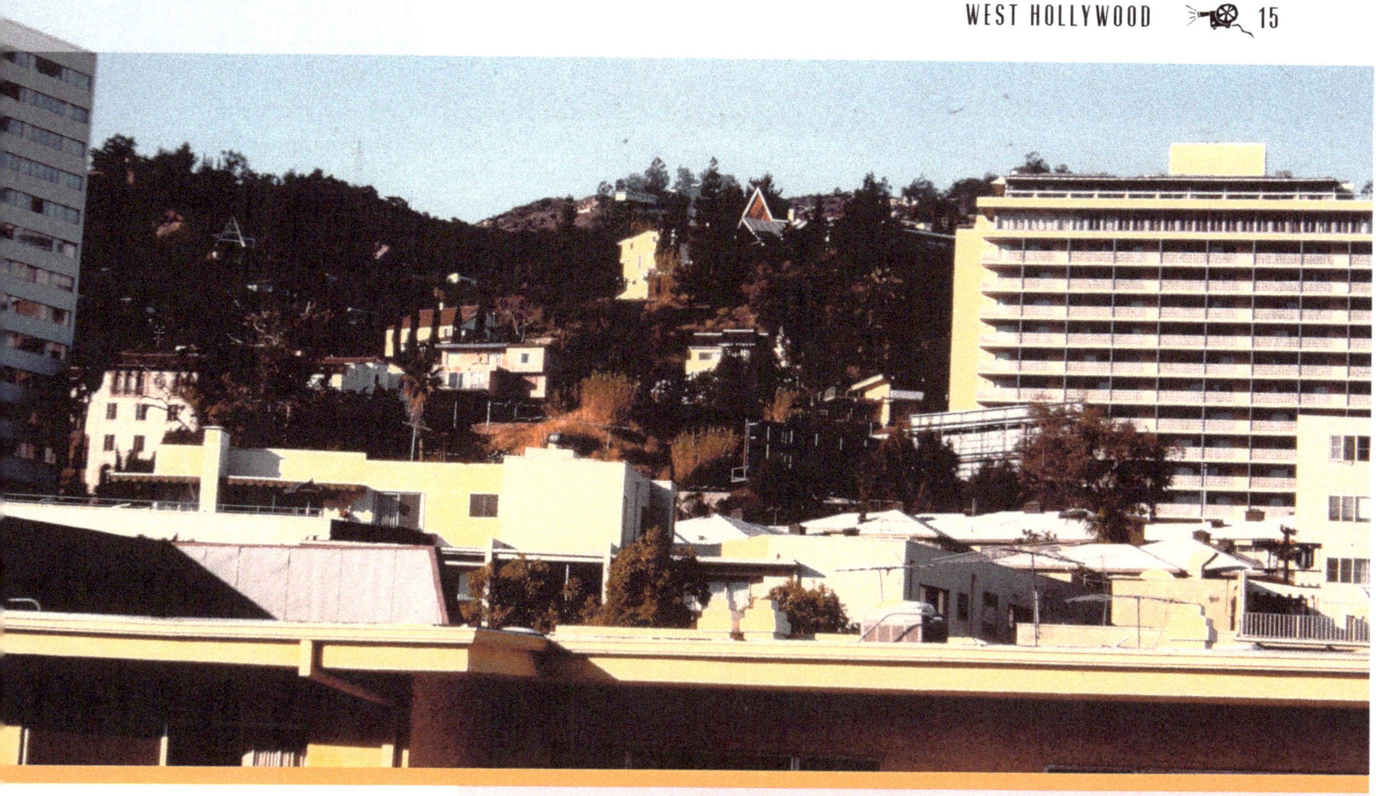

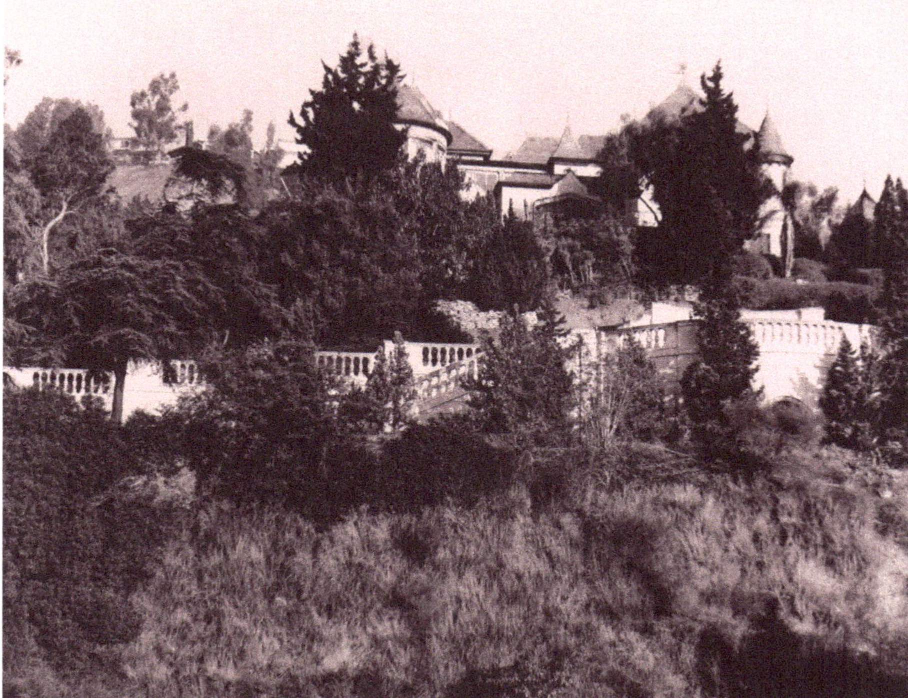

Top: On a rare clear day: The legendary Continental Hyatt House on the right, and the Mondrian Hotel, then apartments, on the left. Dig the A-Frame and the house on stilts. Photo was taken from the roof of 1250 N. Kings Road, West Hollywood. 1974. **Right:** Not the Magic Castle. Not Dracula's Castle. Not Houdini's Castle. Now known as Johnny Depp's Castle, originally called Castle Kalmia 1486 N. Sweetzer, West Hollywood. Elevated 90 feet above Sunset Boulevard on 4 prime acres, completed in 1933 during the Great Depression for $500,000, it took six years to build. Johnny Depp bought the castle in 1995. It remained unidentified in my "vault" until I posted the photo in the "You know you grew up in Hollywood" Facebook group. Time and development on the Strip have made this view history. 1974.

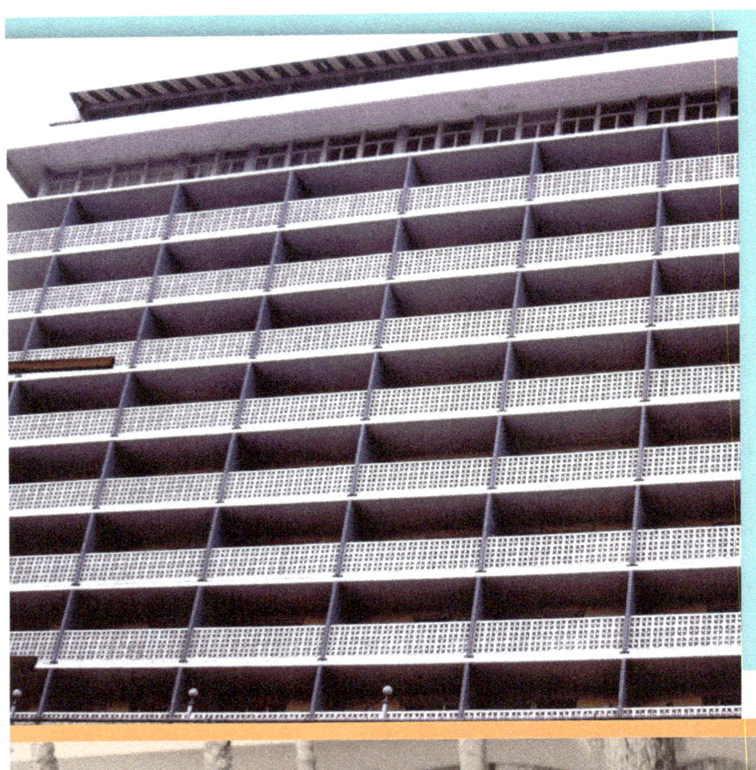

Left: Echoes of Led Zeppelin, the Stones, The Who, and Almost Famous. Watch out for flying televisions and flying bodies. When in concert, the L.A. home of the greatest Hall of Fame rock bands of the '70s, the greatest of all time! The legendary Continental Hyatt House at 8401 Sunset Boulevard was called the Riot House for a damn good reason. The balconies in this classic photo are gone, as is the soul of those crazy times. The Riot House of the 1970s was the ONLY place to stay, and hang out at the rooftop pool, which I was fortunate to do for one memorable teenage summer. 1974. **Bottom:** My favorite corner: Hyatt House Sunset Boulevard and Kings Road, center of the Strip. Ginsberg's Restaurant seems quaint at the same time Led Zeppelin, The Stones, and The Who were partying on the upper floors. 1974. **Right:** Hyatt House Sunset Strip: My universe as a 14-year-old. I lived near the action. The rooftop pool, the Hollywood Hills views. Girls so far out of my teenage league, the A-frame houses in the Hills of Hollywood, and the occasional rock-star sightings. It wouldn't be L.A. without the palm trees. It's now called the Andaz West Hollywood. 1974.

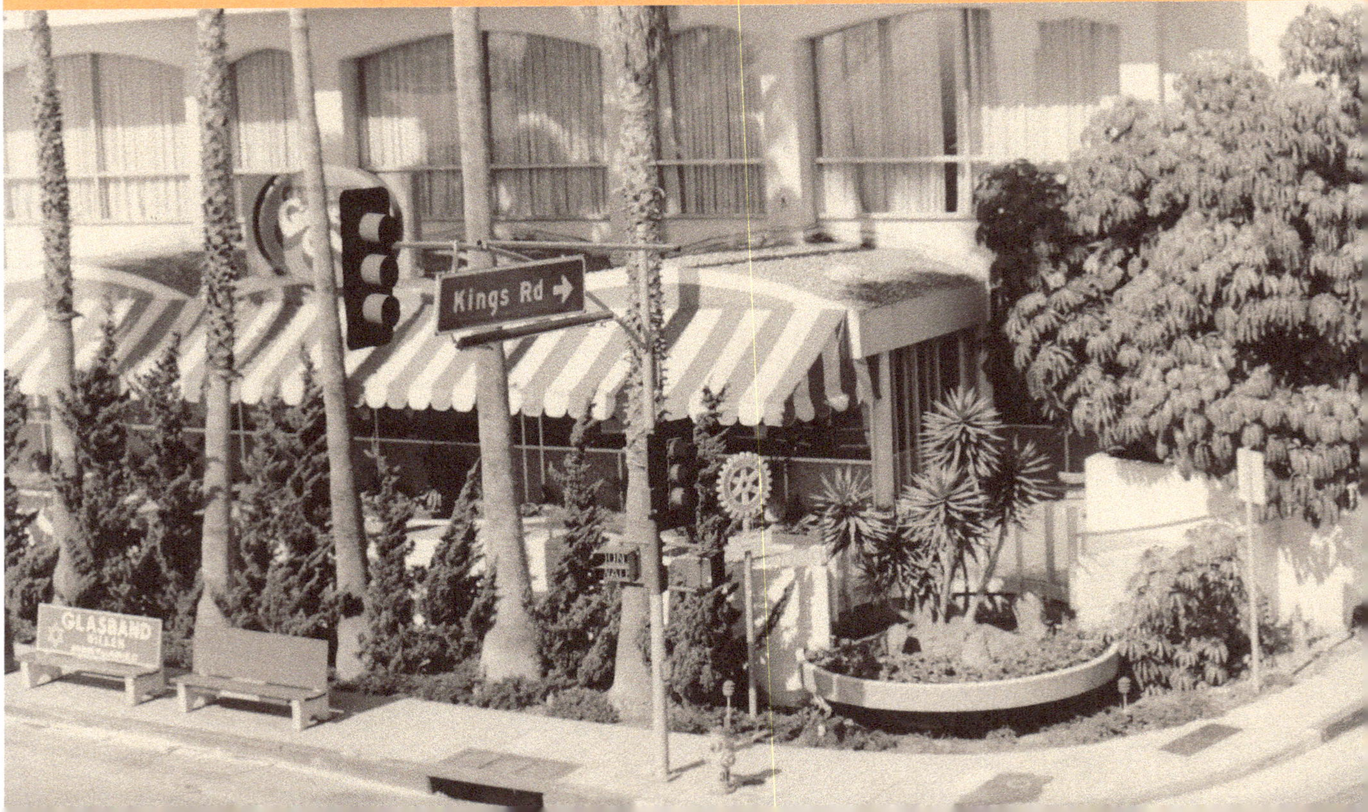

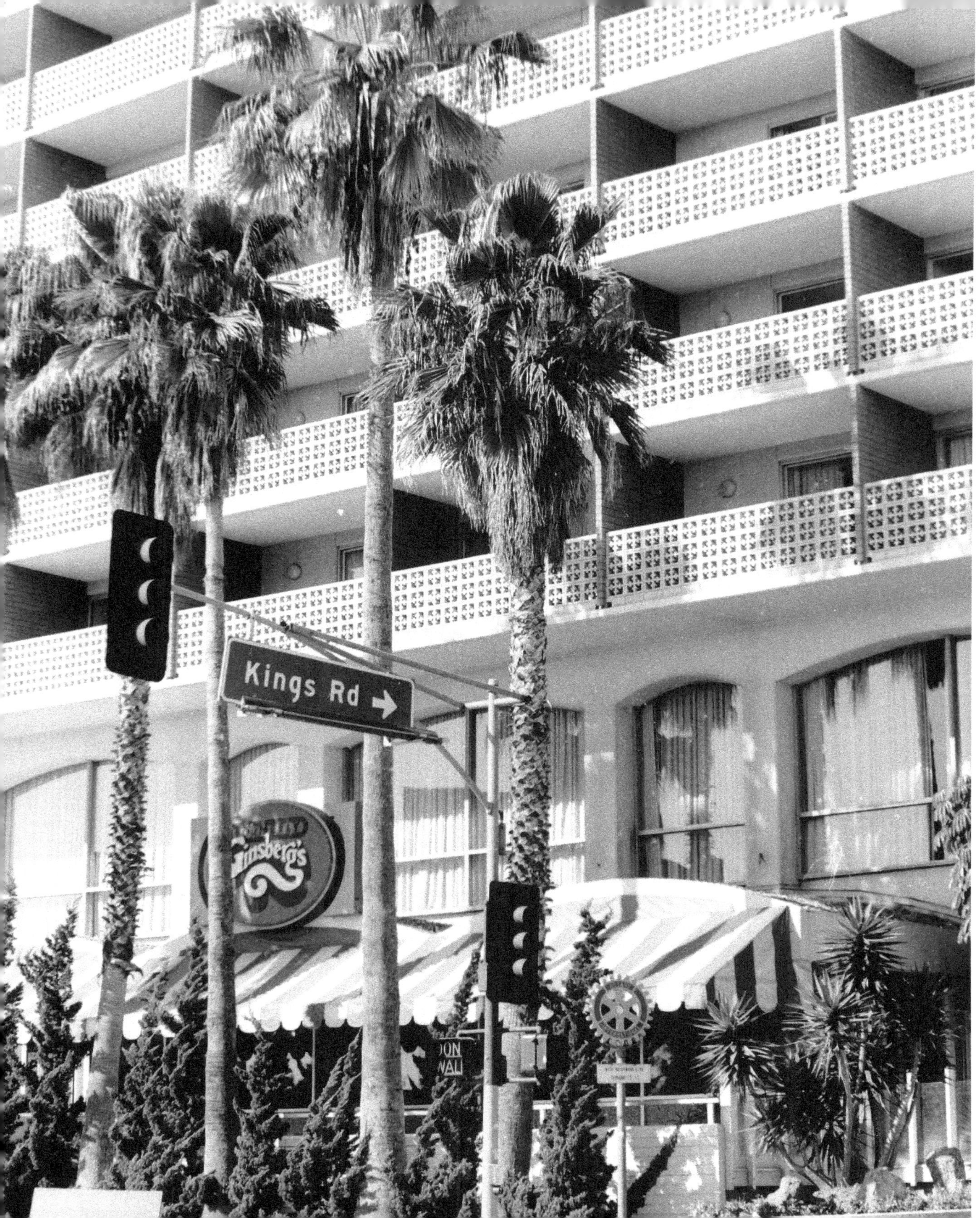

Kings Rd →
Ginsberg's

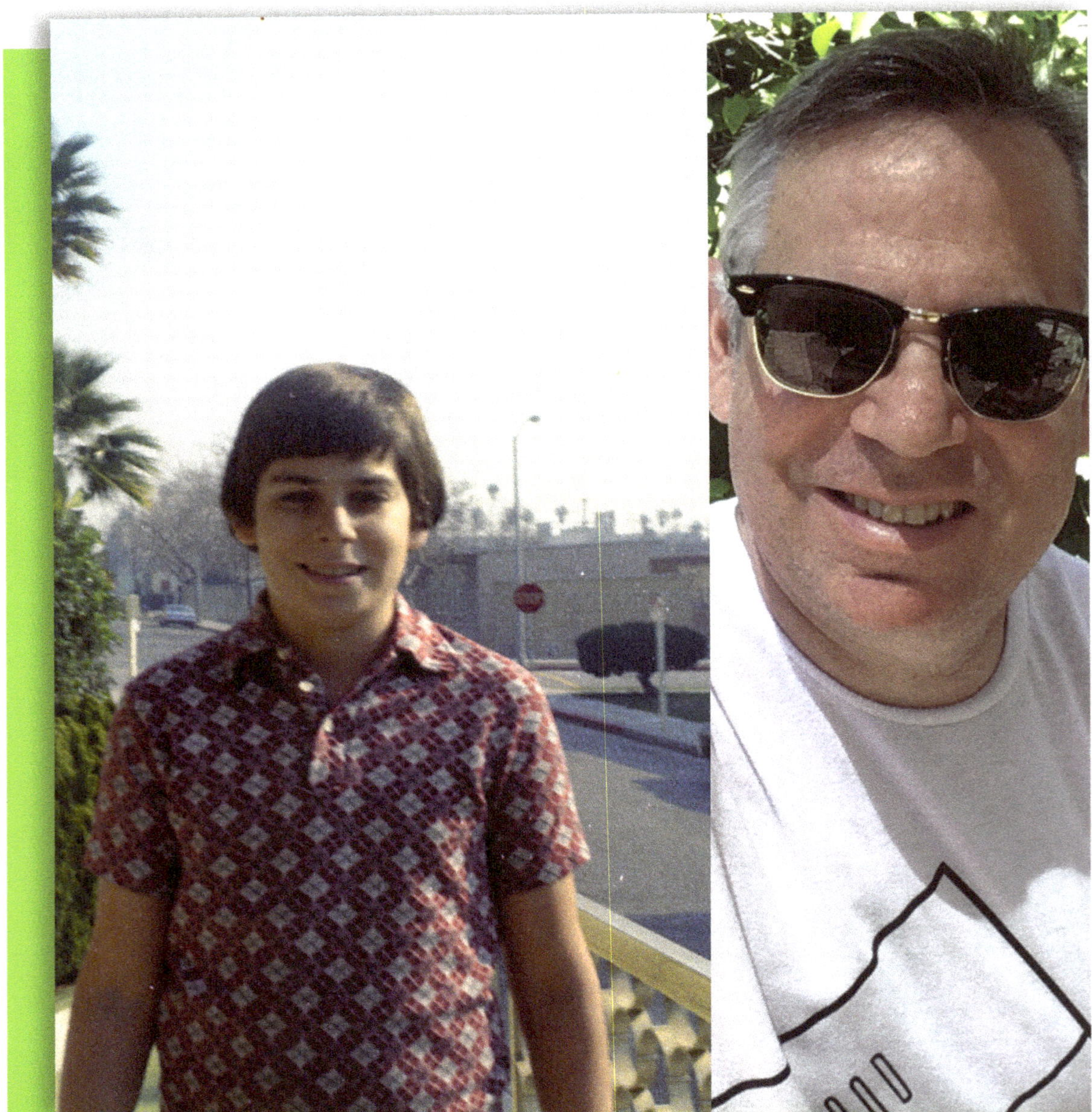

Above: The Author 1972 & 2018. **Bottom:** Jeff at 8011 Romaine: The start of my long-hair and bad-attitude phase. The old-style garages behind me long gone. 8011 Romaine Ave. West Hollywood. 1972.

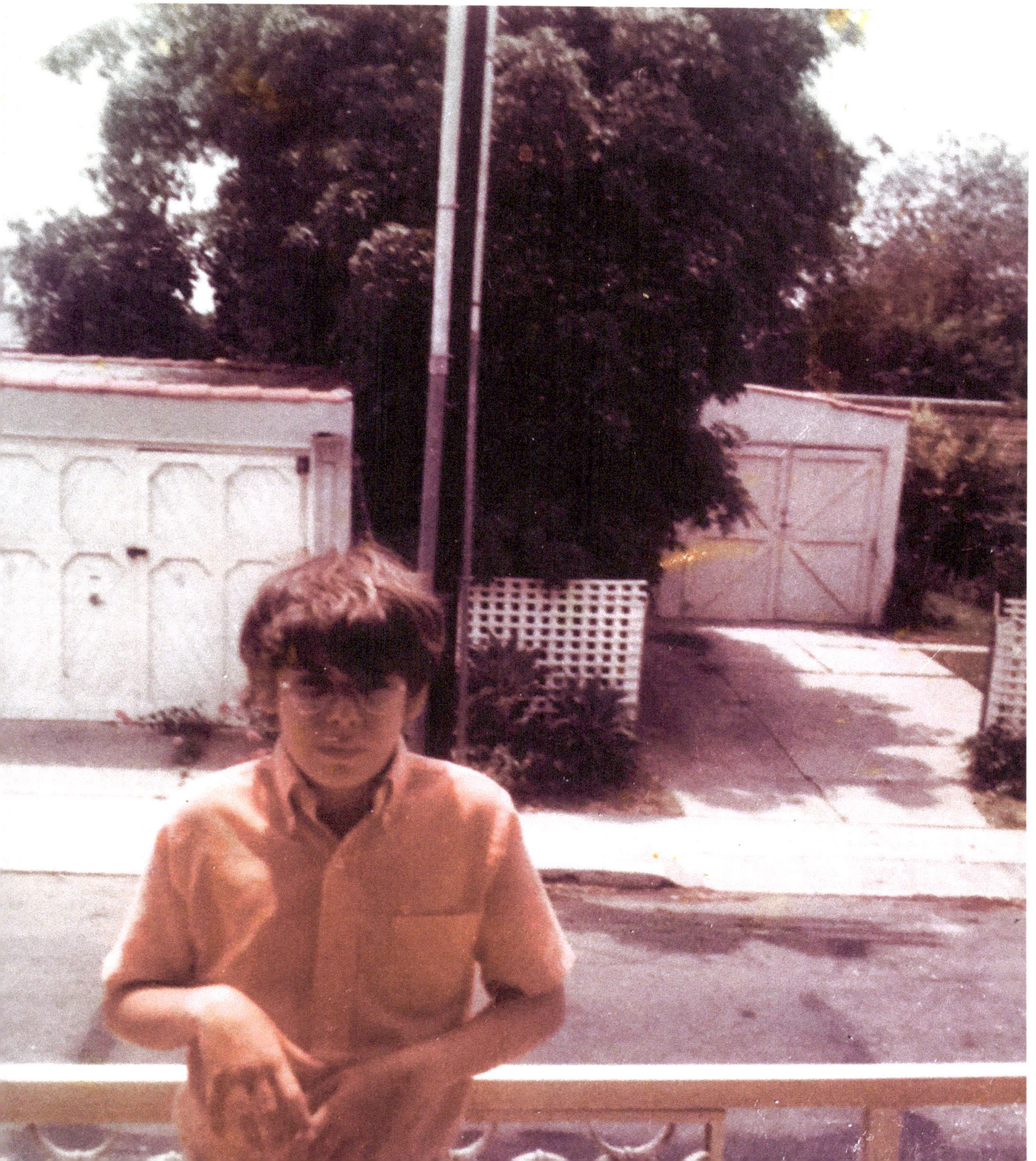

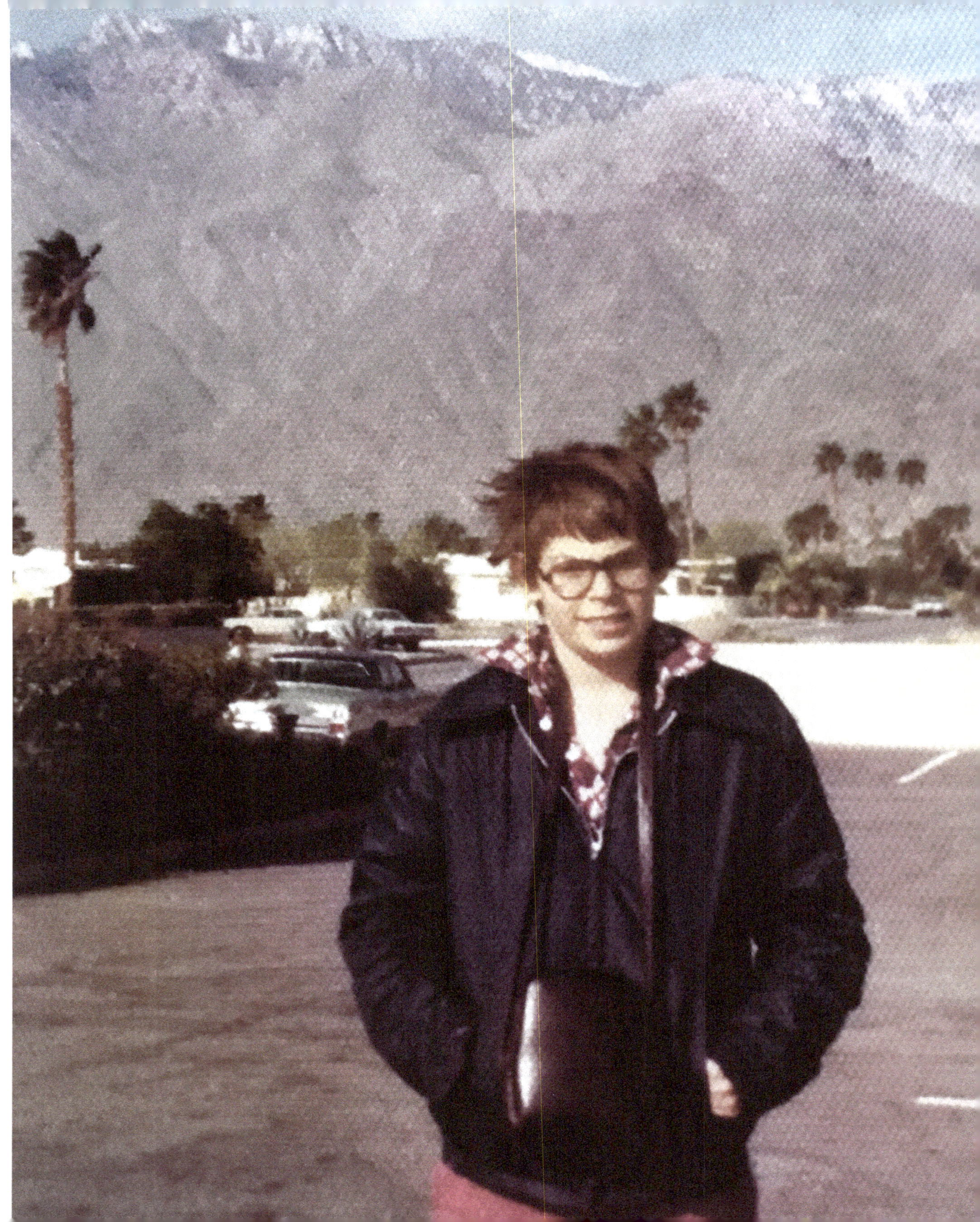

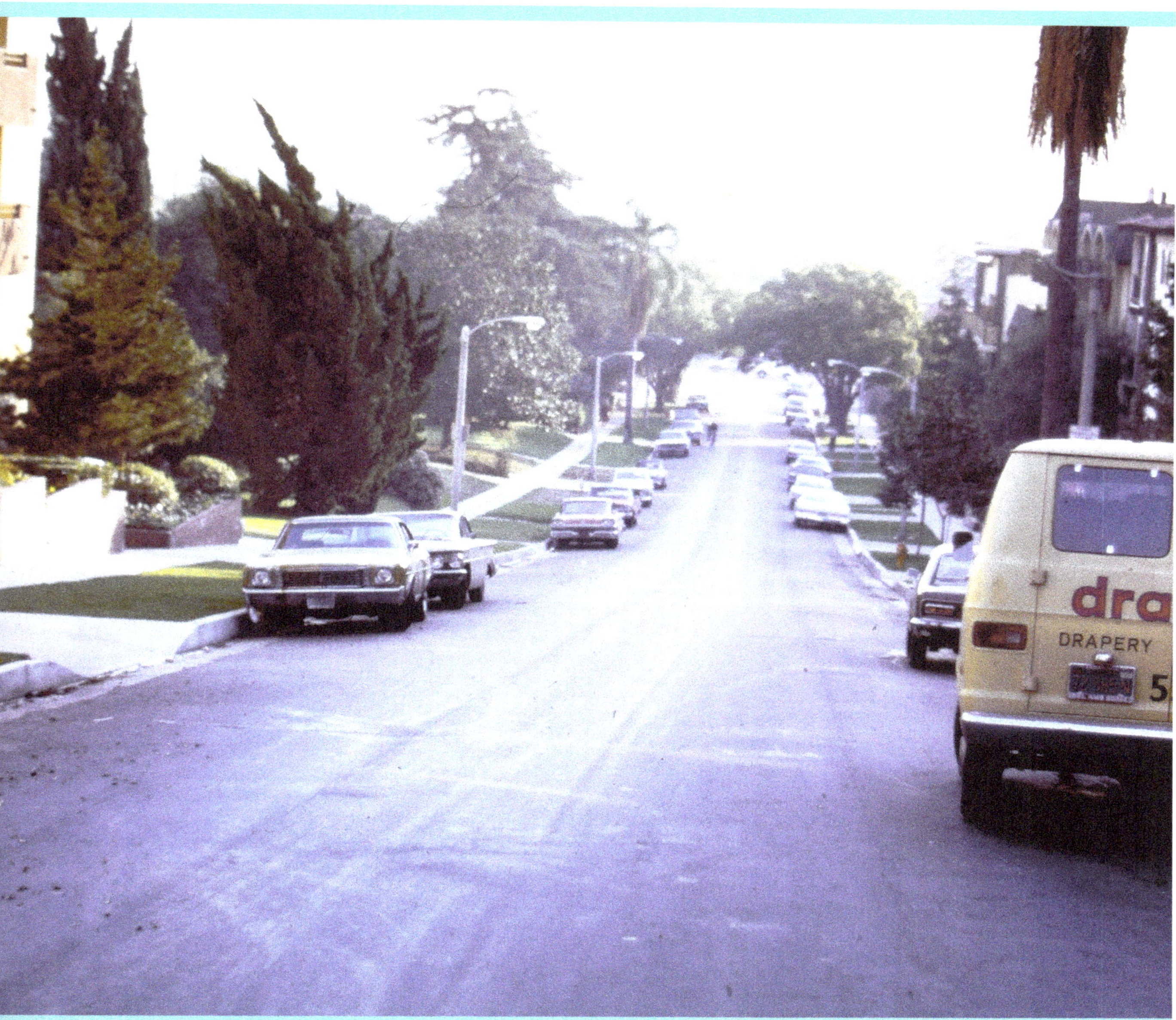

Left: Purple pants and punky hair. I was 14 with my trusty camera bag. Family vacation, Palm Springs, May 1974. **Top:** Looking south toward Santa Monica Boulevard and the smoggy air in the distance, there were still single-family homes on Kings Road, replaced by high-density condos and apartments. Our apartment at 1250 N. Kings Road on the left, were apartments renting for $250 in the '70s, now condos selling for $600,000–$700,000. The late actor Jack Cassidy lived and died in his penthouse apartment at 1221 N. Kings Road, the building just in front of the palm tree on the right. 1975.

Right: I liked the Kings Road sign for some reason. I was 14 and experimenting with framing multiple images with my used 35mm Asahi Pentax. 1974. **Bottom:** The Sunset Tower Hotel was rundown apartments. No longer rundown, respected and restored as the treasure it is. On the National Register of Historic Places, one day I'll stay there. You could practically reach out and touch the Strip from our balcony on Kings Road. 1974.

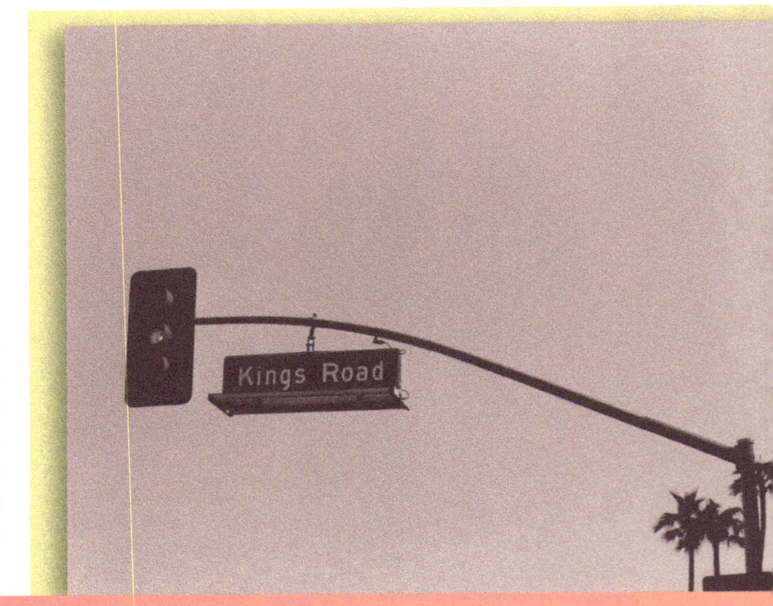

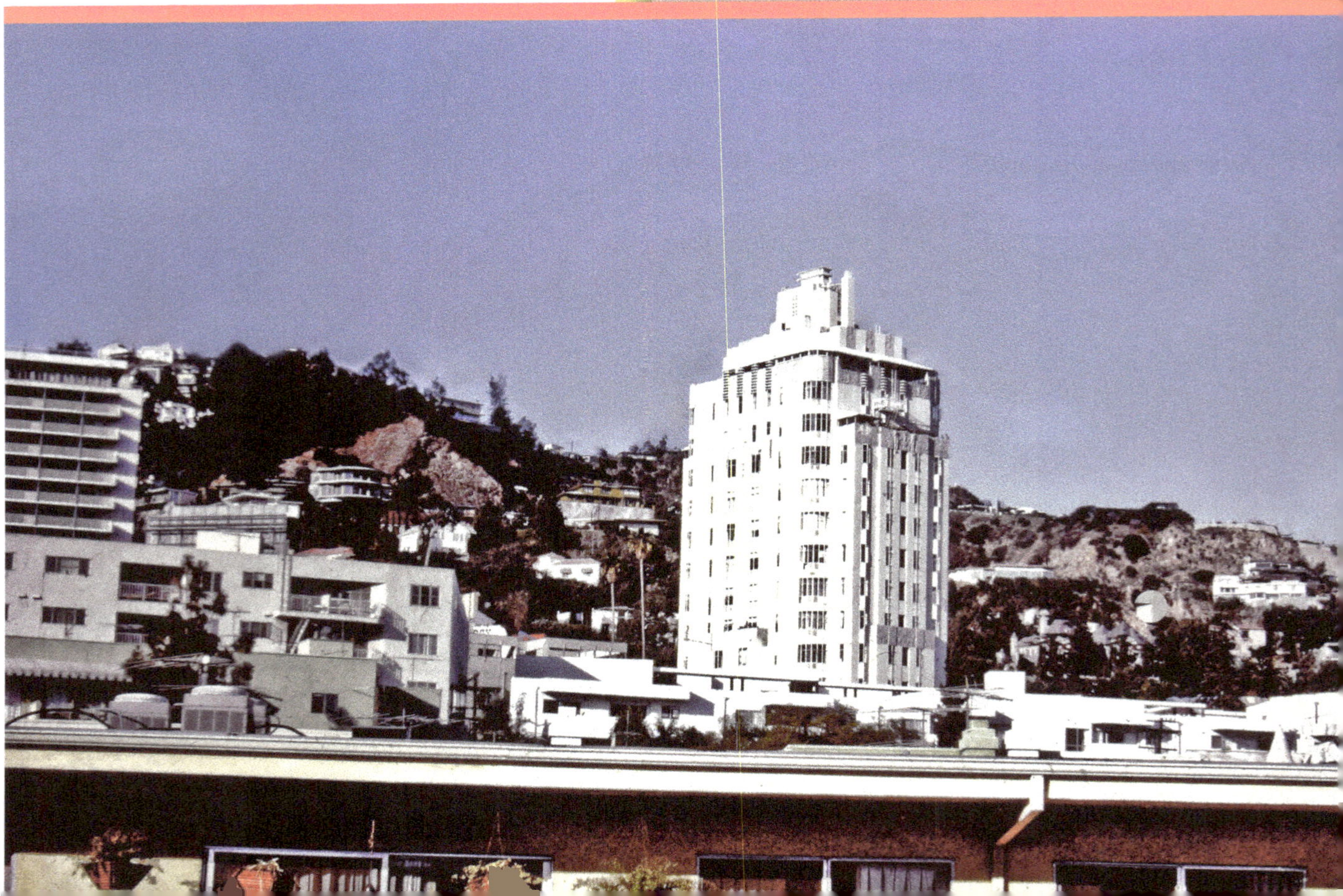

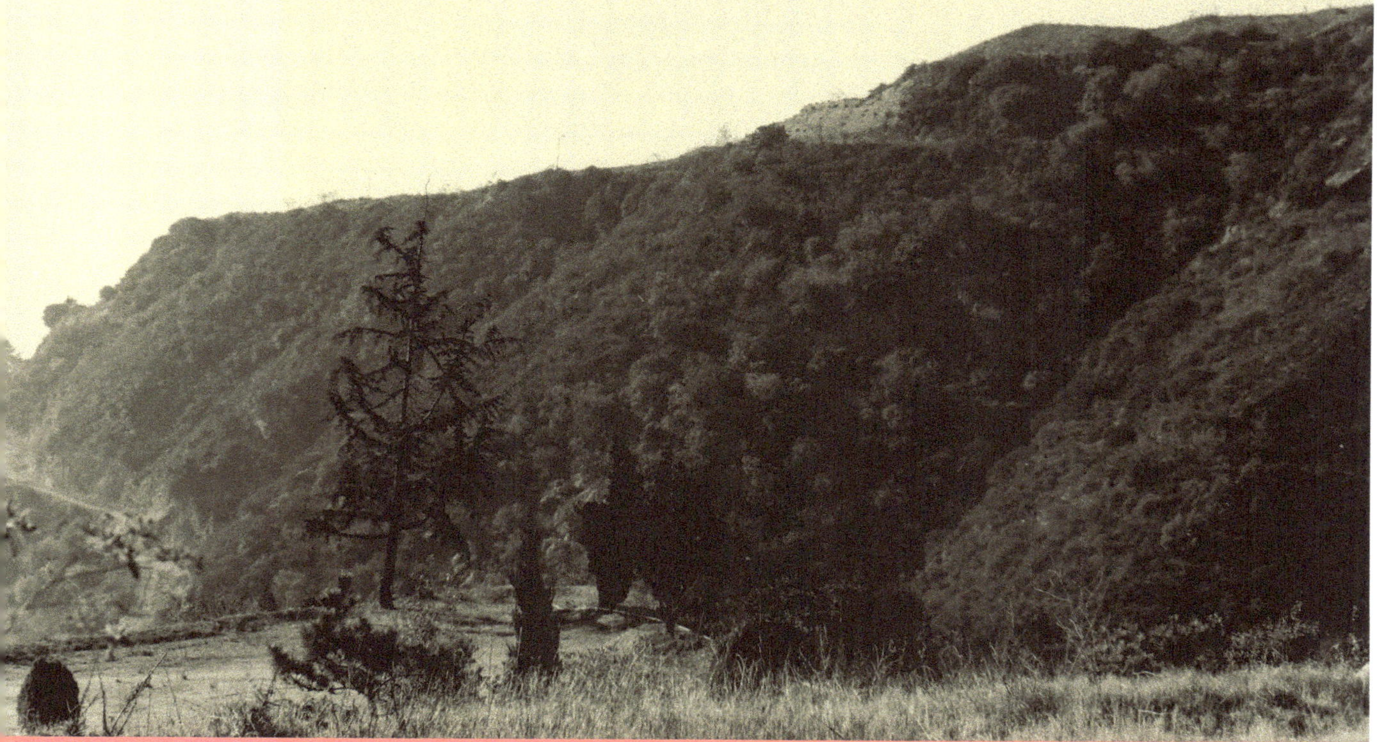

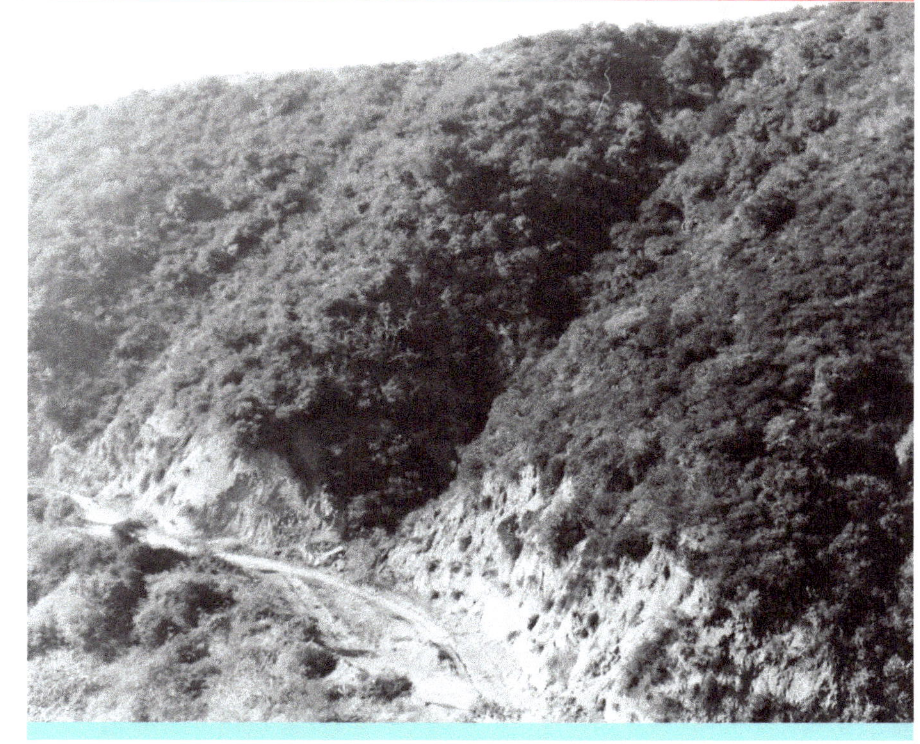

Top: Mt. Olympus subdivision Hollywood Hills was an oasis in the city. Loved to hike up there, catch a breather from the city, and take a few photos along the way. I was into black & white photography at the time. 1974. **Right:** Mt. Olympus was three minutes away from the Sunset Strip! I dreamed of the country, and the sounds of Joni Mitchell were in the air. 1974.

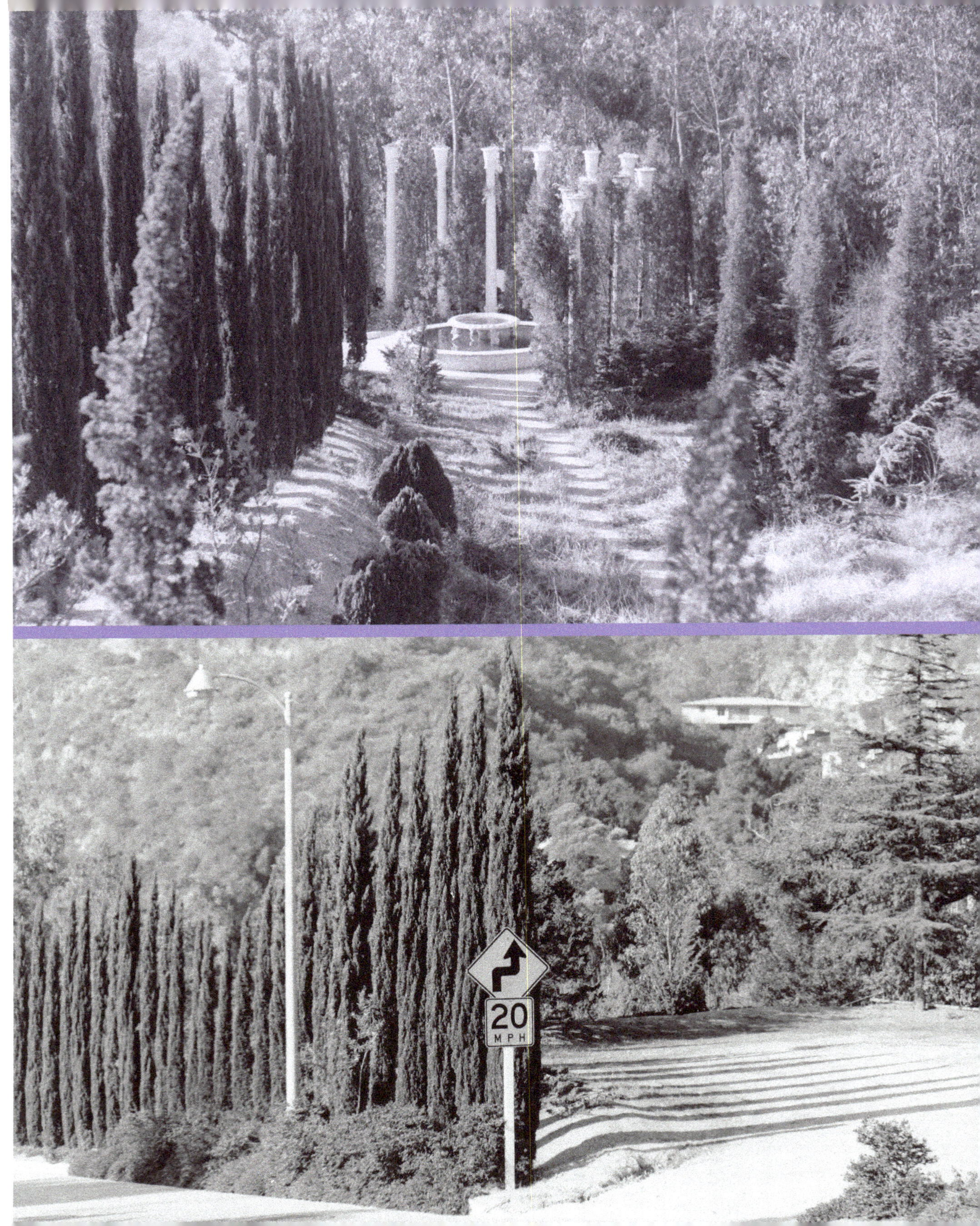
20
M P H

Top Left: Mt. Olympus Fountain: The Cypress trees and marble columns pointing to the Greek gods in the sky. Mt. Olympus subdivision, Hollywood Hills. 1974. **Bottom Left:** Be careful going down that hill. Nice little building lot. Wonder if the Cypress trees are still there? 1974.

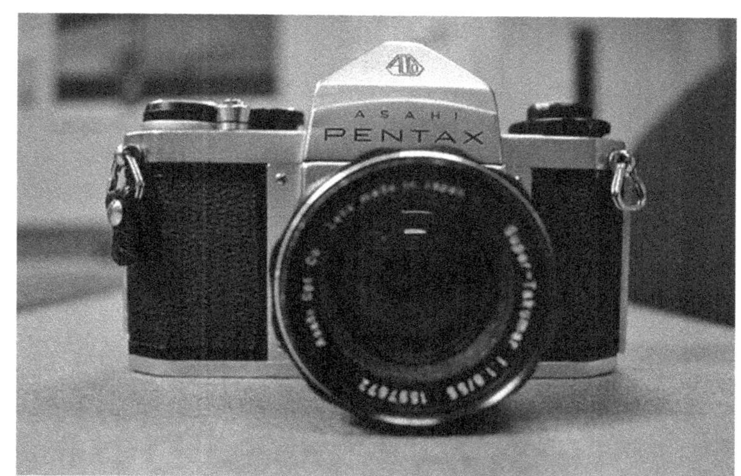

Top Right: My first 35mm camera, a used 1960s ASAHI Pentax, bought for $85 at Elliott Salter's Pawn Shop on Santa Monica Blvd., a large sum of money for a teenager used to carrying forty cents. 1974. Bottom Right: There was breathing room between the houses on the hill. Wasn't that a Joni Mitchell song? Memories of Court & Spark, The Eagles, Jackson Browne, The L.A Express and the Mamas & Papas emanating from the Hills of Hollywood, perhaps from one of these homes at the top or at the bottom of the hill? 1974.

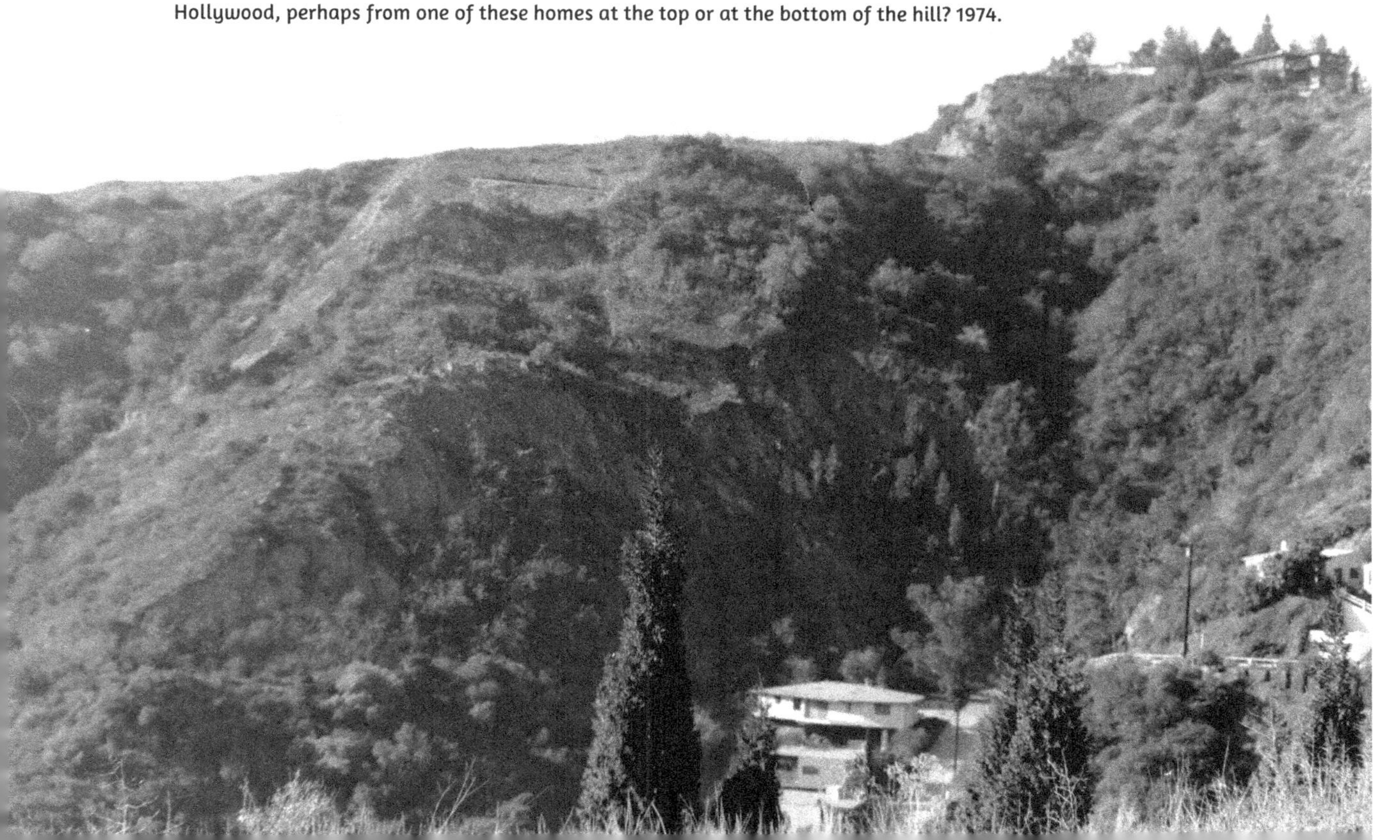

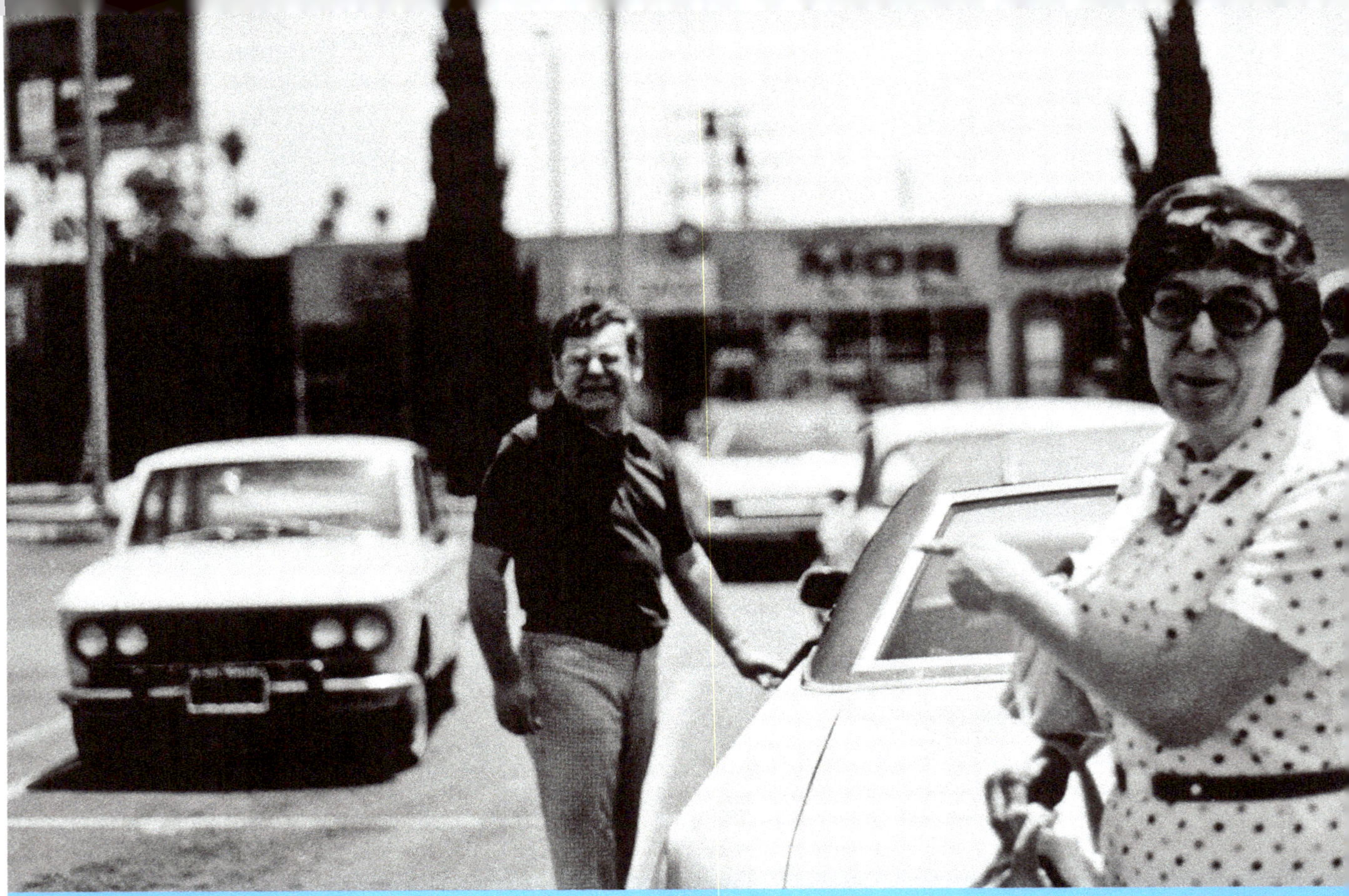

Top: The location is 3rd & Fairfax Town & Country Shopping Center. Mom & Dad having an animated discussion next to Dad's 1972 Buick Electra 225. They were married for 53 years before my mom passed away in 2004. Dad died 10 years later. 1973. **Bottom:** I always sat behind my Dad.   Technically not a great photo but it brings back images of the rare visit to Fisher's and Farmers Market across the street, decades before The Grove. The Safeway is now a Whole Foods, and Sav-on is now a CVS. Current plans for a 26-story residential tower behind the Safeway. 1973.

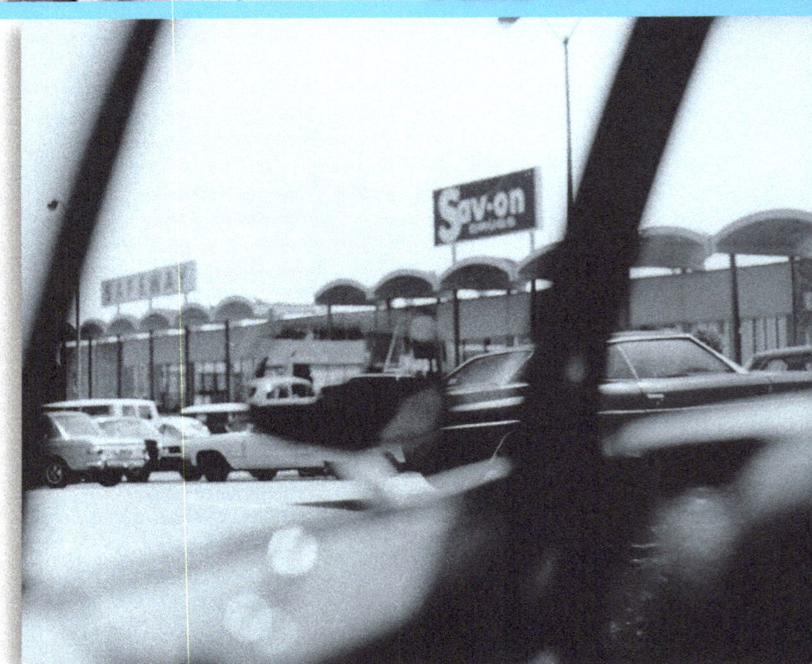

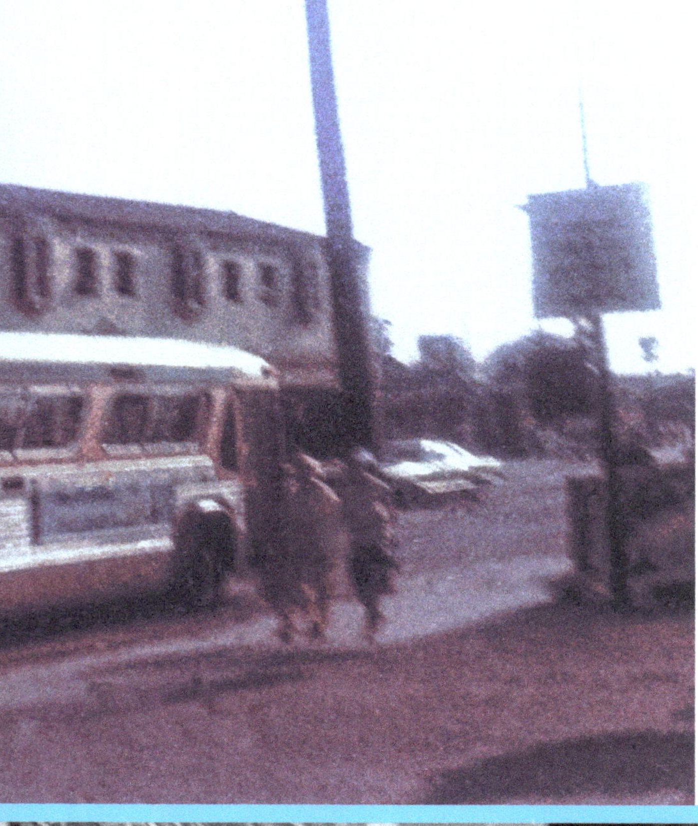

Left: Northwest corner Santa Monica Blvd. & Fairfax. Return from Dodger Stadium on the 91W. The last photo on the 12-exposure roll I had to do something with before taking it to Fotomat, the result is a blurred snapshot of time. That corner is now a Starbucks. 1972.**Bottom:** They were in a better mood. My mom always took off her glasses for photos. My dad was so serious. We lived at 8011 Romaine Avenue, West Hollywood, from 1967 to 1974. Rents were $200–$250 for a 2-bedroom apartment, and houses could be bought in West Hollywood for $25,000. 1973.

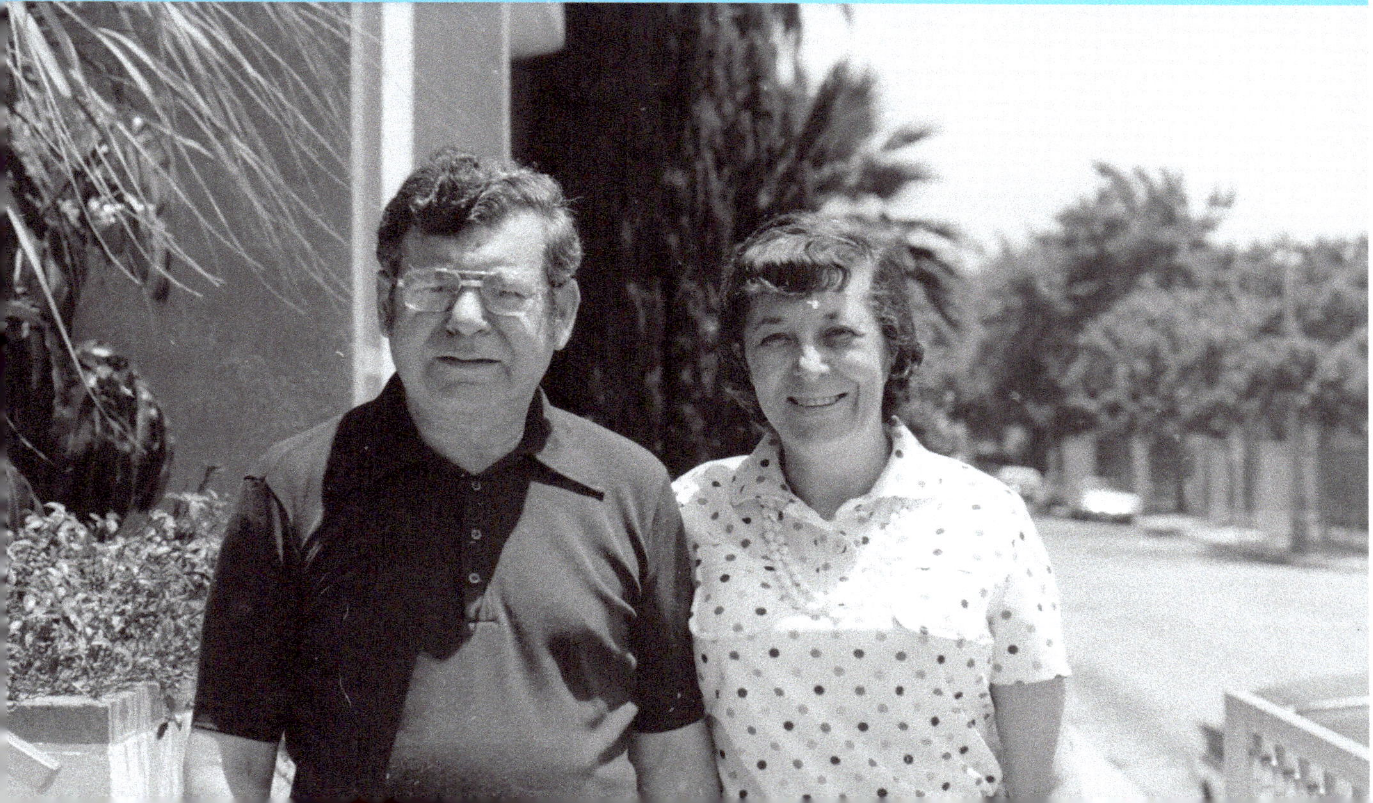

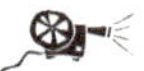

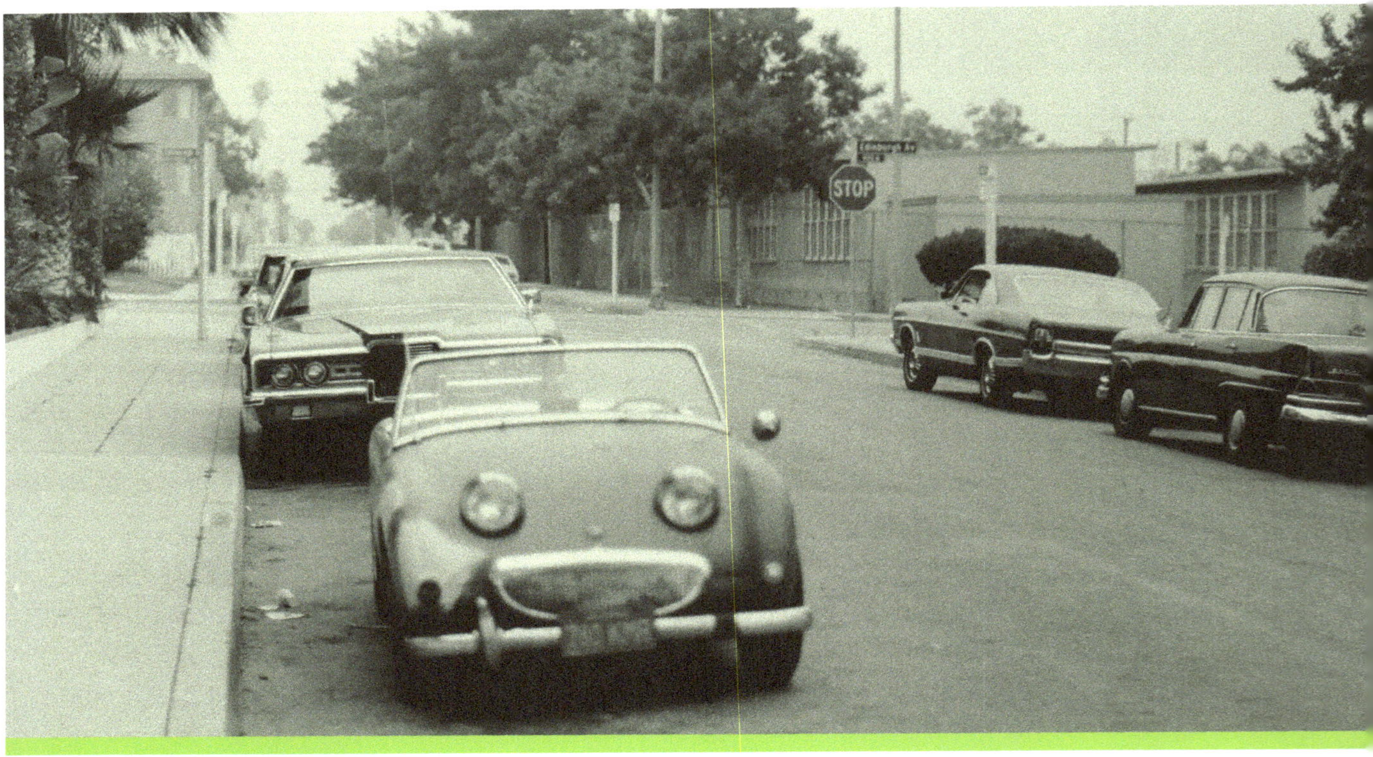

Top: Ordinary street scenes that are interesting decades later. If that car could talk! Romaine Street, West Hollywood. Laurel Elementary School in the background. 1973. **Bottom:** The station wagon was the All-American family vehicle in the decades before SUVs. Looks like a hearse! Parked in front of our apartment on Romaine & Edinburgh, West Hollywood. 1973.

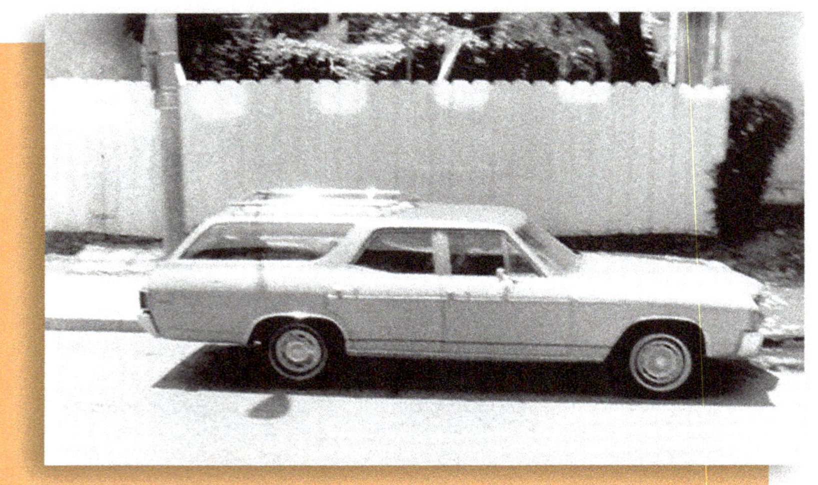

Top Right: My friend Tony lived at Sunset Tower West Apartments 8400 Sunset Boulevard (now a hotel). We were the same age, but he always seemed older. He was 15 in this photo. This was taken in the lobby of the apartments. The old style newspaper racks were easy to kick open even though the *L.A Times* was just 10 cents. 1974. **Bottom Right:** Bentley? Rolls? Lost on Romaine? 1973.

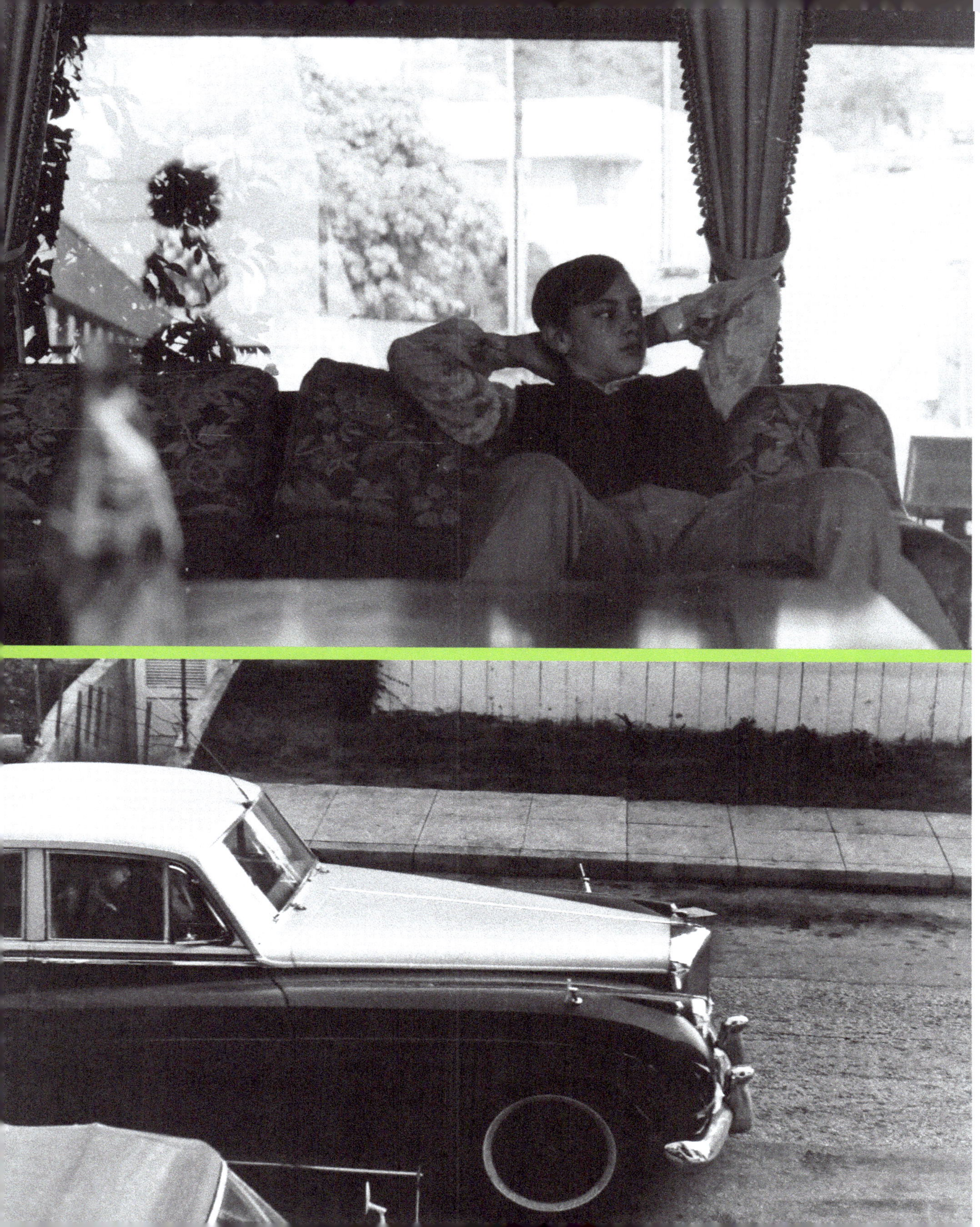

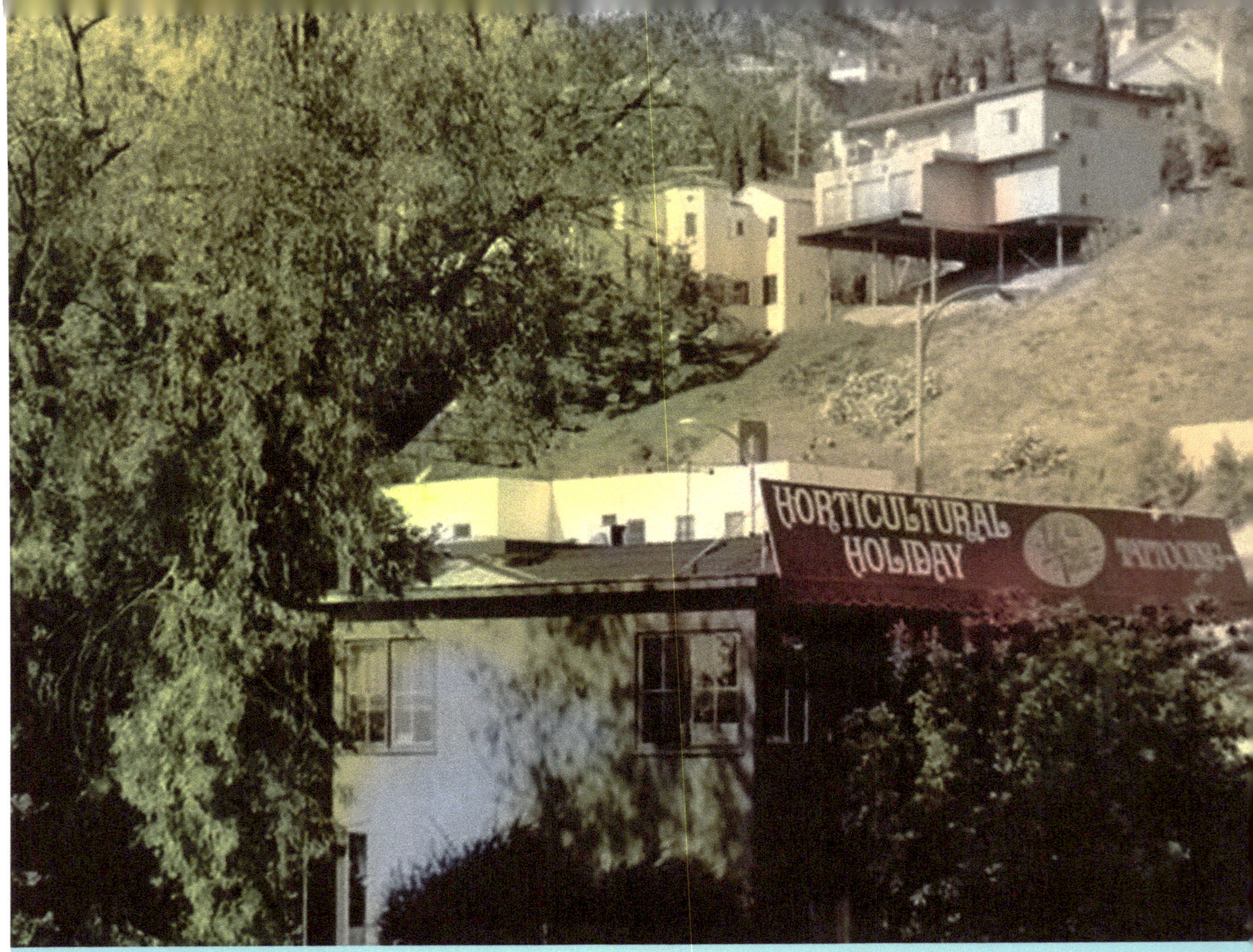

Top: Horticultural Holiday began in the 1970s as an "Environmental Eatery" on Sunset Blvd. just west of Kings Road. All I understood was that it was a cool little building shared with legendary tattoo artist Lyle Tuttle. The house on stilts is classic '70s Hollywood Hills. I was 14 when I took this photo. 1974. **Right:** People came from all over the Westside to buy their classic Schwinn bikes at Harry's, corner of Santa Monica Blvd. & Laurel. I just had to walk or ride up the block. The legendary French Quarter, with its 35 shops, had been open only a short time. Both buildings survive, but the French Quarter, long a community staple, closed in 2015. 1974.

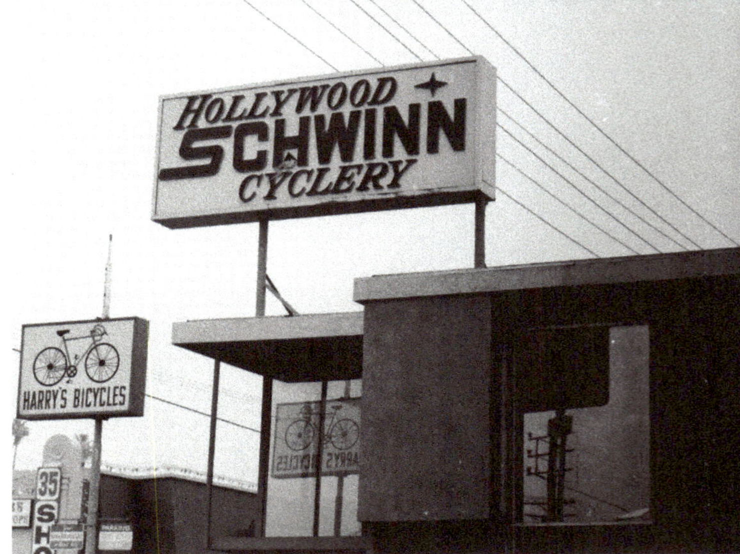

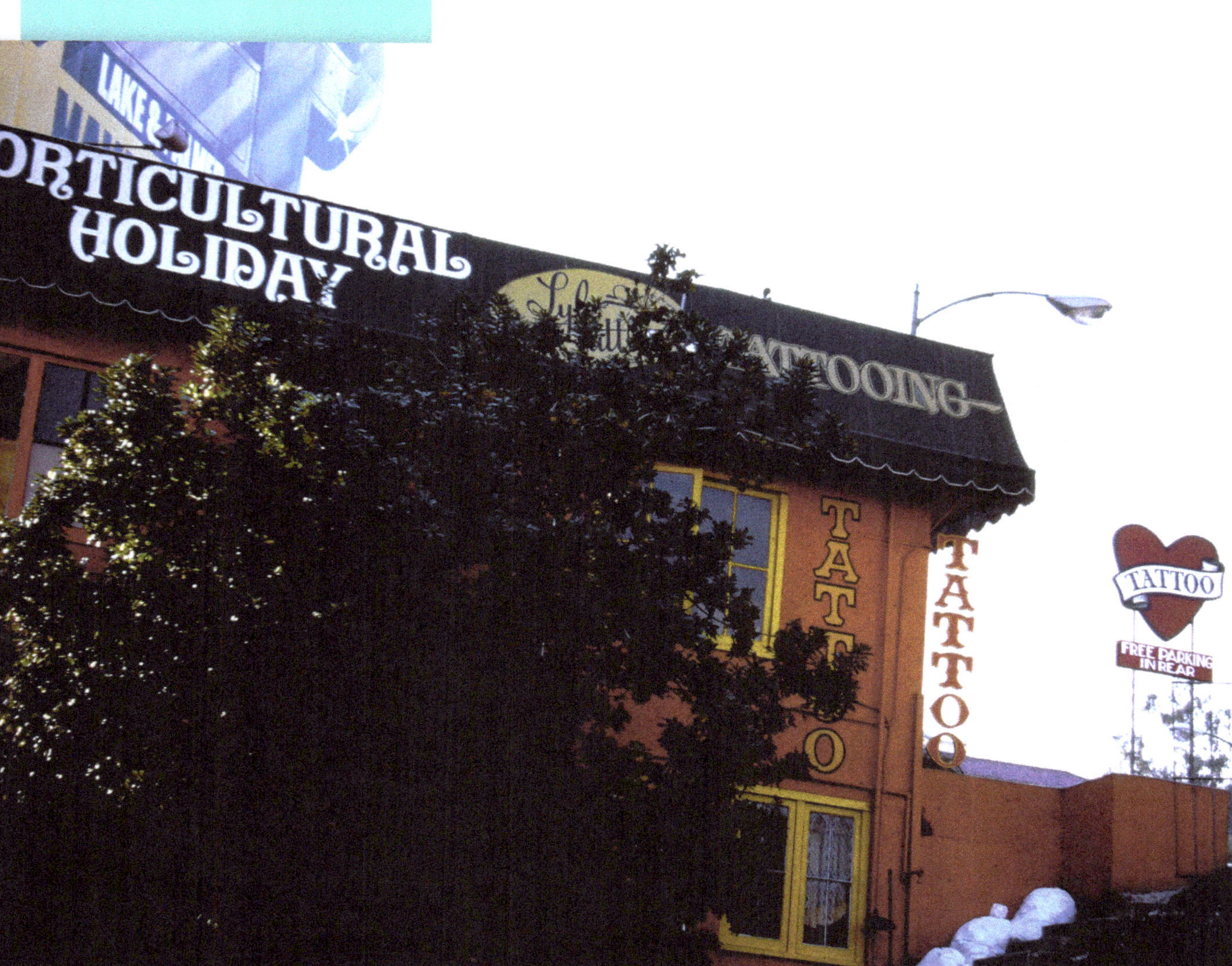

Top: Take a holiday. The vibe of the 1970s Sunset Strip. Hand-painted ELP billboard. 1974.

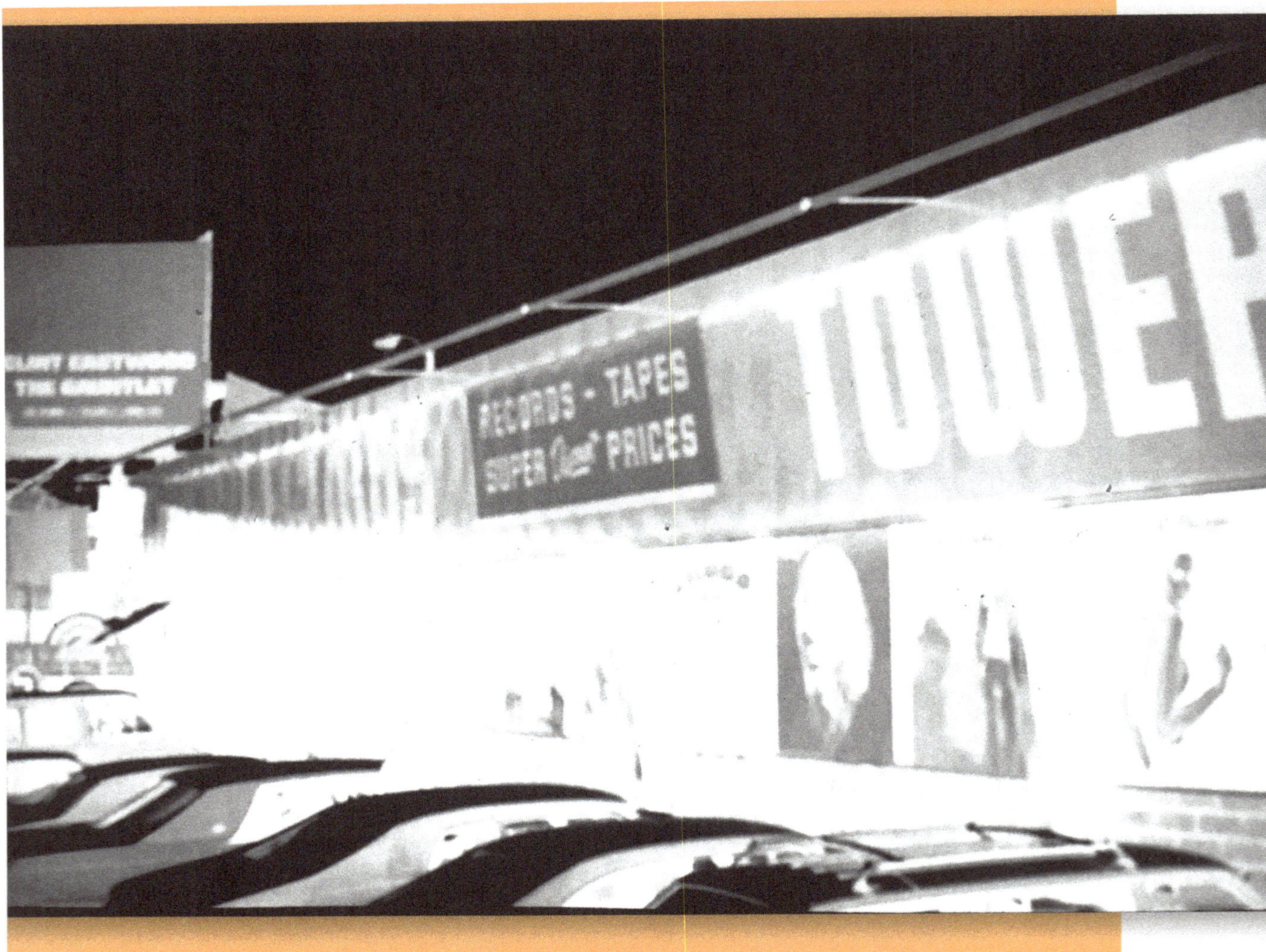

Top: The Sunset Strip and Tower Records are synonymous. Tower and the Hyatt were the centers of my teenage universe. Growing up in West Hollywood in the 1970s gave me a lifetime of interesting stories to share. Taking the way-back machine four decades in time gives me an appreciation for an era and a period of time that I took for granted. 1977.

BASEBALL
TAKE ME OUT TO THE BALLGAME

n 1970, Pepsi-Cola promoted the Dodger Pepsi Fan Club. For $1, you received tickets to six Dodger games and a T-shirt. I scraped a dollar together, and the early photos are the result. Fan Appreciation Day was the one game each year fans could get up close to the players, a thrilling experience for a 10-year-old fanatic.

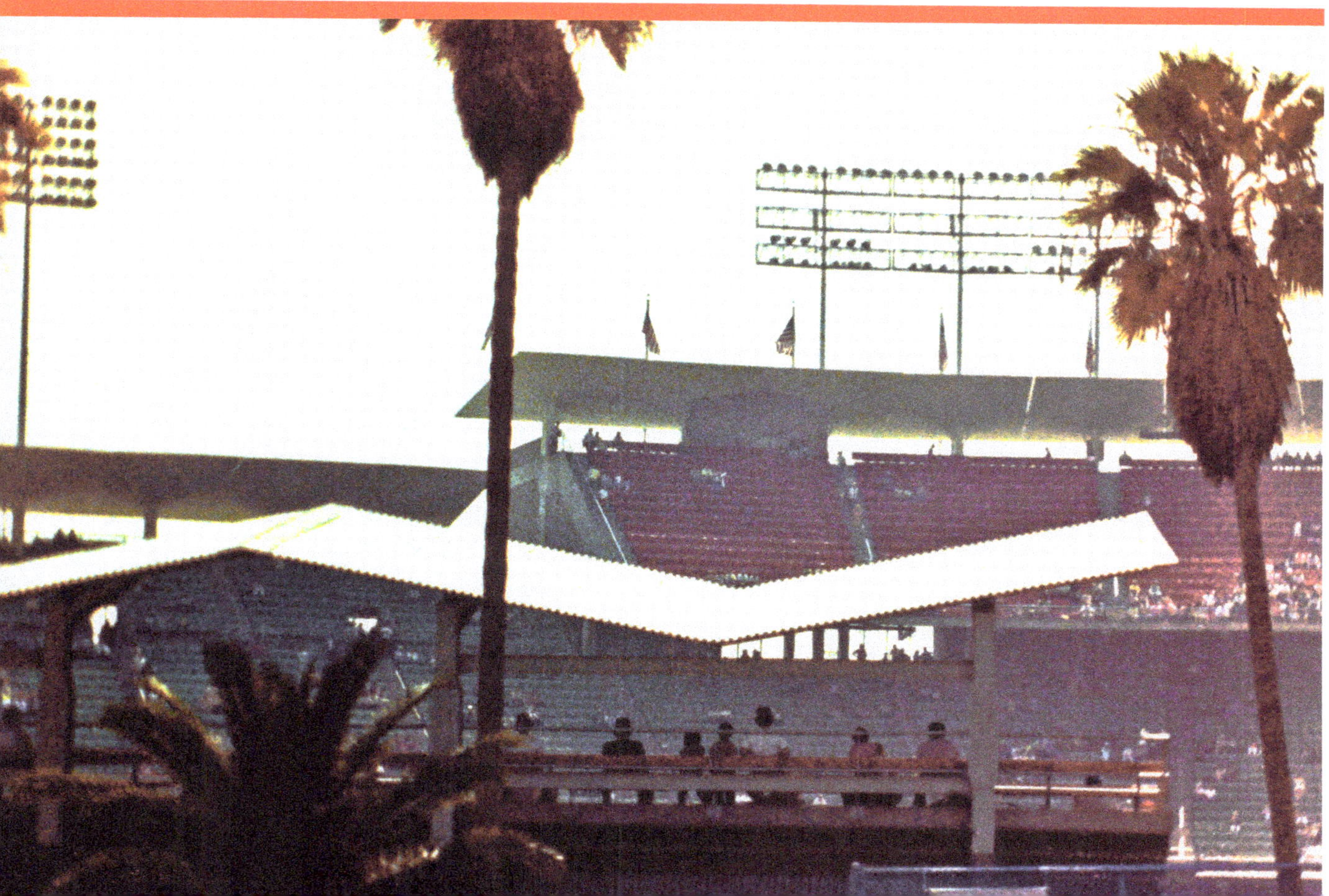

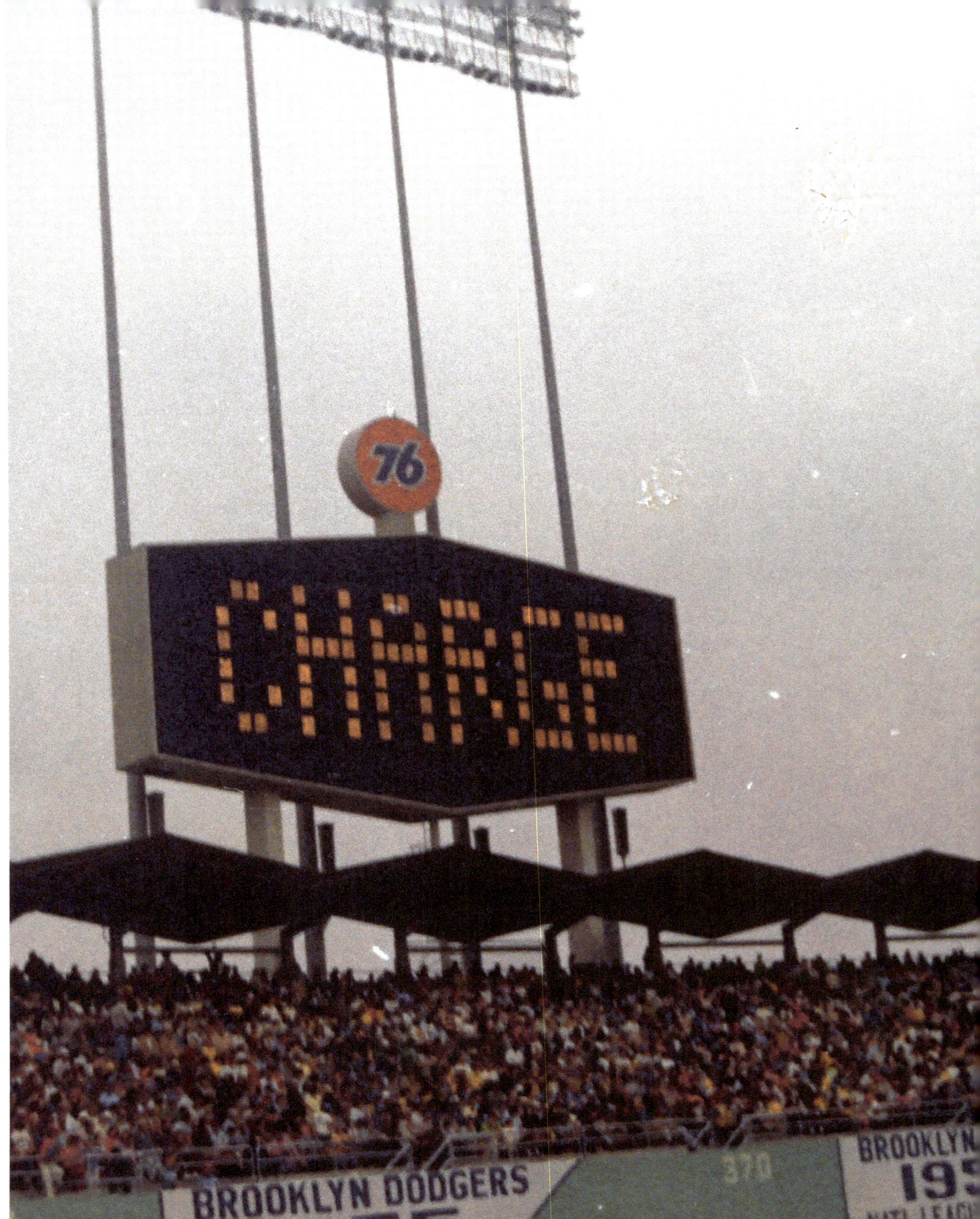
76
MARGE
BROOKLYN DODGERS
370
BROOKLYN
195

A few years later, I was riding the 91E bus from West Hollywood to Dodger Stadium on a regular basis. Sneaking down from the upper deck to the box seats was expected and often successful, as the Dodgers had a lot of empty seats in the '70s.

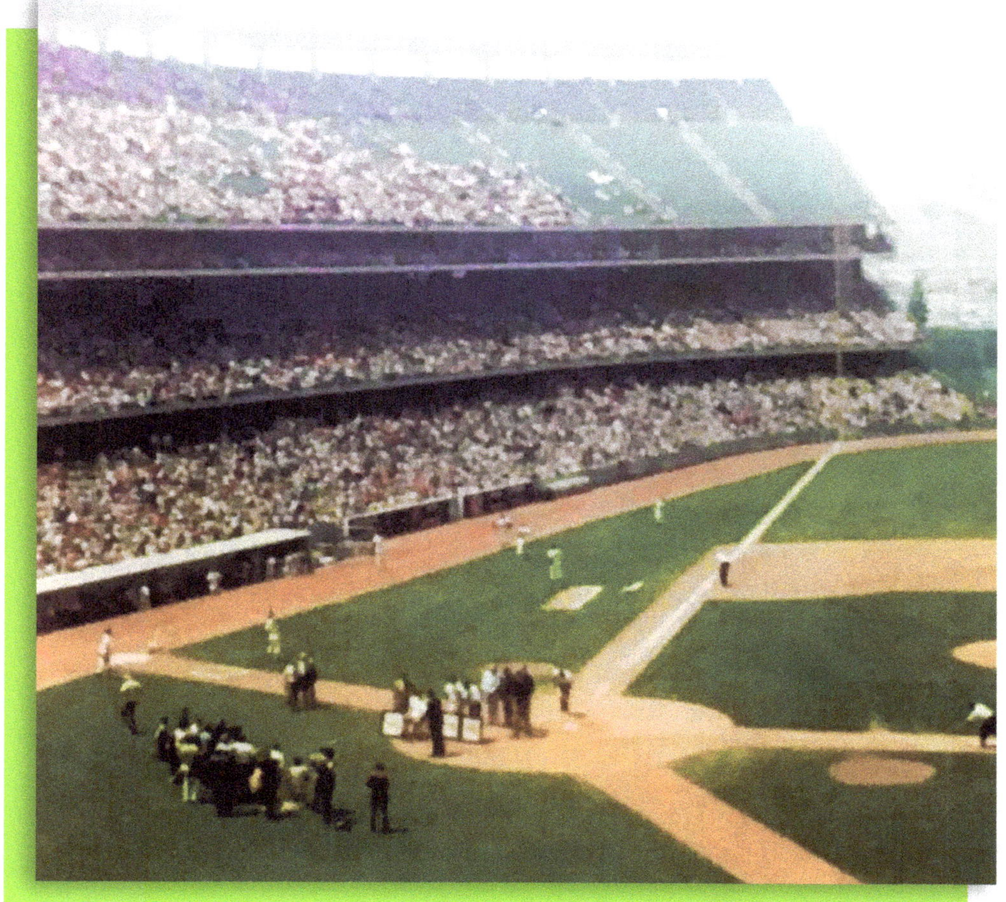

Left: CHARGE! Southern California June gloom weather. '70s L.A. smog made the hills invisible. The old-school original scoreboard commanding the fans to get charged! I caught a foul ball at that game. CHARGE! 1973. **Above:** A historic day viewed from the cheap seats. The jerseys of Dodger Hall of Famers Sandy Koufax (#32), Roy Campanella (#39), and Jackie Robinson (#42) are retired forever. 43,818 witnessed that historic ceremony. No other player in baseball will ever wear #42. It's been retired permanently by Major League Baseball, the only player in baseball history to have that honor. Jackie Robinson died just four months after this ceremony at age 53. June 4, 1972.

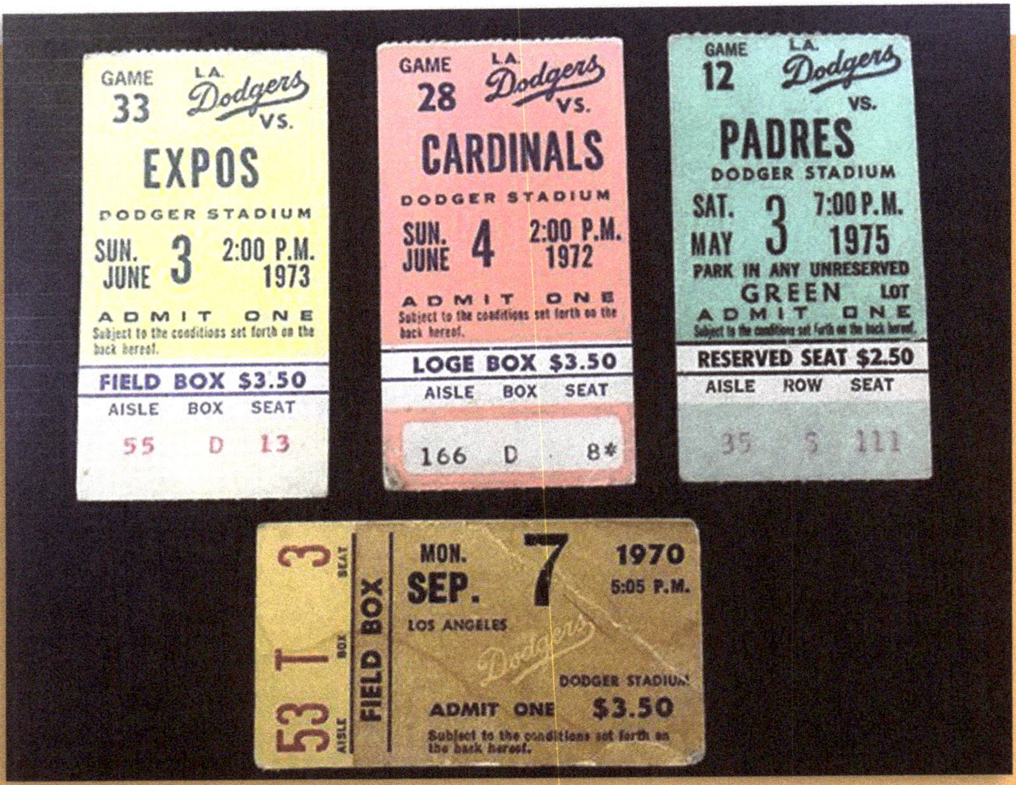

There are some classic but forgotten moments in my collection. The memory of fans flooding the field won't happen today. As a kid, I always remembered the '69 Mets and the image of fans flooding the field at Shea Stadium after winning the World Series. The California Angels of Orange County suffered a lot longer, and in 1979, fans flooded the field after winning their division for the first time (and losing the playoff to the Baltimore Orioles). June 4, 1972, the historic day when the Dodgers retired the numbers of Sandy Koufax, Roy Campanella, and Jackie Robinson. Sadly, the great Jackie Robinson passed away just four months later, age 53.

Top Left: The best tickets were cheap. Cheaper yet when you could sneak down to the box seats, which were $1. 1970. **Right:** July 20, 1970. Bill Singer throws a no-hitter. I was there in the cheap seats, that game being one of the six that were part of the Dodger Pepsi Fan Club promotion. Beginning with Sandy Koufax's perfect game in 1965, if a Dodger pitcher reached the 9th inning without allowing a hit, Vin Scully would record it for "posterity." 1970.

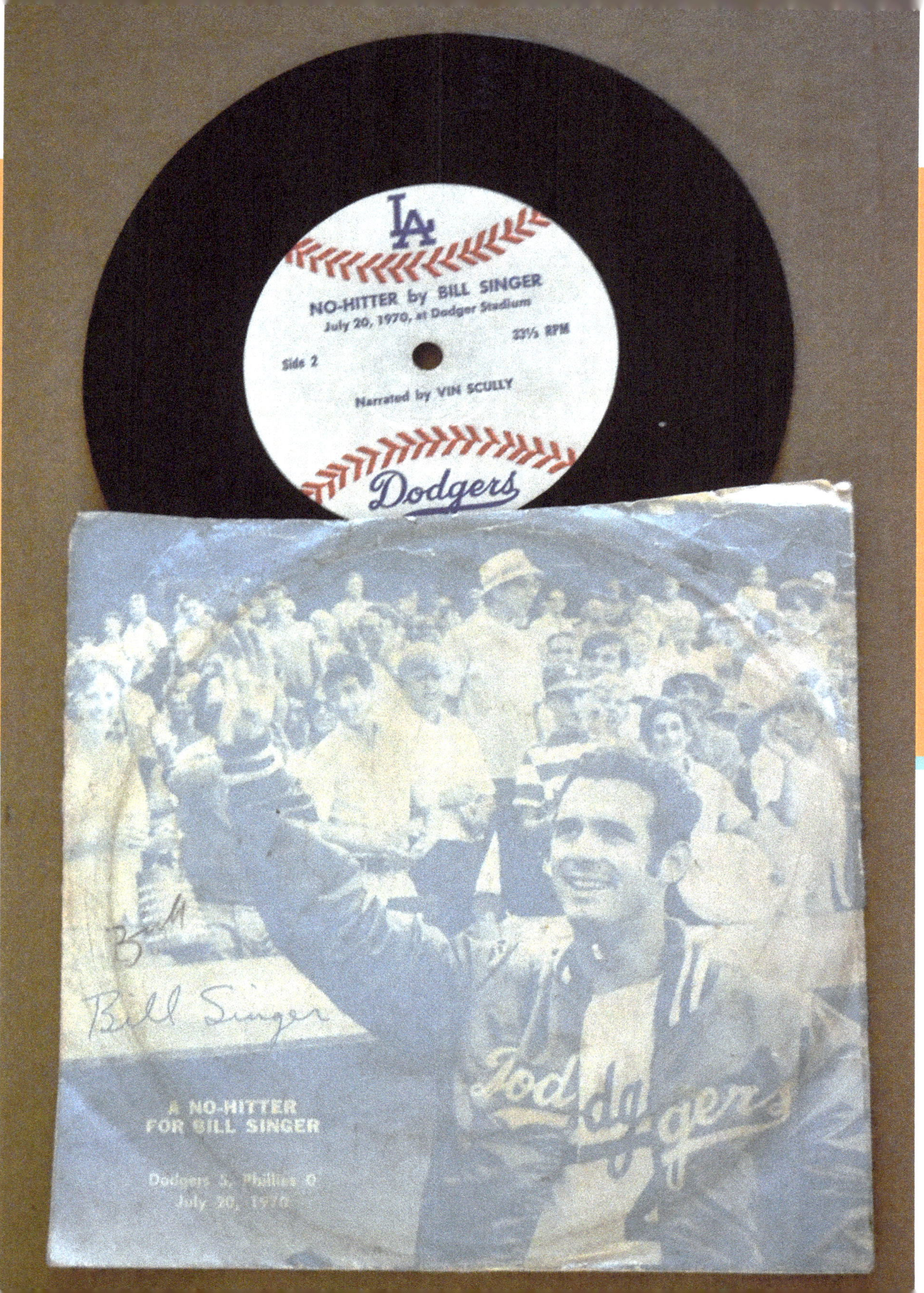

LA

NO-HITTER by BILL SINGER

July 20, 1970, at Dodger Stadium

33⅓ RPM

Side 2

Narrated by VIN SCULLY

Dodgers

Bill Singer

A NO-HITTER
FOR BILL SINGER

Dodgers 5, Phillies 0
July 20, 1970

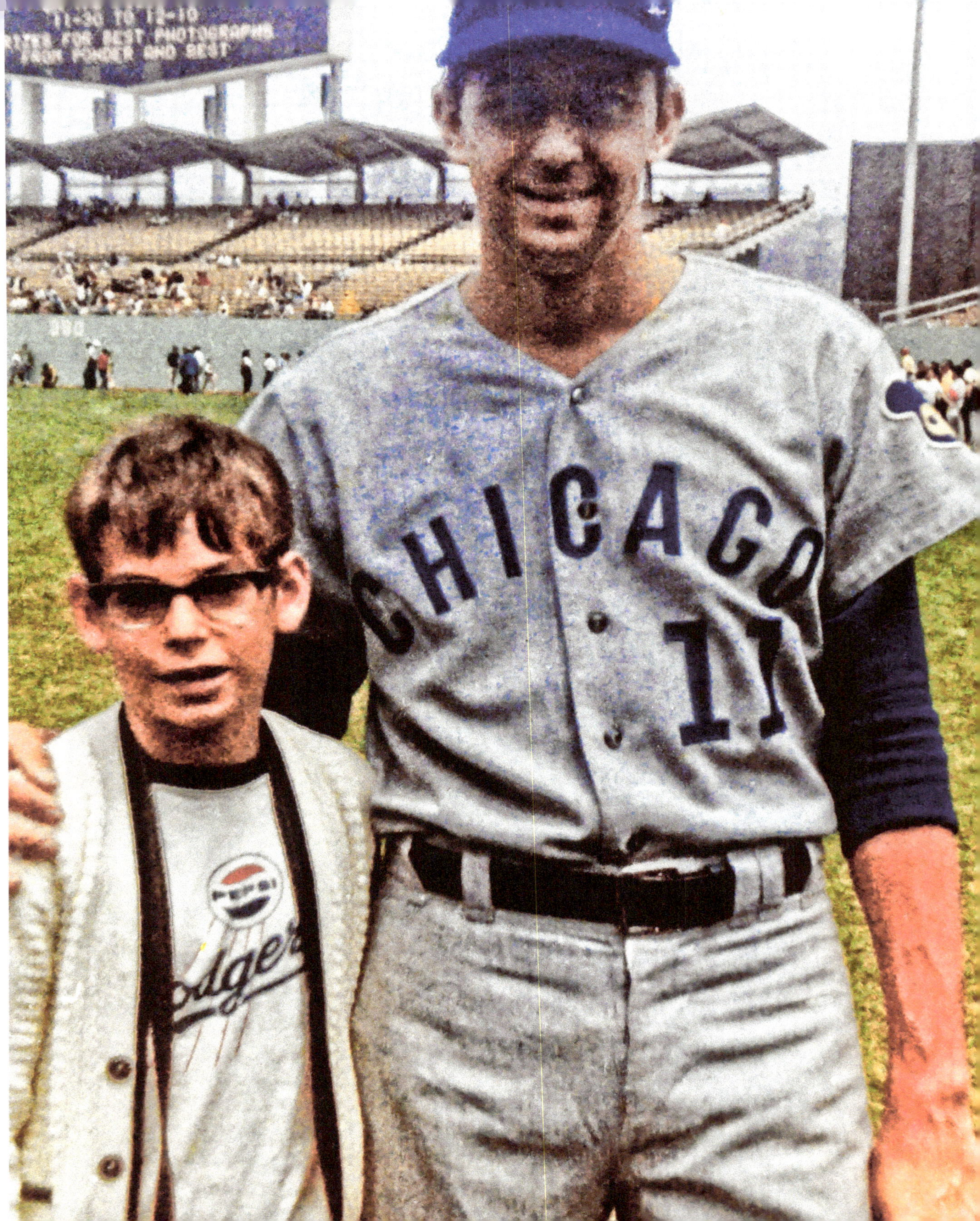

11:30 TO 12:10
TES FOR BEST PHOTOGRAPHS
FROM PONDER AND BEST
CHICAGO
11
PEPSI
odgers

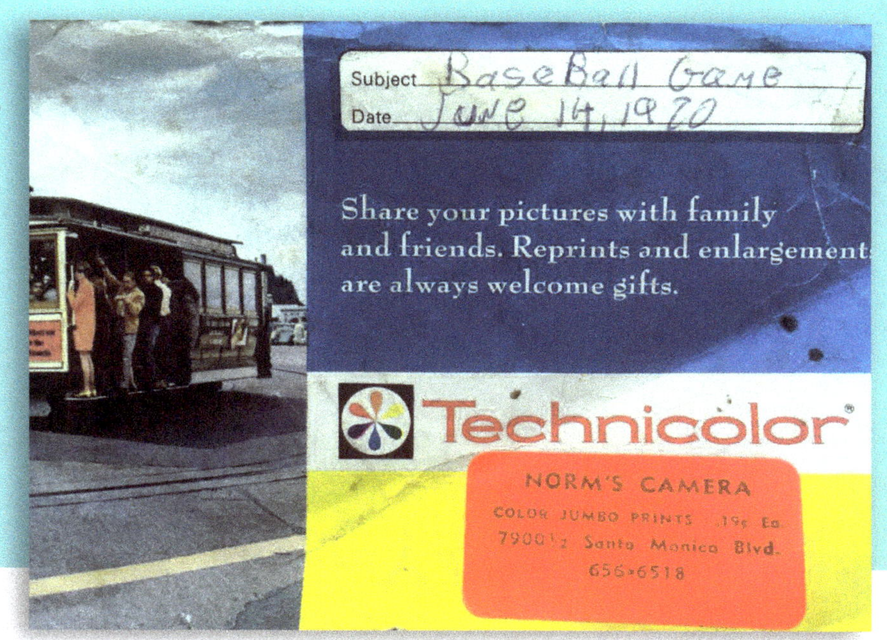

July 20, 1970, with another Dodger-Pepsi Fan Club ticket, I witnessed Bill Singer's no-hitter in front of a sparse crowd of 12,454. Win or lose, the best part of being at Dodger Stadium in the '70s was the echo and cadence of Vin Scully emanating from the thousands of transistor radios in unison in Dodger Stadium and throughout Los Angeles.

Left: Fans get up close to their heroes on Fan Appreciation Day. Chicago Cubs shortstop Don Kessinger was a 6-time all-star. Going on the field at Dodger Stadium was a dream come true for this kid, and for one dollar I received a T-shirt, six Dodger tickets, and membership in the Dodger Pepsi Fan Club! 1970. **Top Right:** You have to take the film somewhere! Digital photography was decades away! 1970.

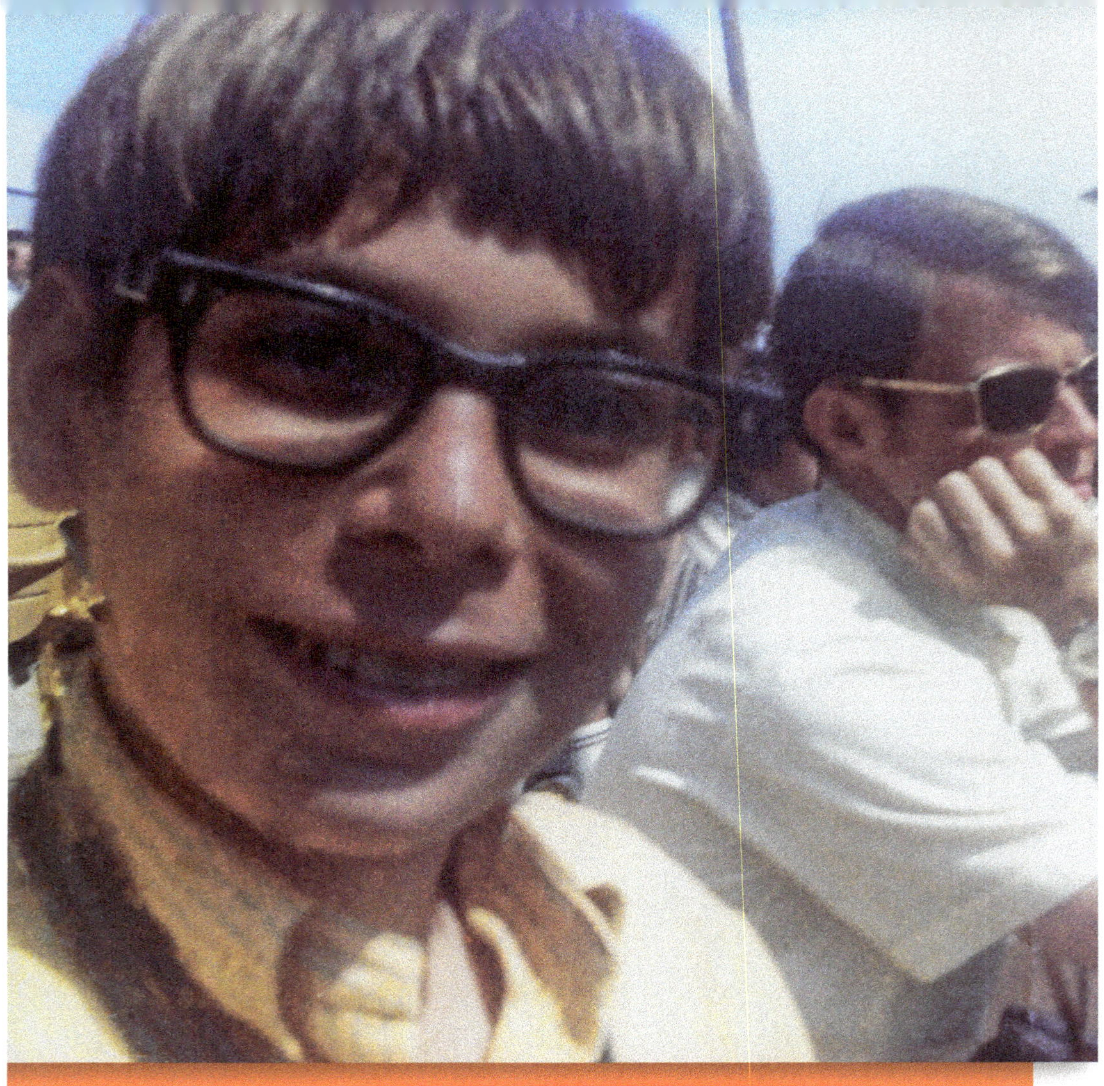

Top Left: Those super-cool glasses I wore weren't so cool when I was 13, when this picture was taken. Not many kids in those days wore glasses. Now the guy sitting next to me at Dodger Stadium, those are cool frames! 1972. **Right:** Old Timers Day: Dodger pitcher Larry Sherry, MVP of the 1959 World Series as a rookie, was an L.A. native and Fairfax High graduate. He died in 2006. Old Timers Day was one of those "special" games, like Fan Appreciation Day, that I looked forward to. 1973.

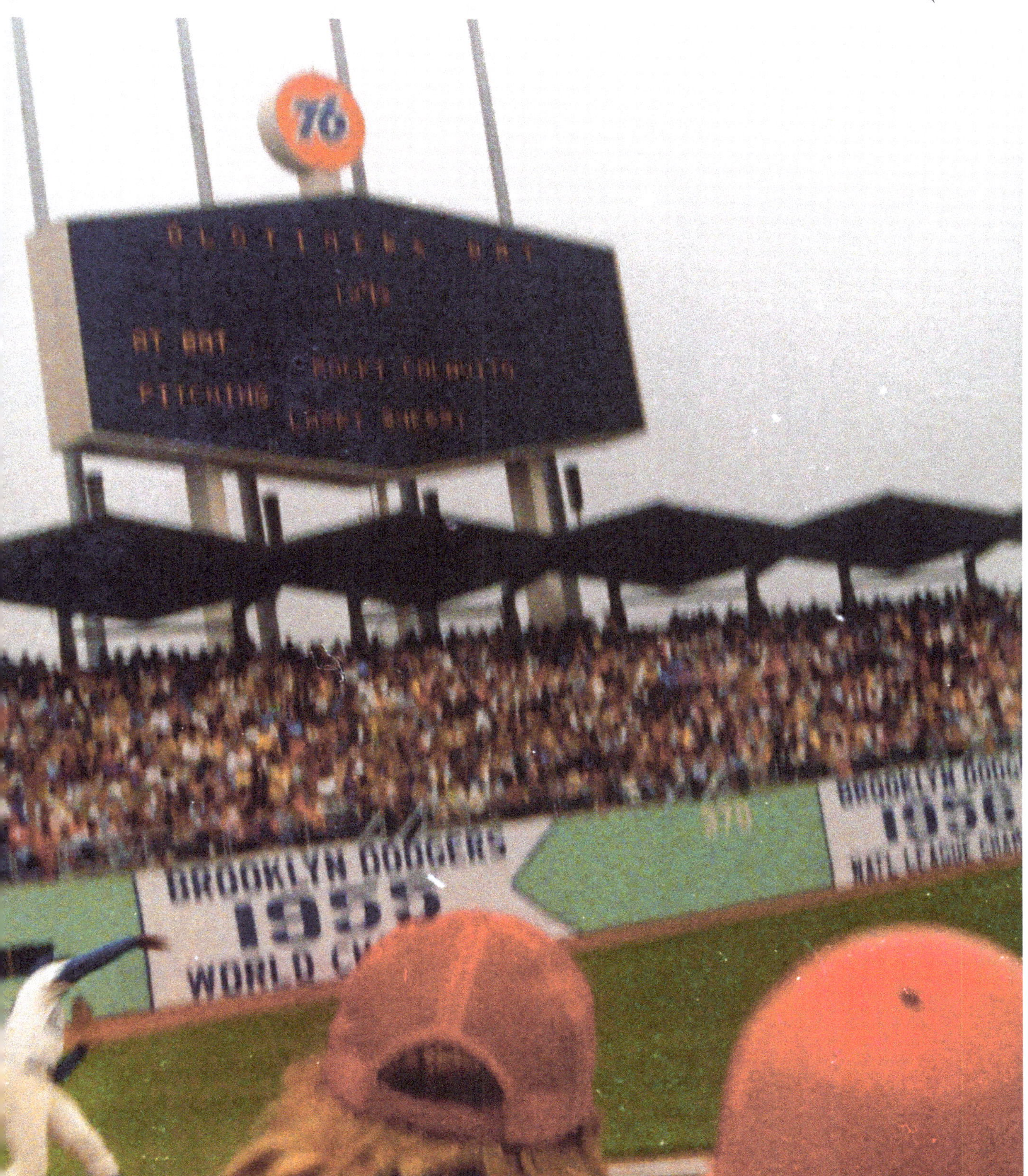
76
OLDTIMERS DAY
1978
AT BAT
PITCHING
BROOKLYN DODGERS
1955
WORLD CH
BROOKLYN DODGERS
1956
NAT'L LEAGUE CHAM

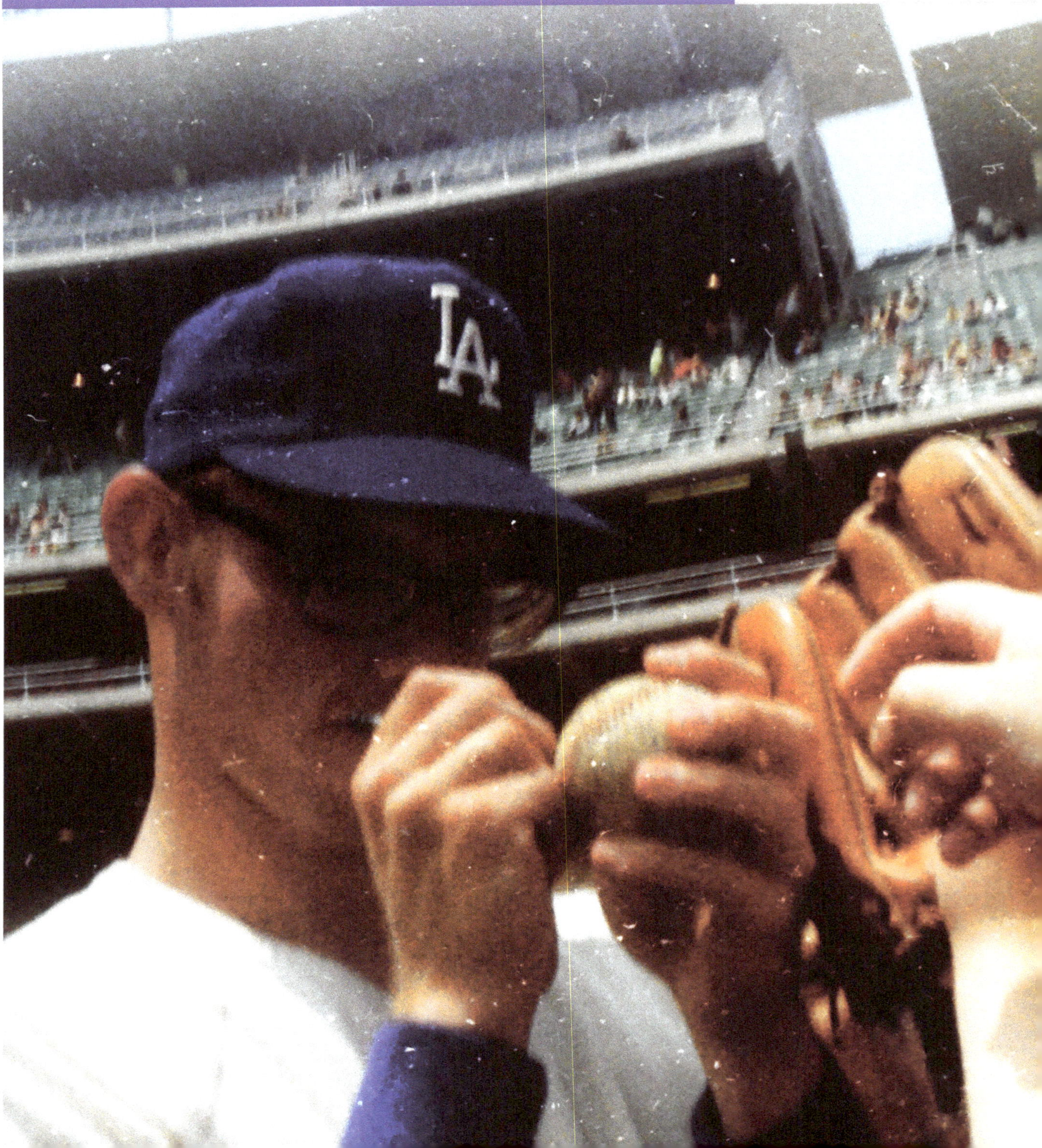

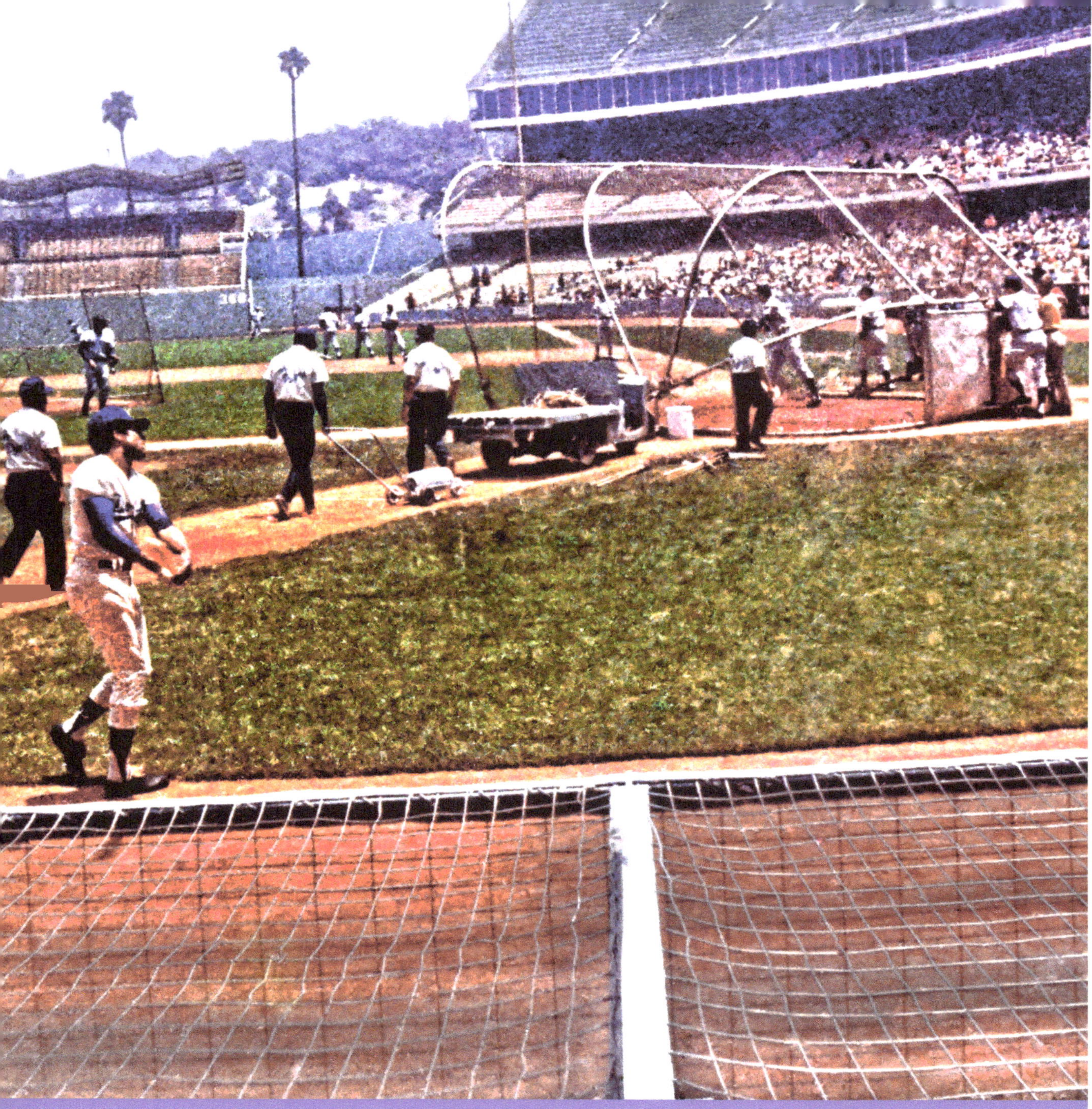

Left: *Please sign my ball! 1970.* **Top Right:** *Pregame.* The Dodger in the photo was #3 Willie Davis (1940-2010). He still holds Dodger records for most hits, runs, at-bats and extra-base hits, along with a 31-game hitting streak in 1969 that no Dodger has matched. Crowds were sparse in the early 1970s, but, for a 10-year-old kid, what could be better than a box seat at beautiful Dodger Stadium on a summer day. 1970.

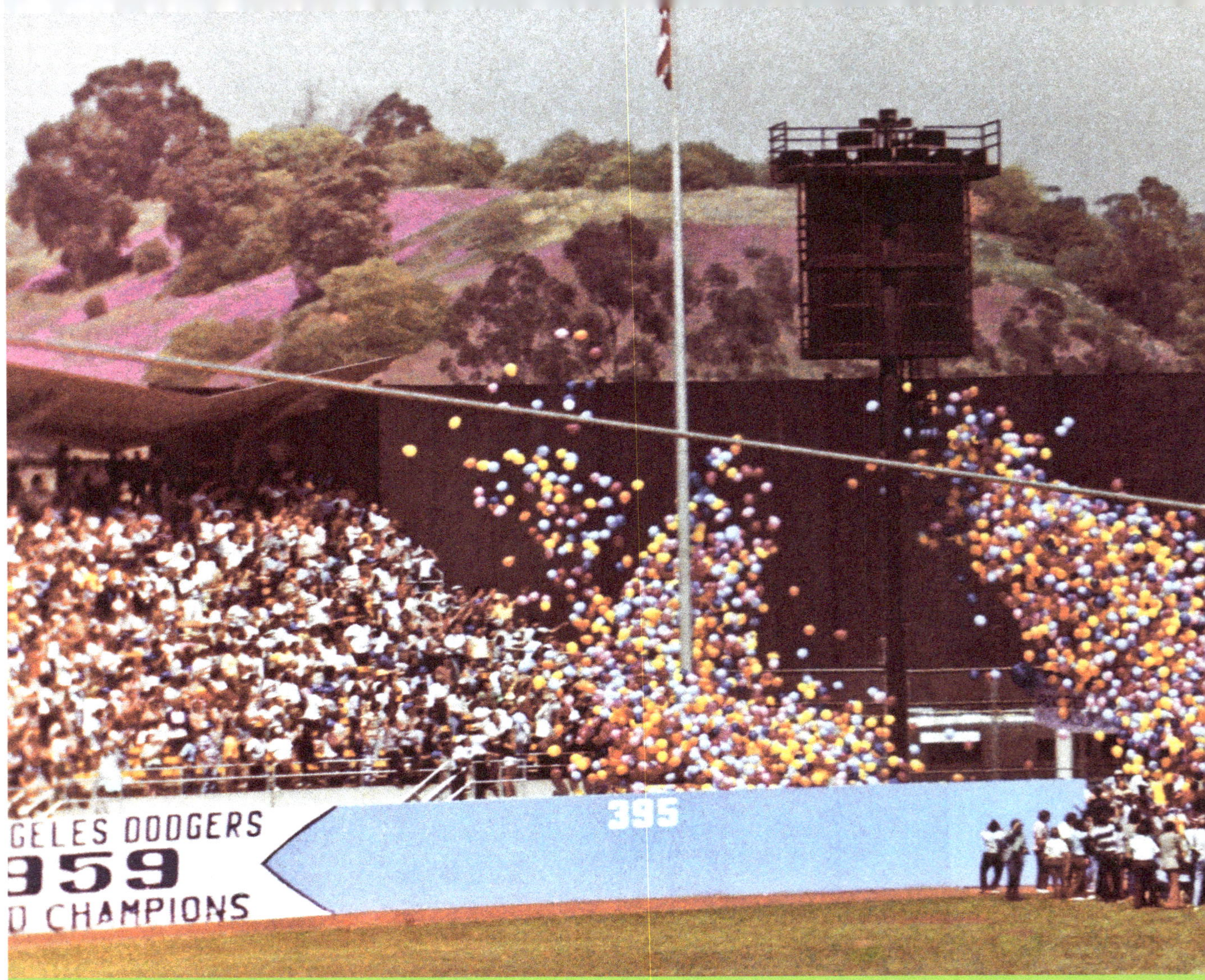

Top: Opening day! Hello, baseball fans, and welcome to Dodger Stadium. Thousands of transistor radios tuned into KABC 790 and the cadence of Vin Scully reverberates throughout Dodger Stadium and Los Angeles on Opening Day 1975. The Dodgers had won the National League pennant the prior year but lost to the Oakland A's in the World Series. 1975.

Bottom: The California Angels, long a sorry second to the Dodgers in terms of Southern California baseball, after 18 years of futility, win their division for the first time, and fans flood the field. I was in that flood. They lost the divisional playoff to Baltimore, and the following year came in dead last in their division—just my bad luck to buy season tickets. 1979.

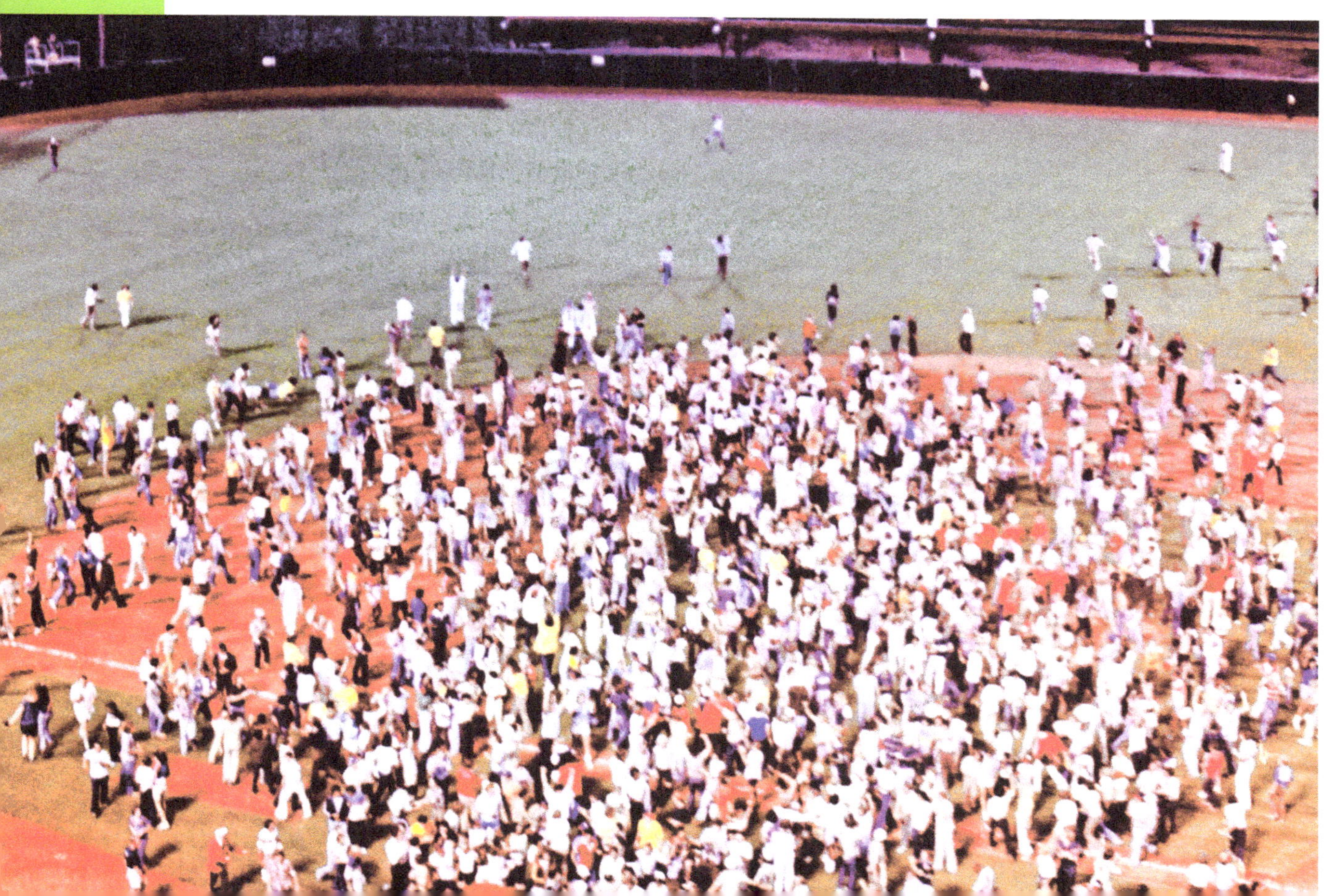

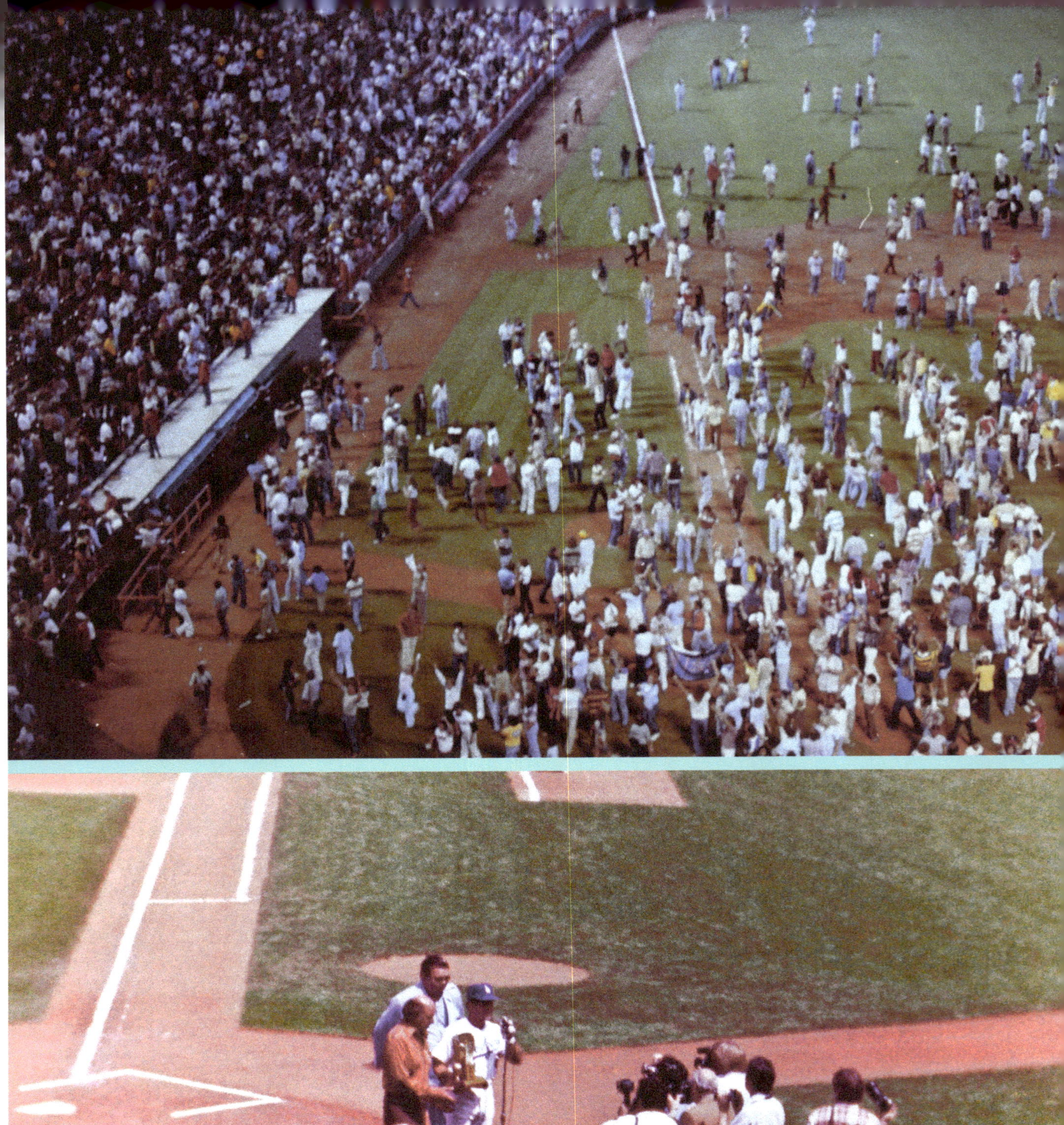

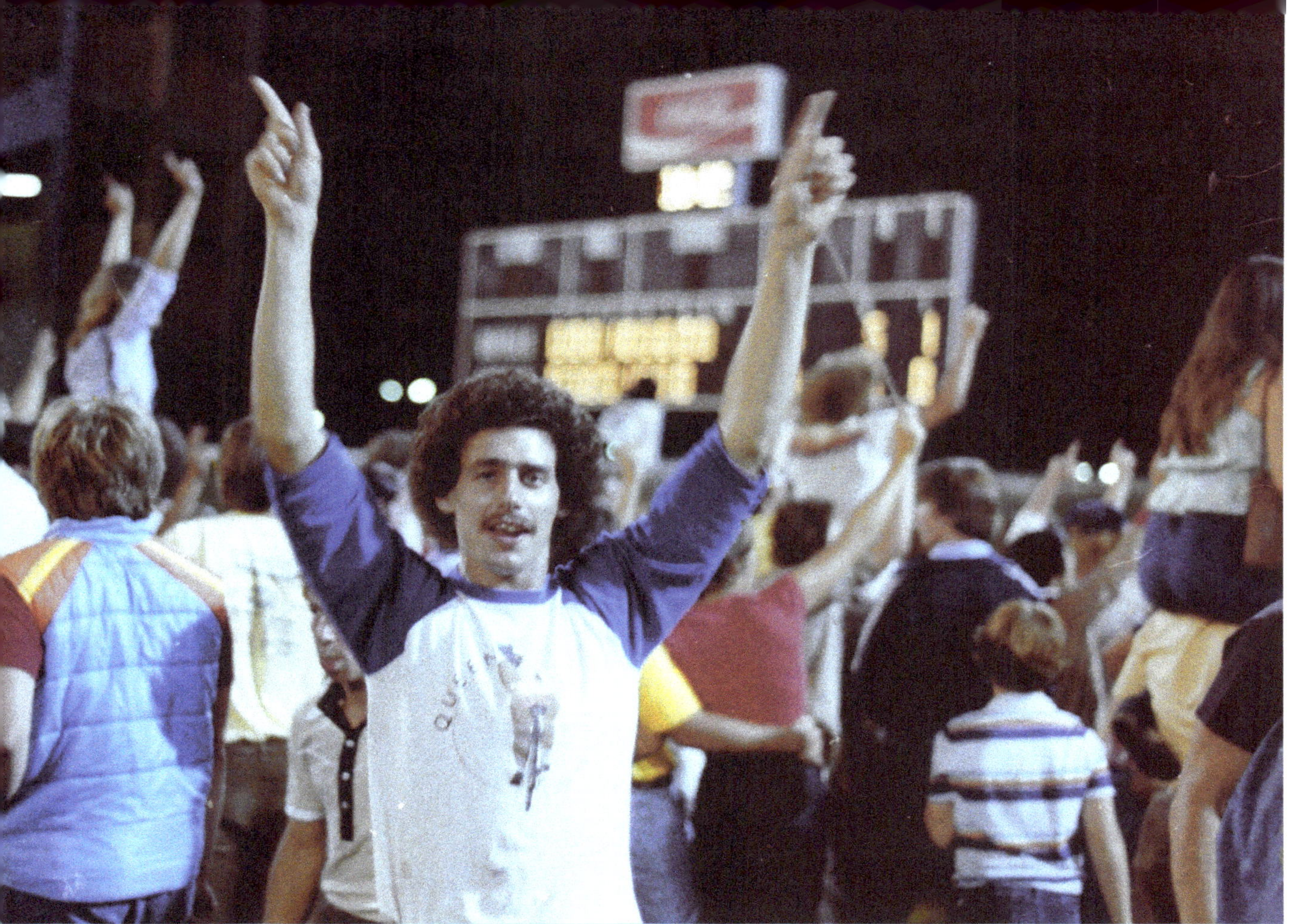

Top Left: Exuberant Angels fans had waited 18 years through mostly losing teams to jump onto the field, the ushers standing on the dugout feeling overwhelmed. Unlikely this scene will play out again in Southern California baseball. 1979. **Bottom Left:** Dodger first baseman Steve Garvey accepts his 1974 Gold Glove award on opening day 1975, the first of four consecutive Gold Gloves, to go along with his 1974 NL MVP award. In my opinion, Garvey should be in the Hall of Fame. Dig the polyester suits and bell bottoms. 1975. **Top Right:** Even this New Yorker was happy for the Angels. I wish I had kept some of my rock 'n roll t-shirts. 1979.

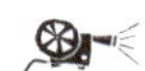

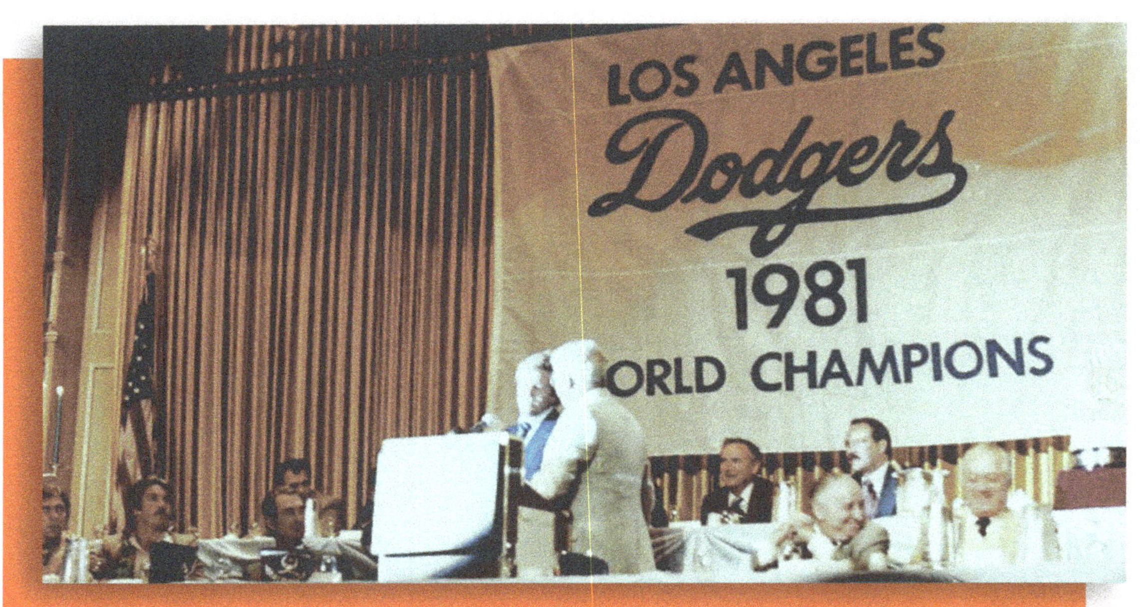

LOS ANGELES
Dodgers
1981
WORLD CHAMPIONS

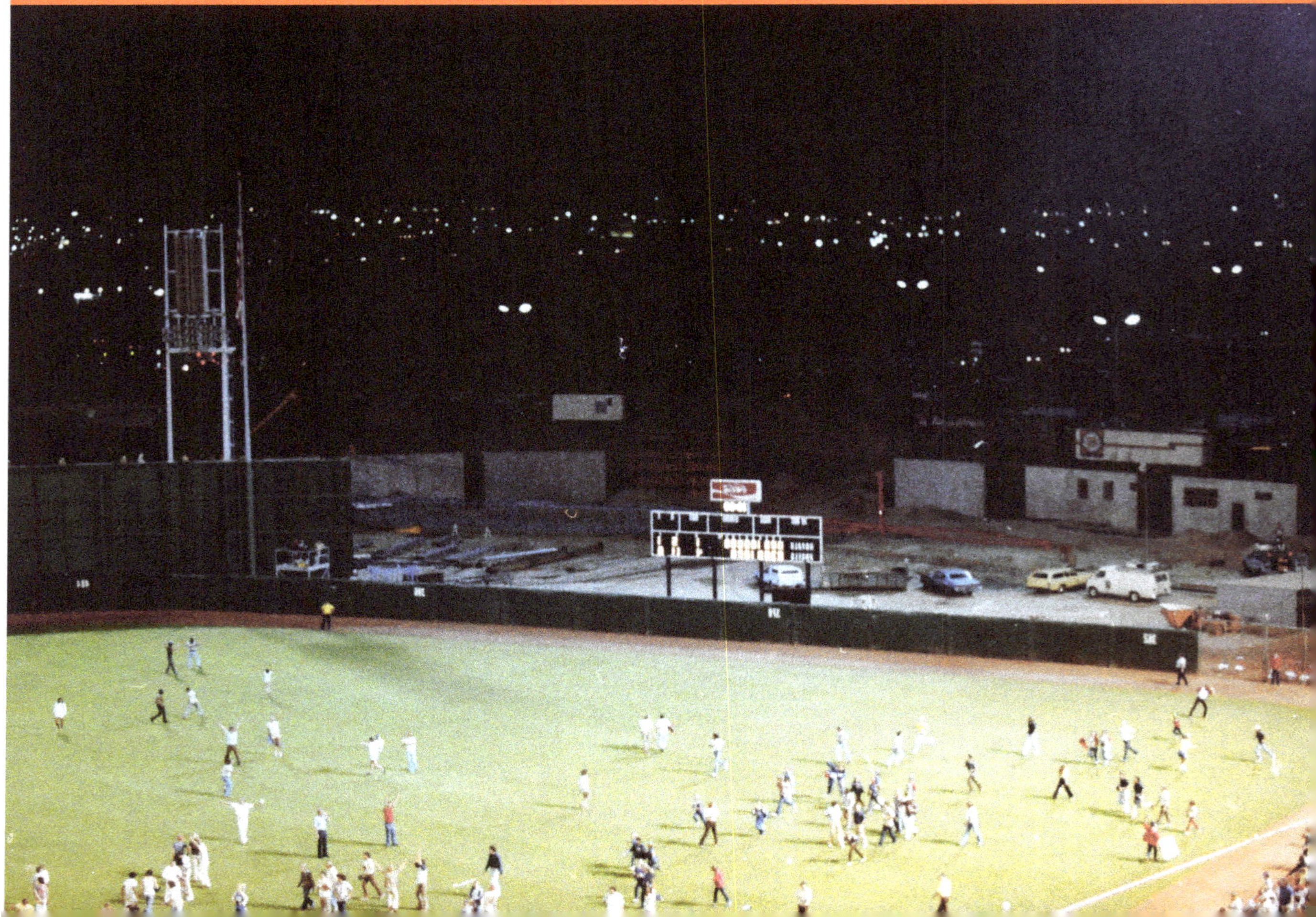

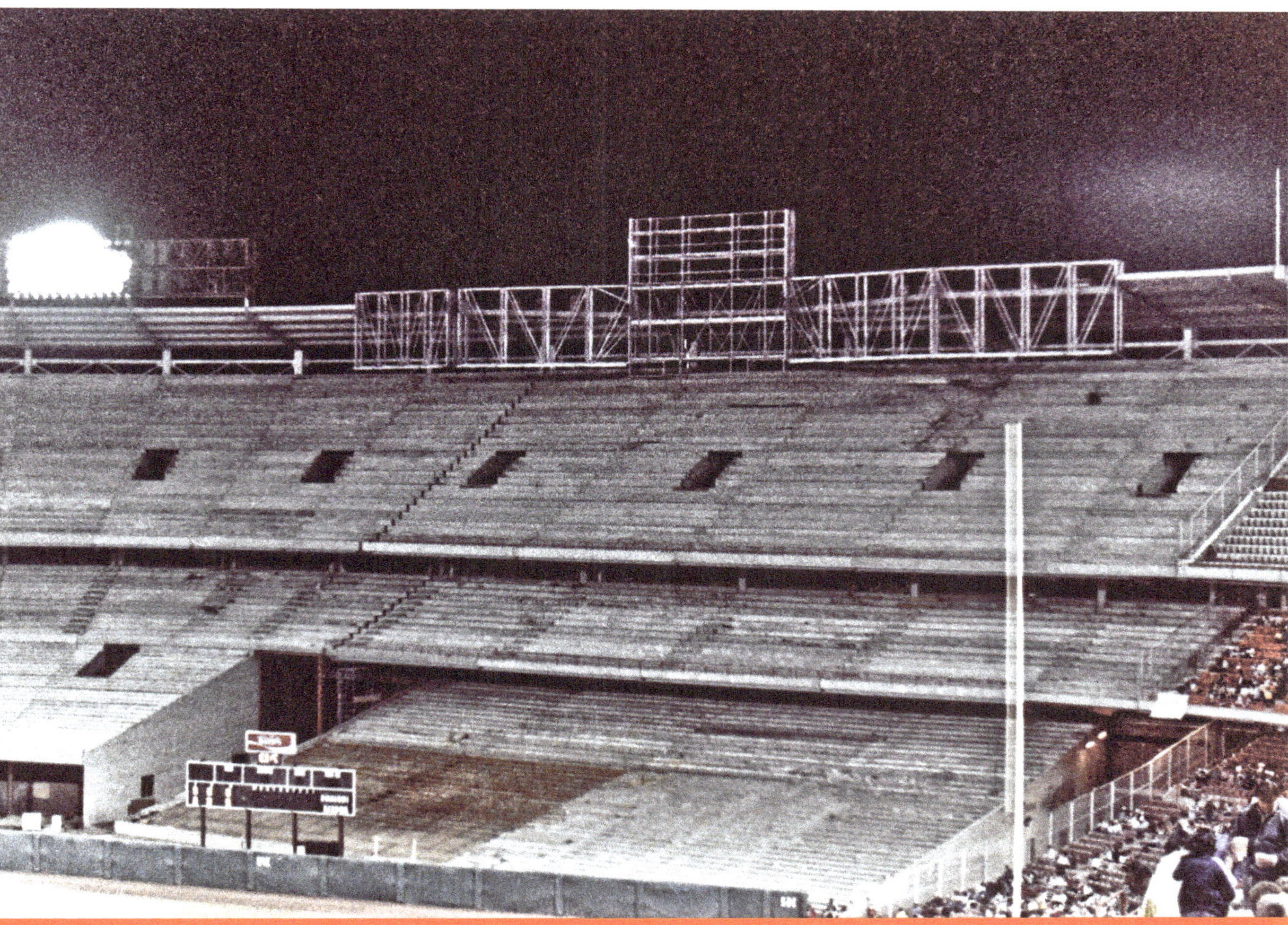

Top Left: A rare sight was seen only twice in the past 40 years in Los Angeles: The Dodgers celebrating a World Series victory. Old-school Shriner's roast. My father was a member of the Westwood Shrine Club. 1982. **Bottom Left:** An odd sight: Fans on the field, right field a construction zone, the scoreboard high school quality. The character of the original "Big A" demolished. High-density Orange County is not far in the future. 1979. **Top Right:** Los Angeles Rams move to Anaheim. When you make a baseball stadium into a multi-purpose football and baseball stadium, you lose the view, and you lose the soul (see the previous photo). Rams played at Anaheim until 1994 and then bailed for St. Louis. 1980.

SCHOOL
THE CONCRETE JUNGLE

School from 1971 to 1974 was Bancroft Junior High in Hollywood and, after that Fairfax High on Melrose Avenue. Like most schools in urban Los Angeles, Bancroft was a concrete jungle school, surrounded by factories, industrial plants, and movie studios. The old main brick building, built in 1929, lasted one semester after the 1971 Sylmar earthquake condemned it, and prefabricated "bungalows" with no air conditioning were brought in, squeezing what was left of the concrete playground and making a challenging learning environment . . . well . . . challenging.

Above: My High School senior photo. By that time I'd had enough of school and crowded Los Angeles, and it was time to move to the leafy suburbs of Orange County. 1977.

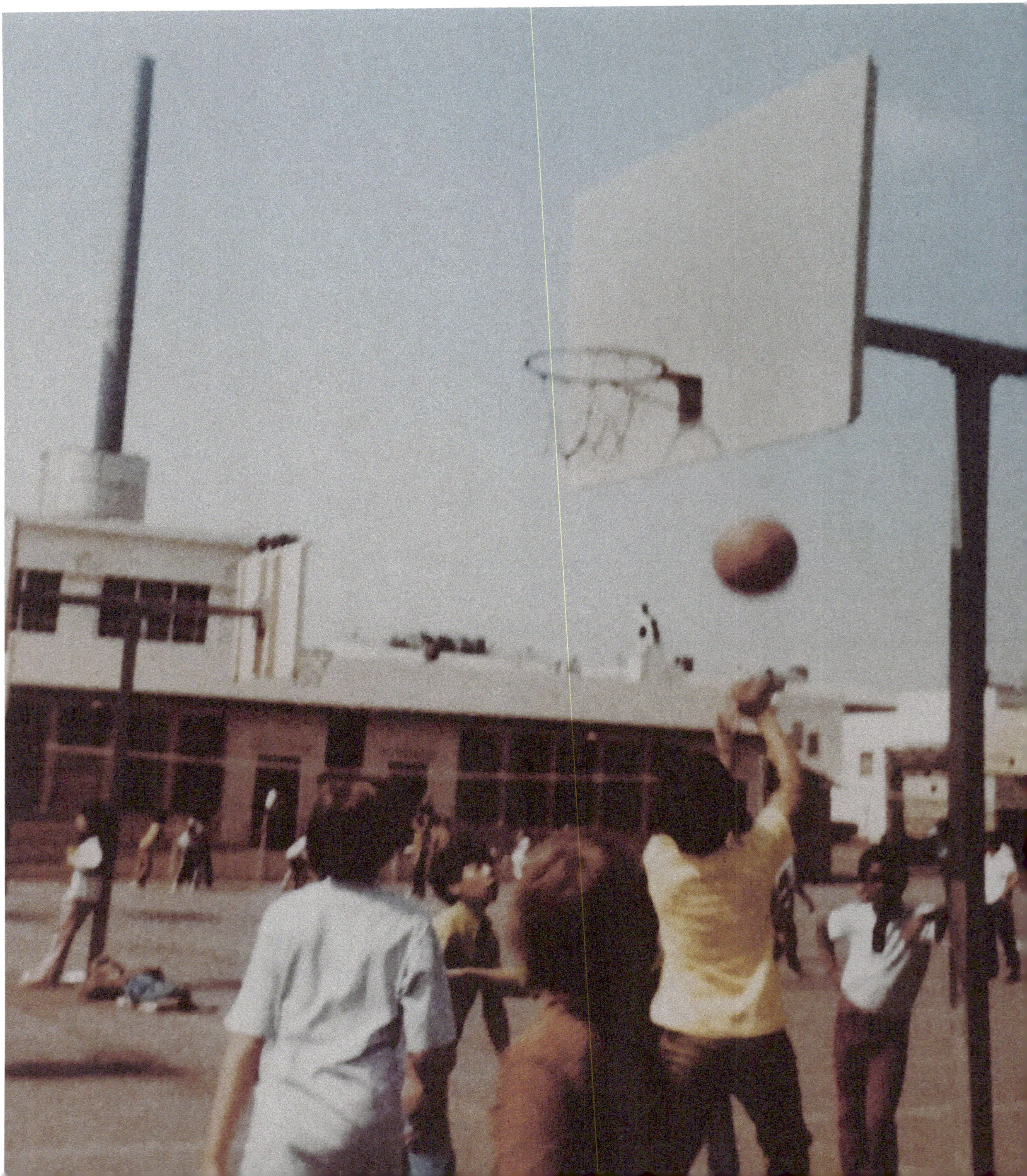

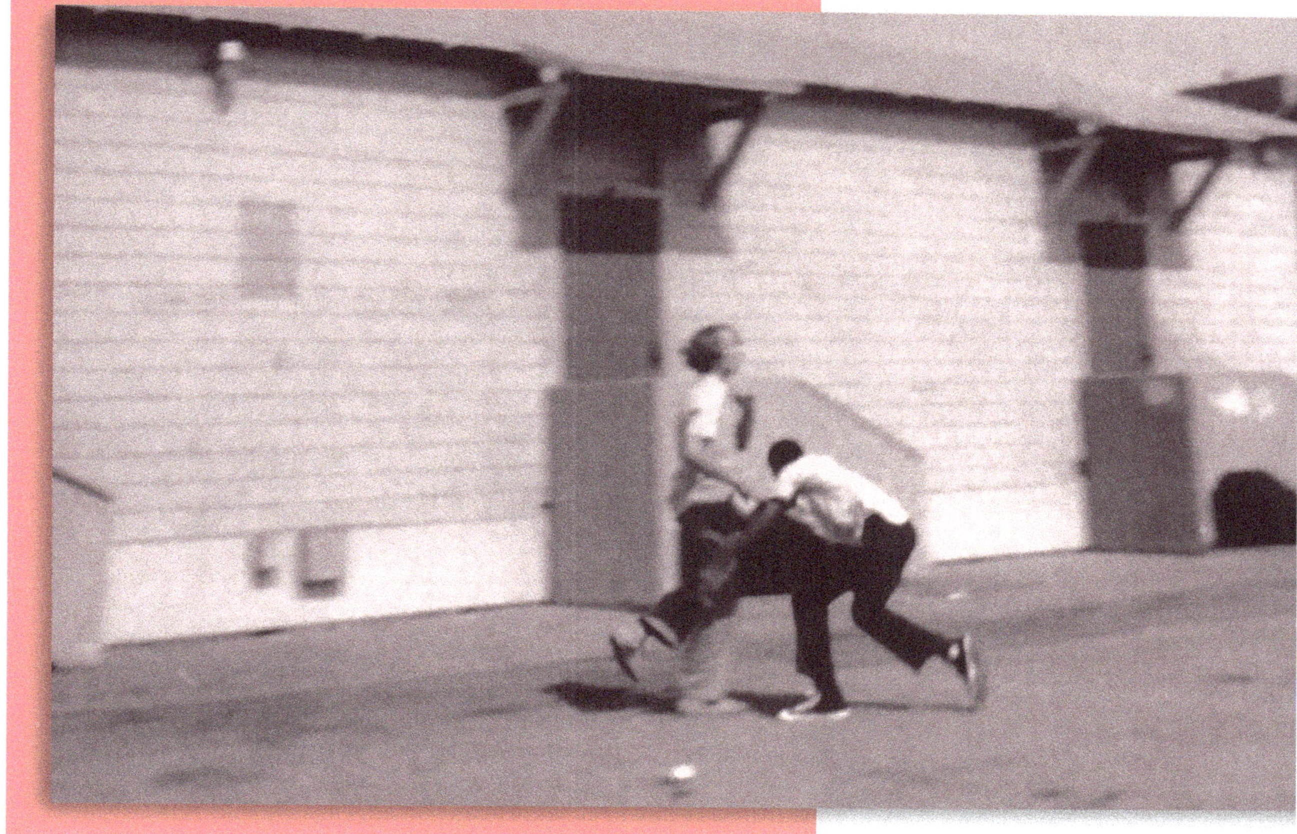

The old main building at Bancroft Junior High's claim to fame is the final scene in the final episode of *The Fugitive* in 1967. More than 70 million people viewed that episode, the highest-rated TV show until *Roots* 10 years later.

Left: Hoops and Stacks: American Linen Supply Company is still there, stacks are long gone. Unlike football, basketball is meant for the street. 1972. **Top:** Rush the passer? You bet. Take-no-prisoners tackle football on the concrete playground. Bancroft Junior High. 1973.

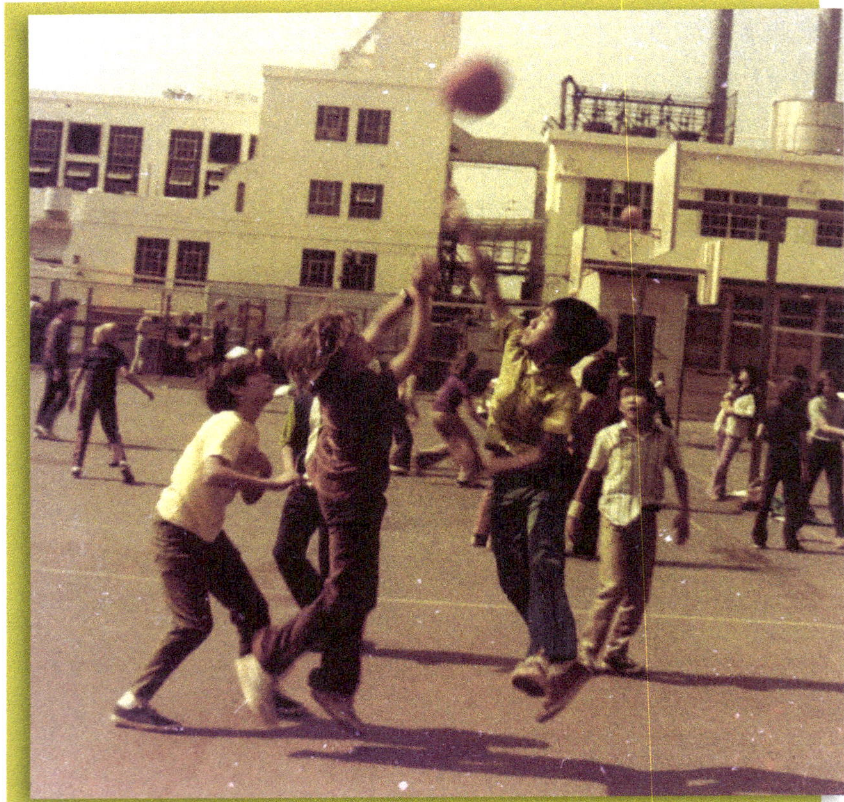

Left: The essence of the concrete-jungle playground: One of my favorite photos, taken with the Kodak Instamatic. American Linen Supply 900 N. Highland Avenue made a great industrial photo background but was a noisy neighbor. 1973. **Right:** Time to huddle: We took our tackle football seriously at Bancroft Junior High School in Hollywood, and we were not afraid to hit the ground. 1973.

The photos I took when I was 13 and 14 years of age were from a 126mm Kodak Instamatic, my first real camera. Yes, many of the "action" photos are grainy, but looking back almost 50 years, these grainy photos capture a school with a lot of diversity, when kids still held books, no backpacks, and no shorts worn except at gym. In these early photos, there is a playful seriousness and intensity that comes with urban living. Fairfax High class of '77 finished off my Los Angeles Unified School District education.

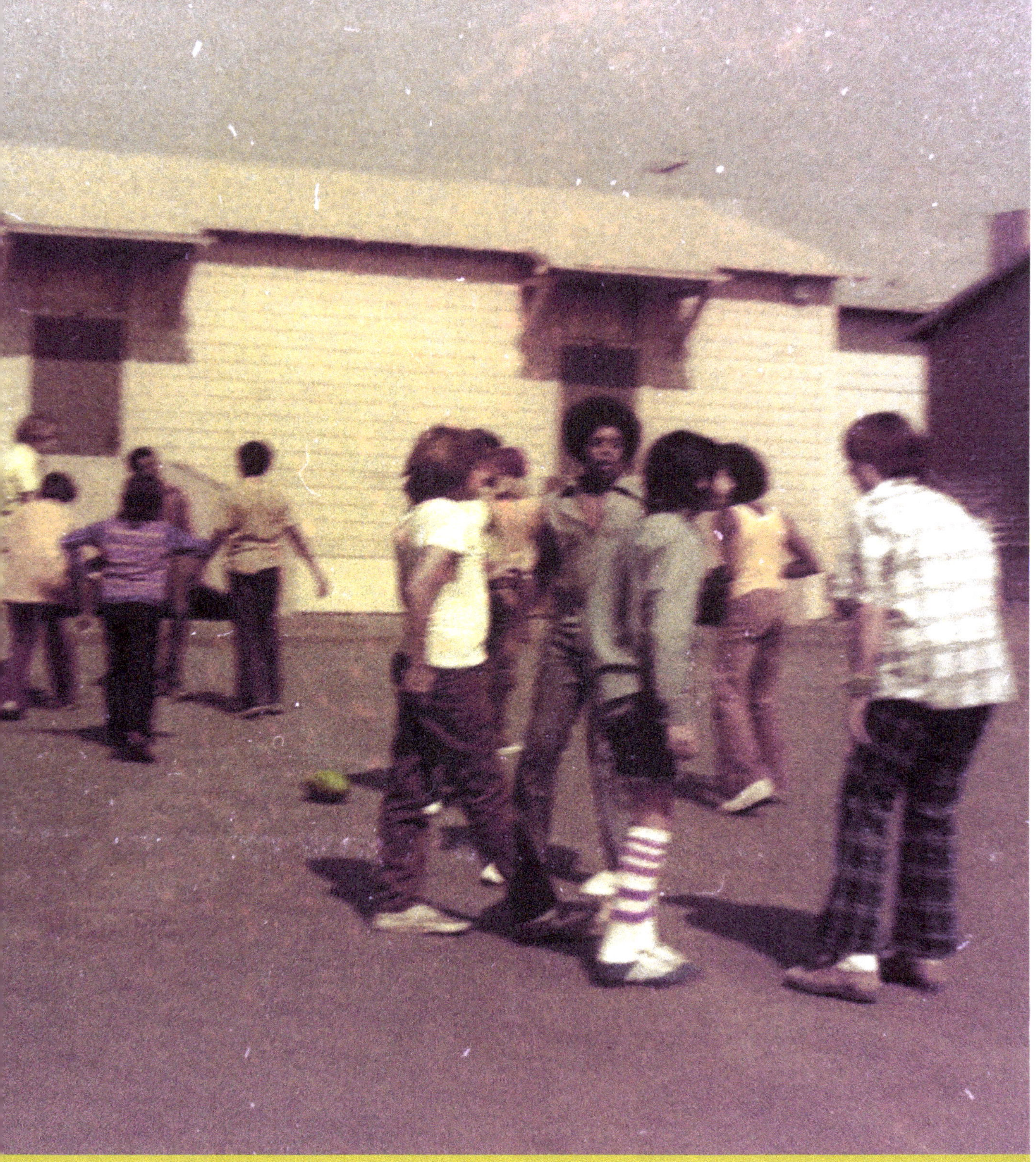

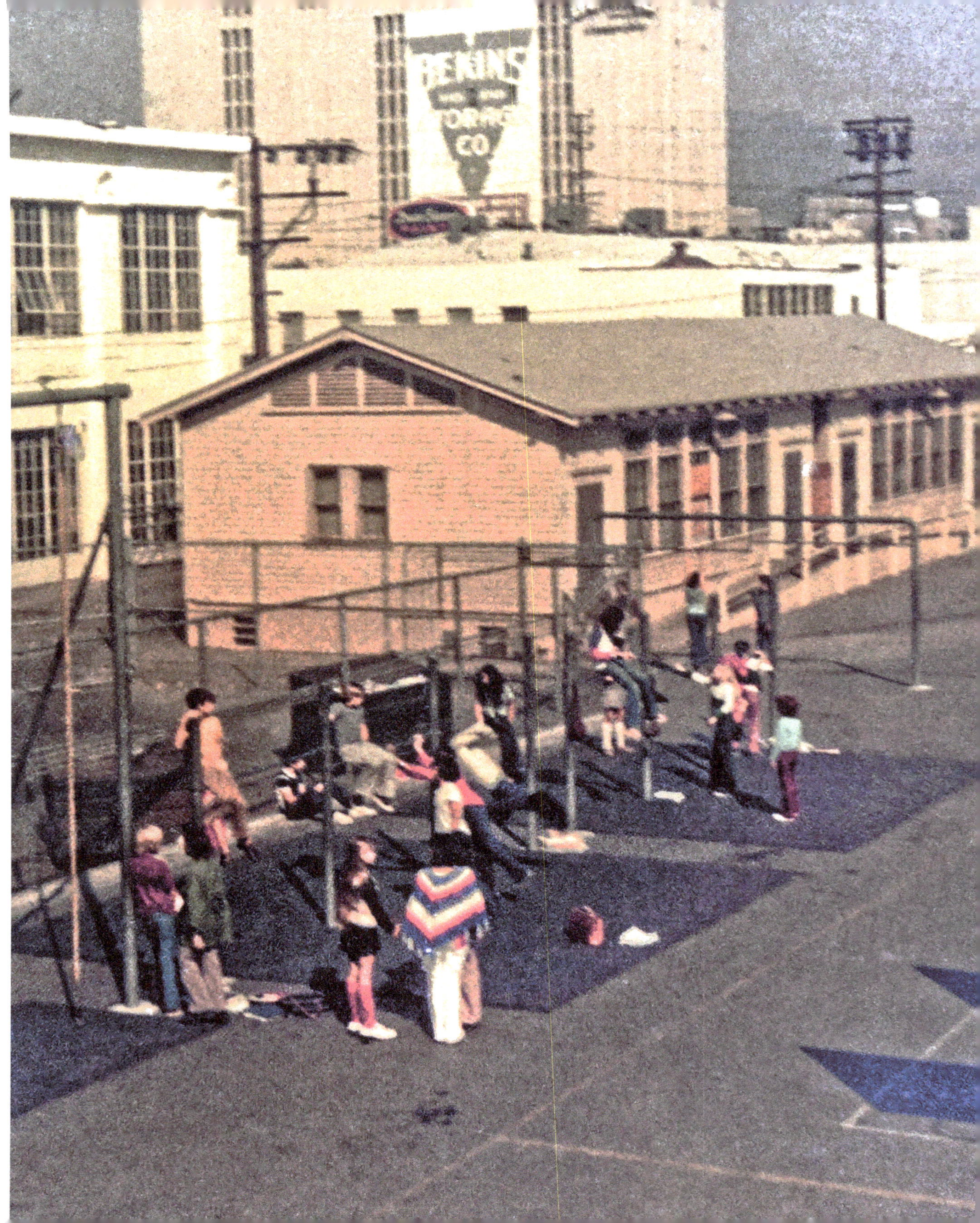
BEKINS
STORAGE
CO

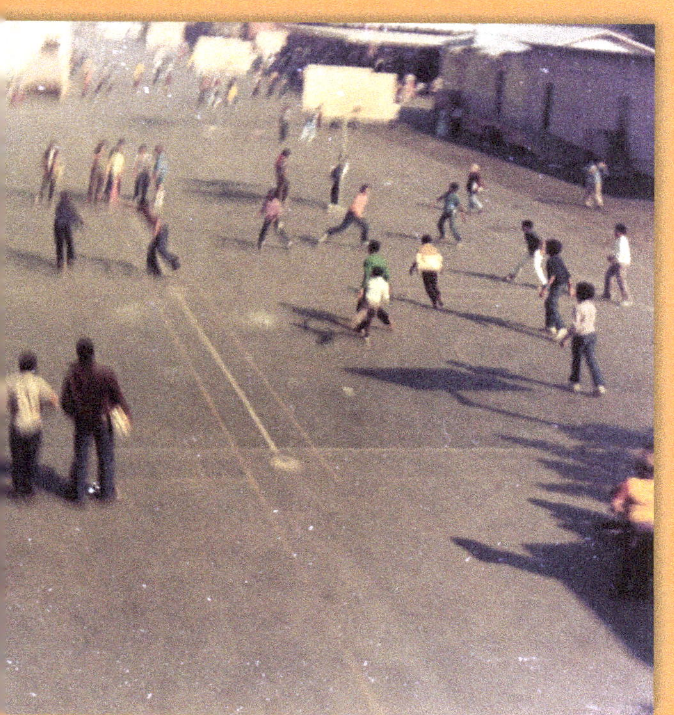

Far Left: A multitude of stories in this photo. Old-school playground with monkey bars; temporary "bungalows" installed after the 1971 Sylmar quake destroyed the main building. School policy was if the temperature hit 100 degrees, the school would close. Naturally, it never got above 99, and the bungalows had no air conditioning or heating; American Linen Supply building, a loud and stinky neighbor; the fortress-like Bekins Storage building, 1025 N. Highland, was the tallest building in Hollywood in 1925 when it was built. 1973. **Left:** Concrete jungle playground in motion. 1973. **Bottom:** The legendary English teacher Mr. Greenspan kept smiling for the camera. It was hard to get a good composition with the very basic Instamatic, but hey, I was only 14 and still learning! 1973.

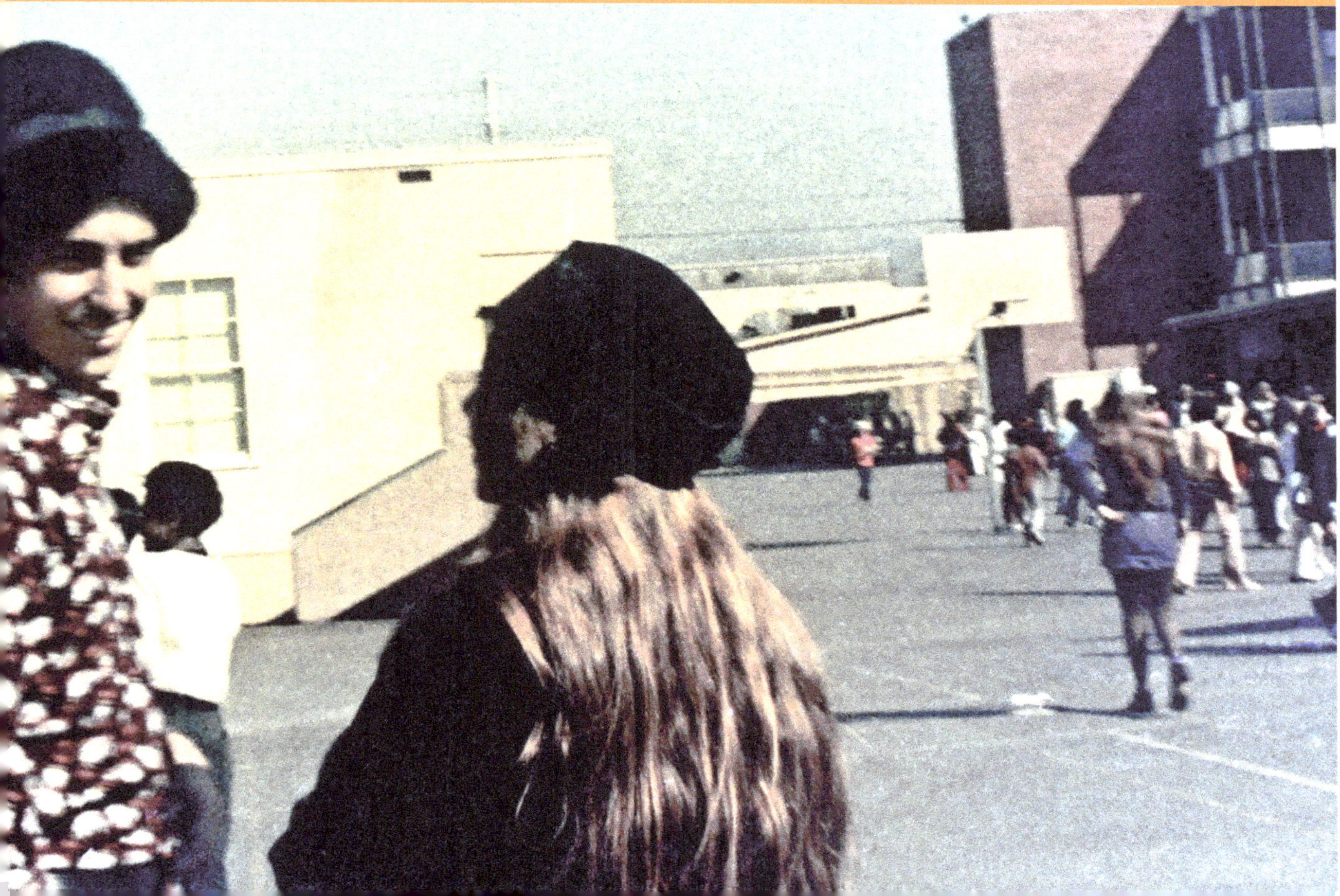

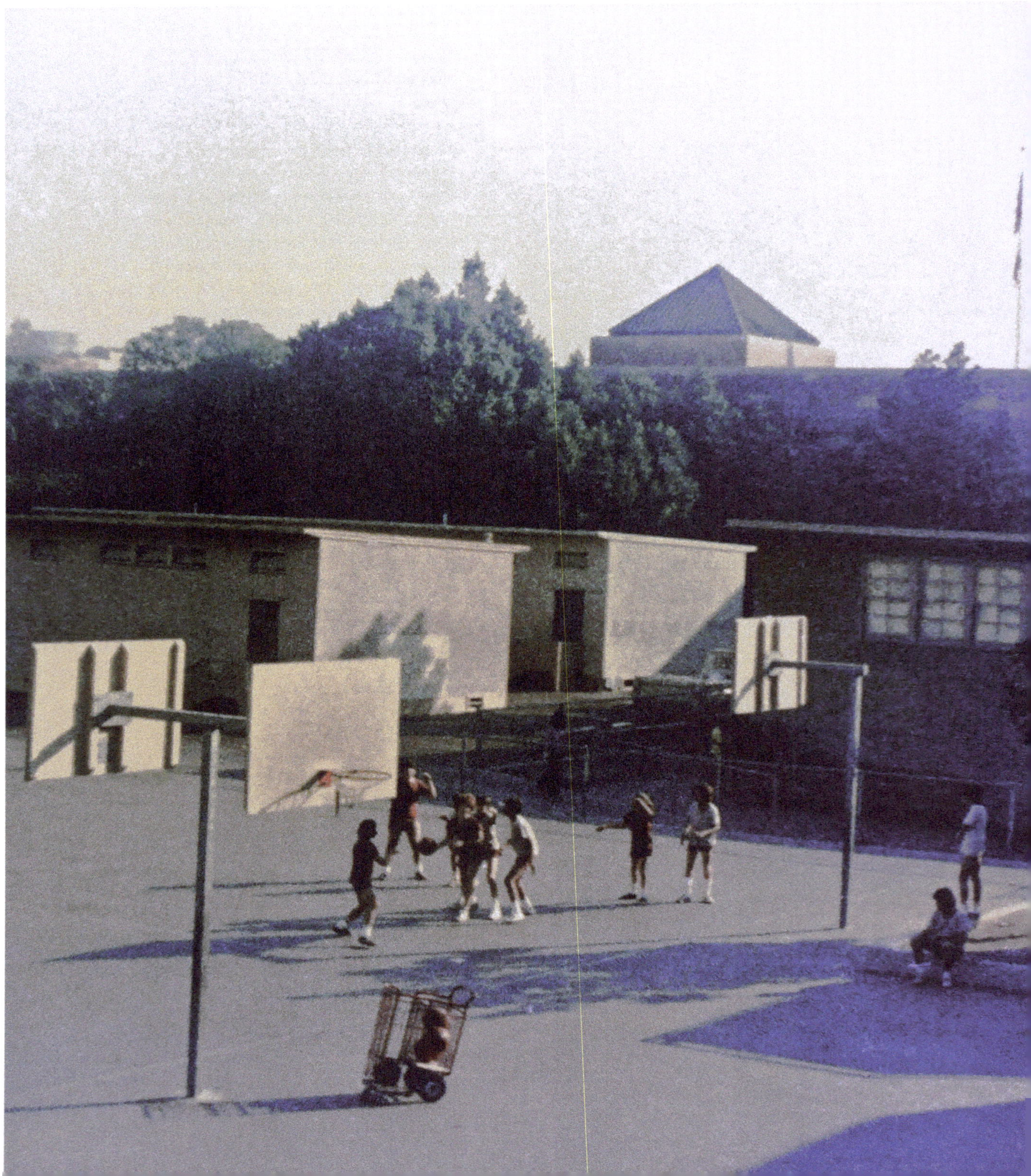

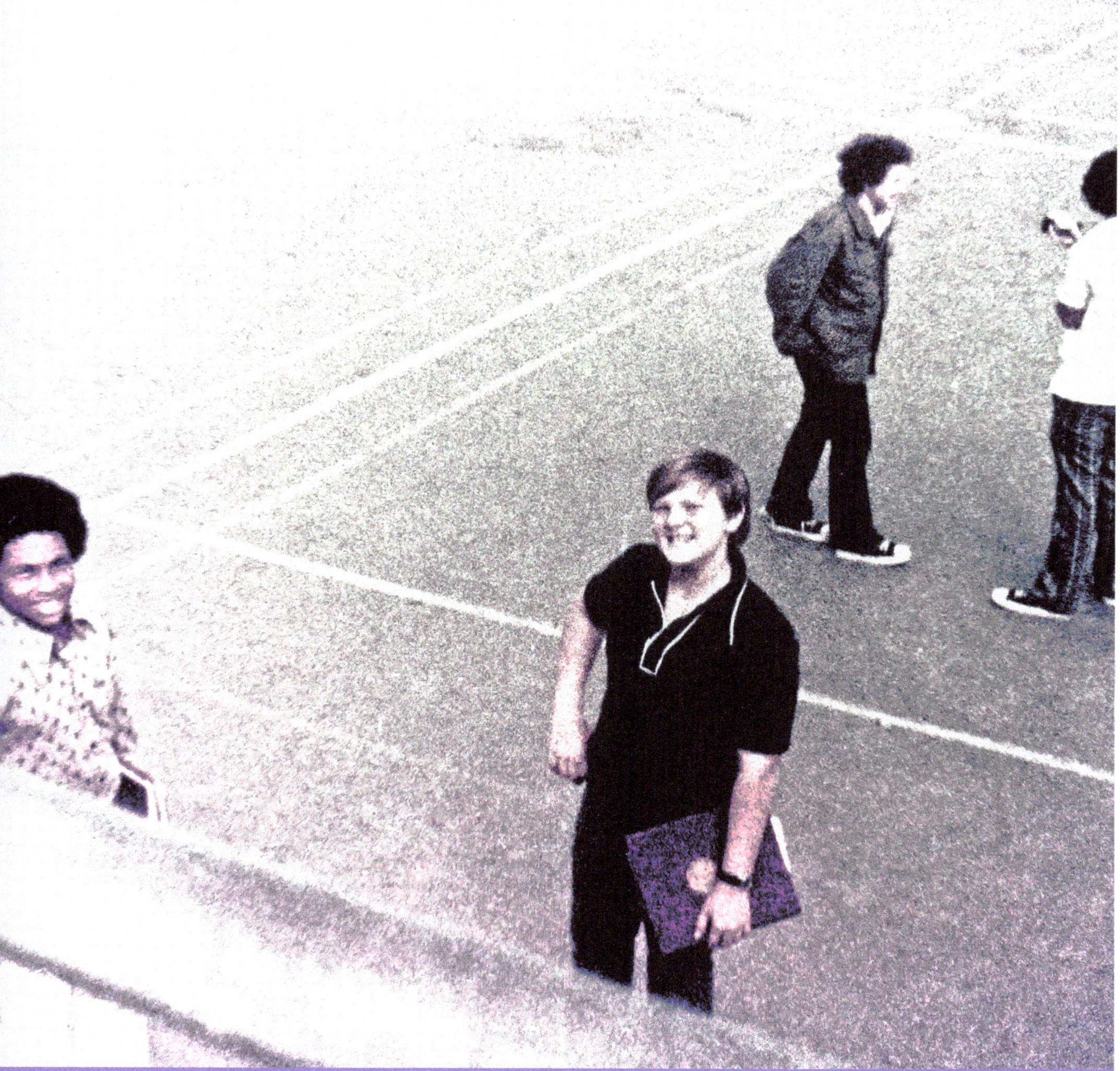

Left: The building with the pyramid-shaped roof was the original brick main building that opened with the school in 1929. It lasted one semester after the February 9, 1971, Sylmar quake; then it was permanently closed and demolished. The all-concrete playground was squeezed further by the addition of portable "bungalows." The basketball courts with the plywood backboards and the sound of clanging wire netting were typical city-style courts. 1972. **Top:** '70s gritty playground style: Afro, polyester, Converse, carrying your books. 1972.

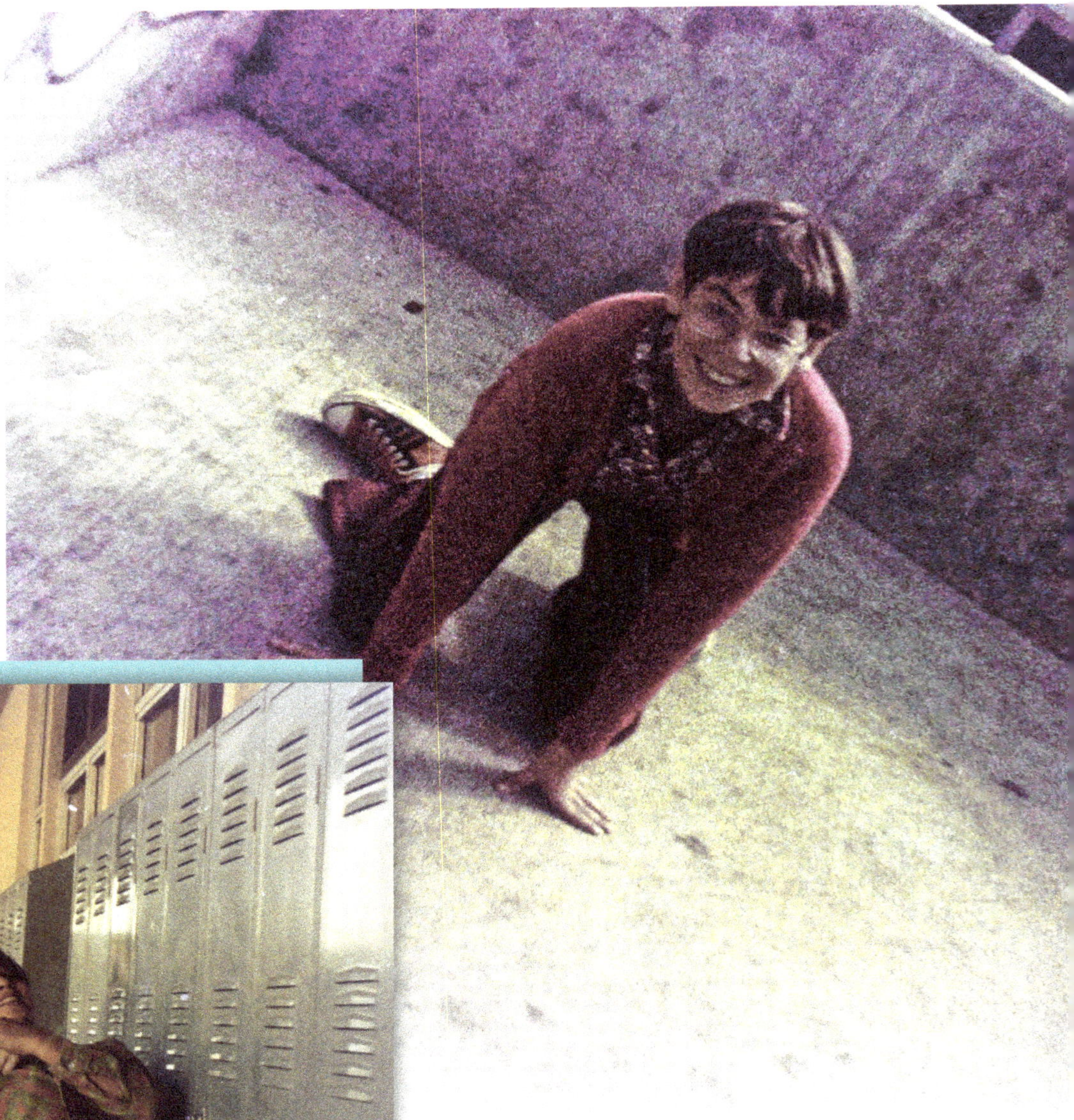

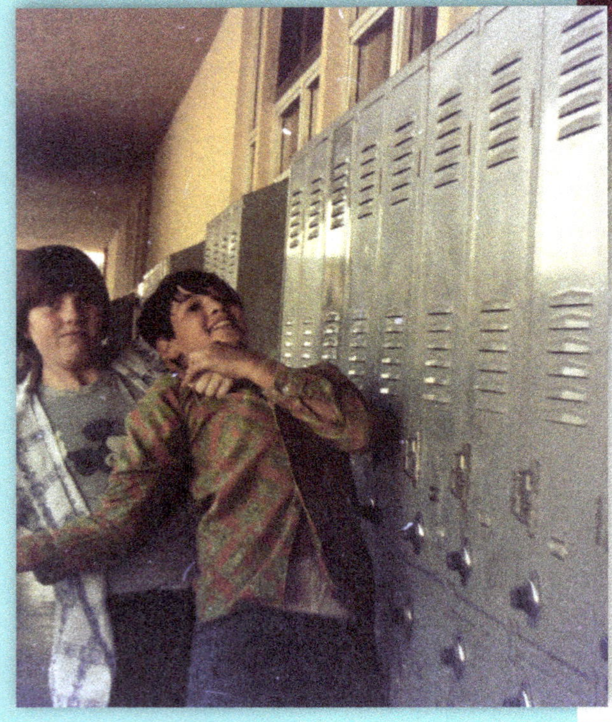

Left: The bully gets bullied. My friend Richard took care of this bully for me. I soon learned the art of fighting back, goodbye bullying. Bancroft Junior High in Hollywood was a tough inner-city school like so many others in the Los Angeles Unified School District. 1972. **Top:** The Boy Who Took the Photos: Except for the gold Converse shoes, I wasn't exactly stylin' in the decade that fashion forgot. 1973.

HARDWARE STORE EAST LOS ANGELES MY EDUCATION IN STREET

My experience in East L.A. was an experience few of my teenage peers shared: a white Jewish teenager working in Dad's hardware store in a tough neighborhood on Whittier Boulevard.

I worked in East Los Angeles for five years beginning in the summer of my 10th grade (1975) significantly enhancing my street and business education. Our stores—my Dad also brought the clothing store next door from old Mr. and Mrs. Heller—were jam-packed with merchandise, and in those pre-computer days, I knew every item in the store, inventory, how much they cost, and our retail price, all 20,000 items, all in my head. I had a natural inclination for business. It was also my job to get new business for the store, and my father asked me to take

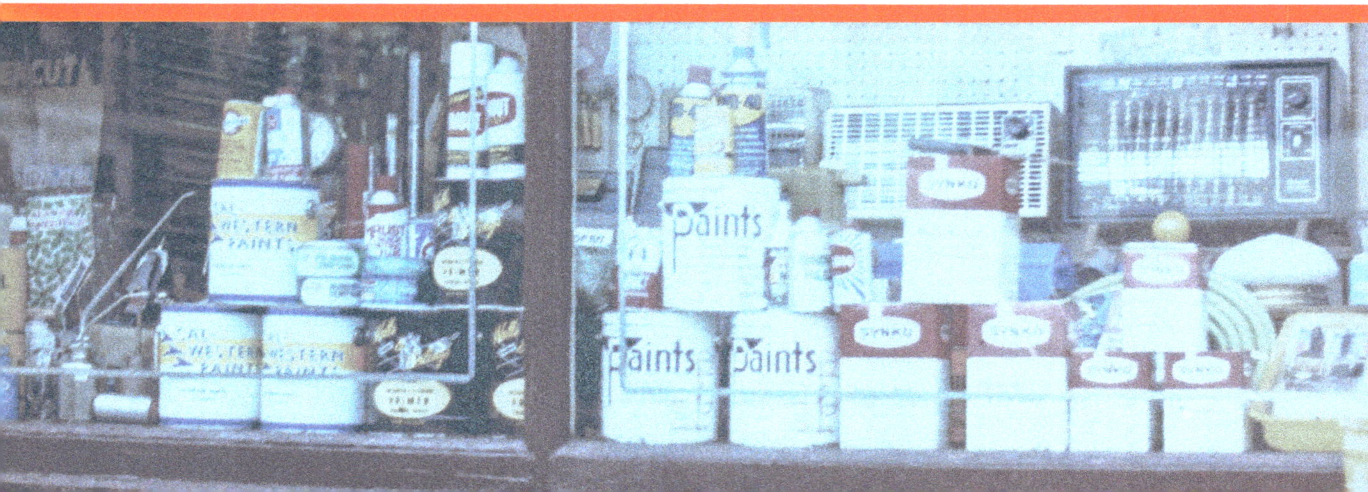

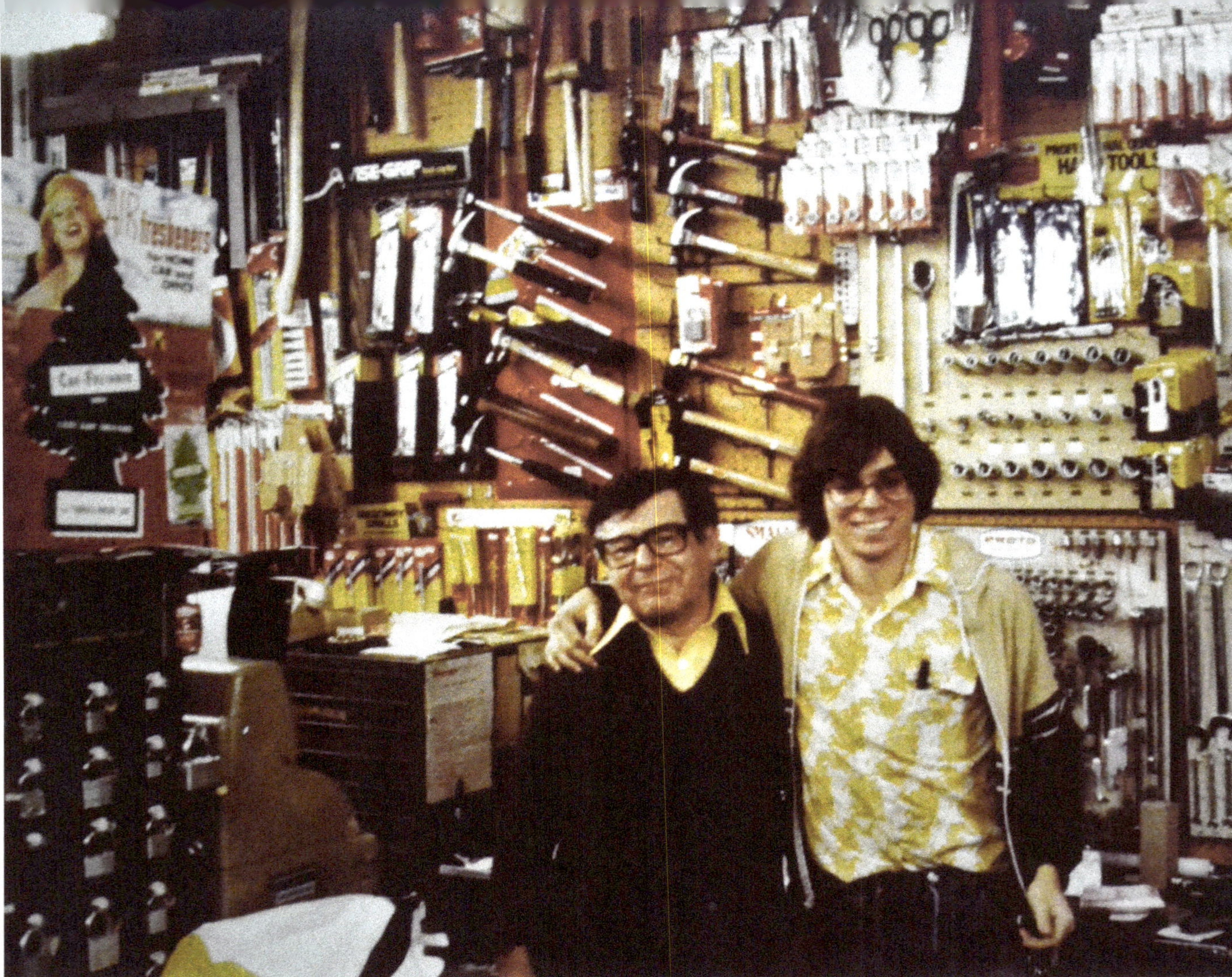

photos of the store for a "portfolio" that I would take around to local factories and industrial plants and show my photos in an effort to drum up business. I took the photos in this chapter in 1977, when I was 18.

These photos are meaningful because the business was thriving. Dad bought the store ten years earlier from the widow of the owner, Mr. Gordon, who had dropped dead in the store. My father's first-day sales in his new business on March 22, 1967 was $39.37. My dad was the last wave of Jewish merchants, many of them who were Holocaust Survivors, in East L.A. and Boyle Heights in the '70s, and he

Left: Me and Dad: He was a serious person. Our relationship revolved around business and the store. By this time, business was good, every square foot in the small store covered with merchandise, so Dad should have been smiling. The action was behind the counter. Pop was the hardest-working person I ever met, and I was fortunate to inherit his work ethic. I was hustling and making money for the business. I was 18, still a longhaired smartass in this photo. 1977.
Bottom: There were always customers in the store, and the rotary dial phone AN8-0743 behind Sam was usually ringing. And by the way, cash or credit card, no checks, please. 1977.

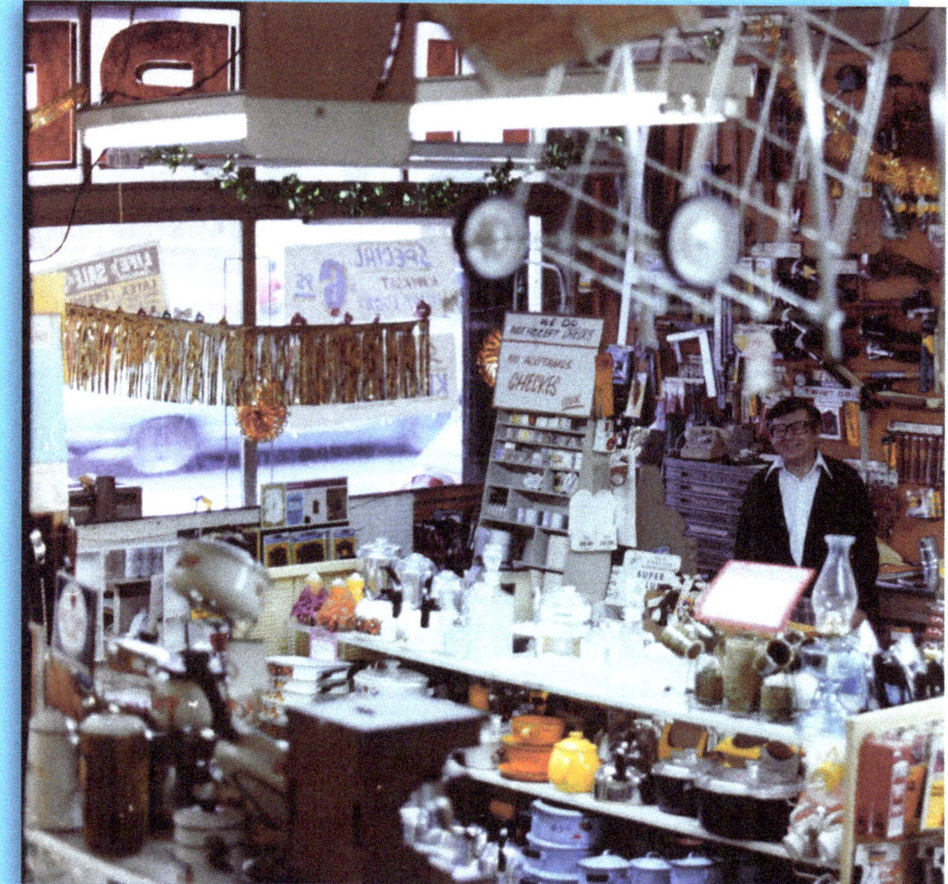

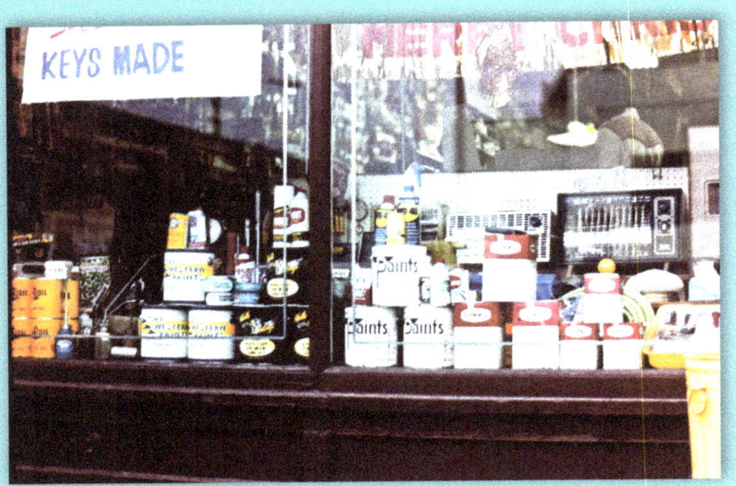

Left: My biggest regret is not taking a photo of the front of the building. I was too lazy to walk across Whittier Blvd. Instead the front-window shot does not say much other than our store was in a 1928 vintage brick building, we made keys for .49 cents, and oil was 69 cents a quart! We used all our window space! 1977. **Bottom:** Our tool wall: Mostly made-in-USA tools in those days. I would show this photo to prospective customers and tell them "if we don't have it we will get it." This sales approach coming from an 18-year-old was not sophisticated, but it worked! 1977. **Right:** Anita was a wonderful employee who worked for my dad for many years. Next door to the hardware store was a clothing store my father had purchased from the old couple who'd owned it since the 1930s. That is how we got into the clothing business. I wish I had kept a few original Made in USA Levi's 501 jeans I recently saw in an L.A. boutique for $169. We sold them for $9.95! 1977.

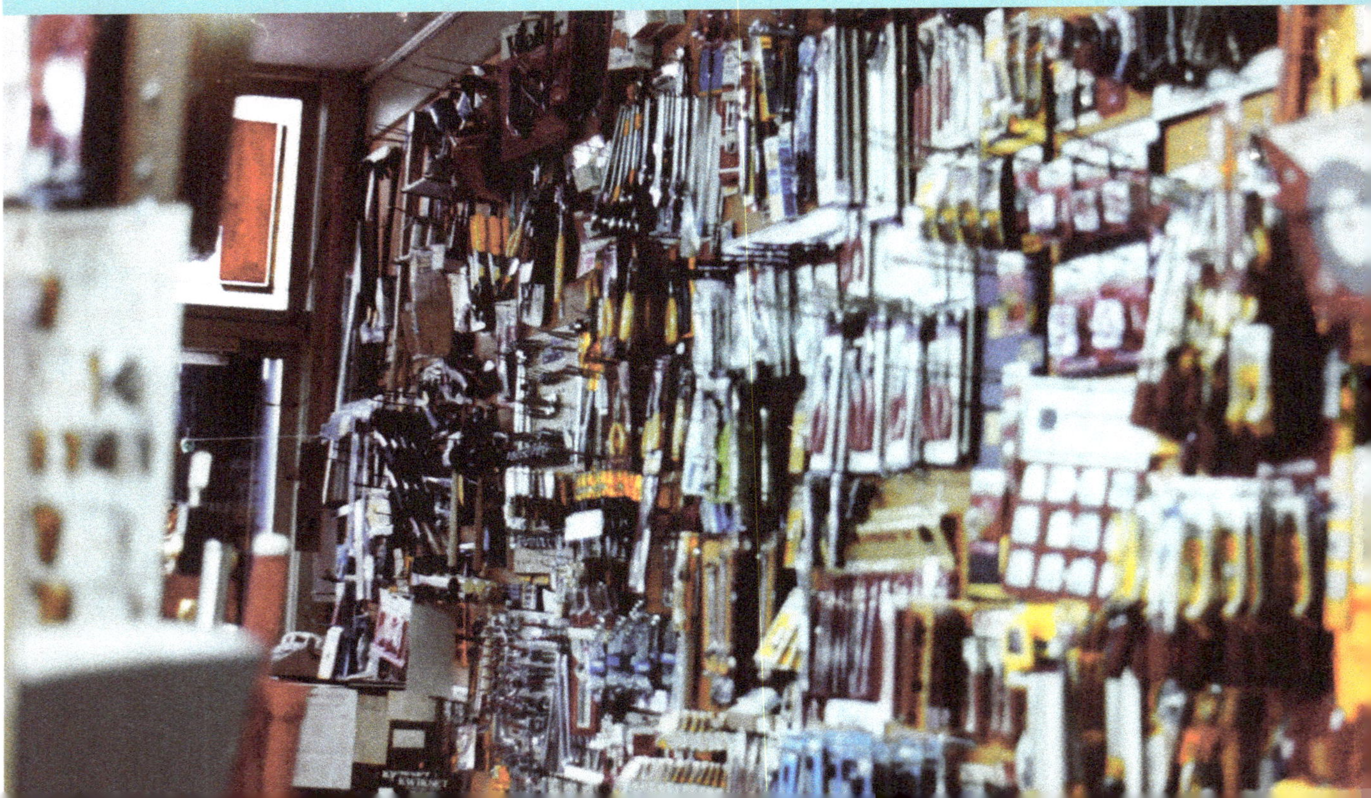

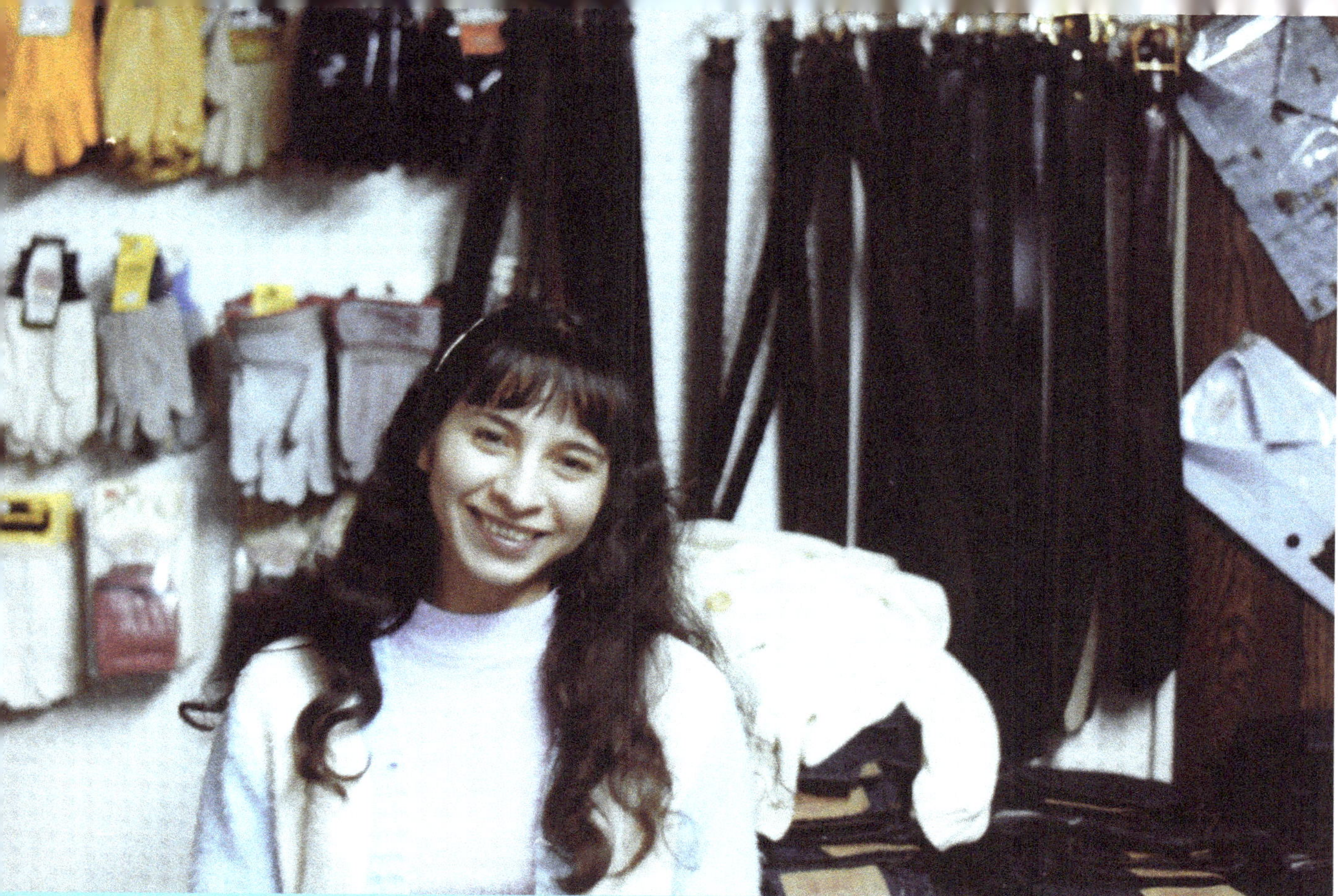

learned Spanish, adding to the other languages he spoke. East Los Angeles was intense during the mid-1970s. It carried over from the many anti-war protests against the Vietnam War of the early '70s, and Dad's' store was in the center of the death and chaos the day of the Chicano Moratorium riots August 29, 1970, another long hot summer in Los Angeles.

My father owned the store for 16 years before selling it and opening up another store in Orange County, where we had moved to after my graduation from Fairfax High in 1977. I had finally returned to the suburbs.

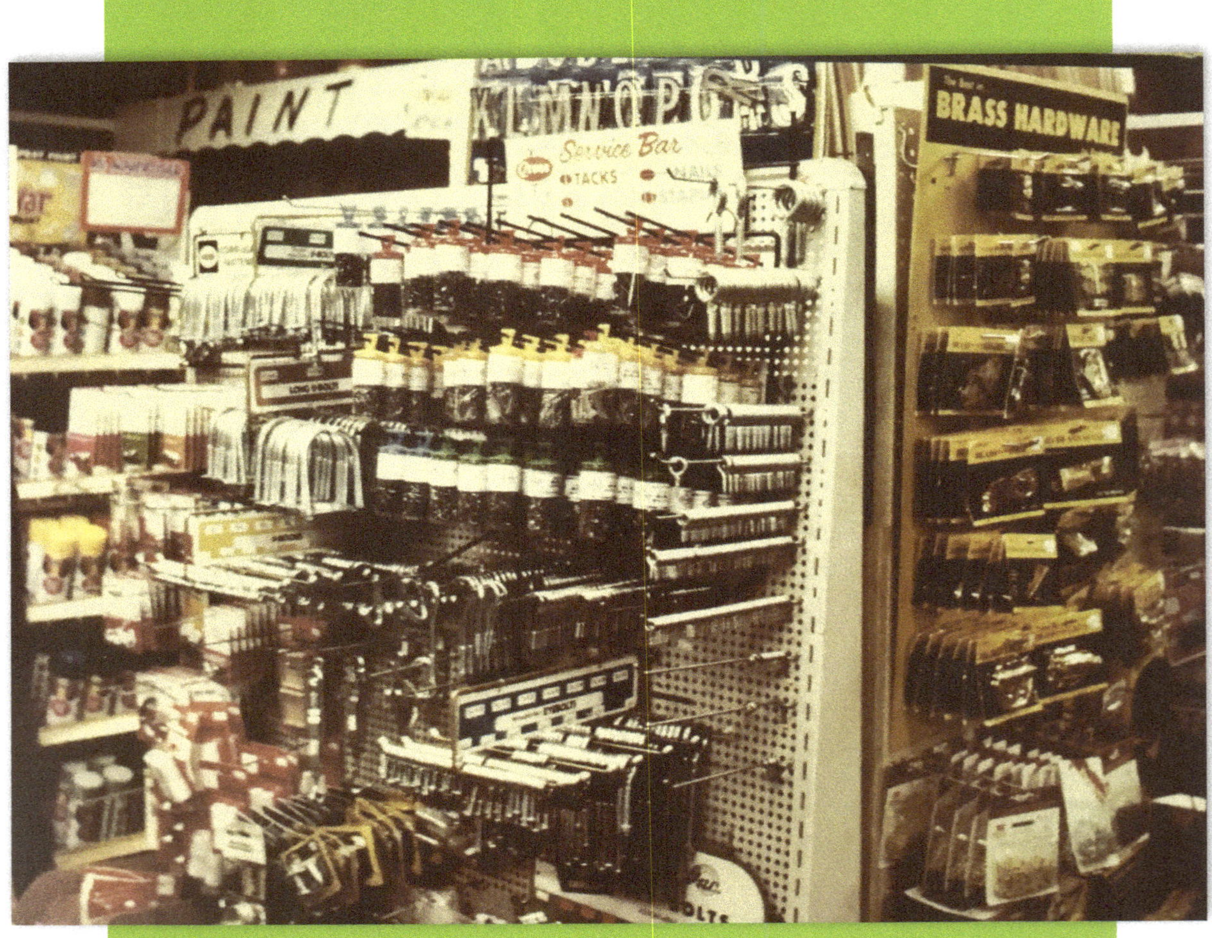

Top Left: When I showed these photos to prospective customers, I would tell them we were small in size but big in inventory; there was hardly a square foot in this old-fashioned hardware store that was not covered in merchandise. 1977.

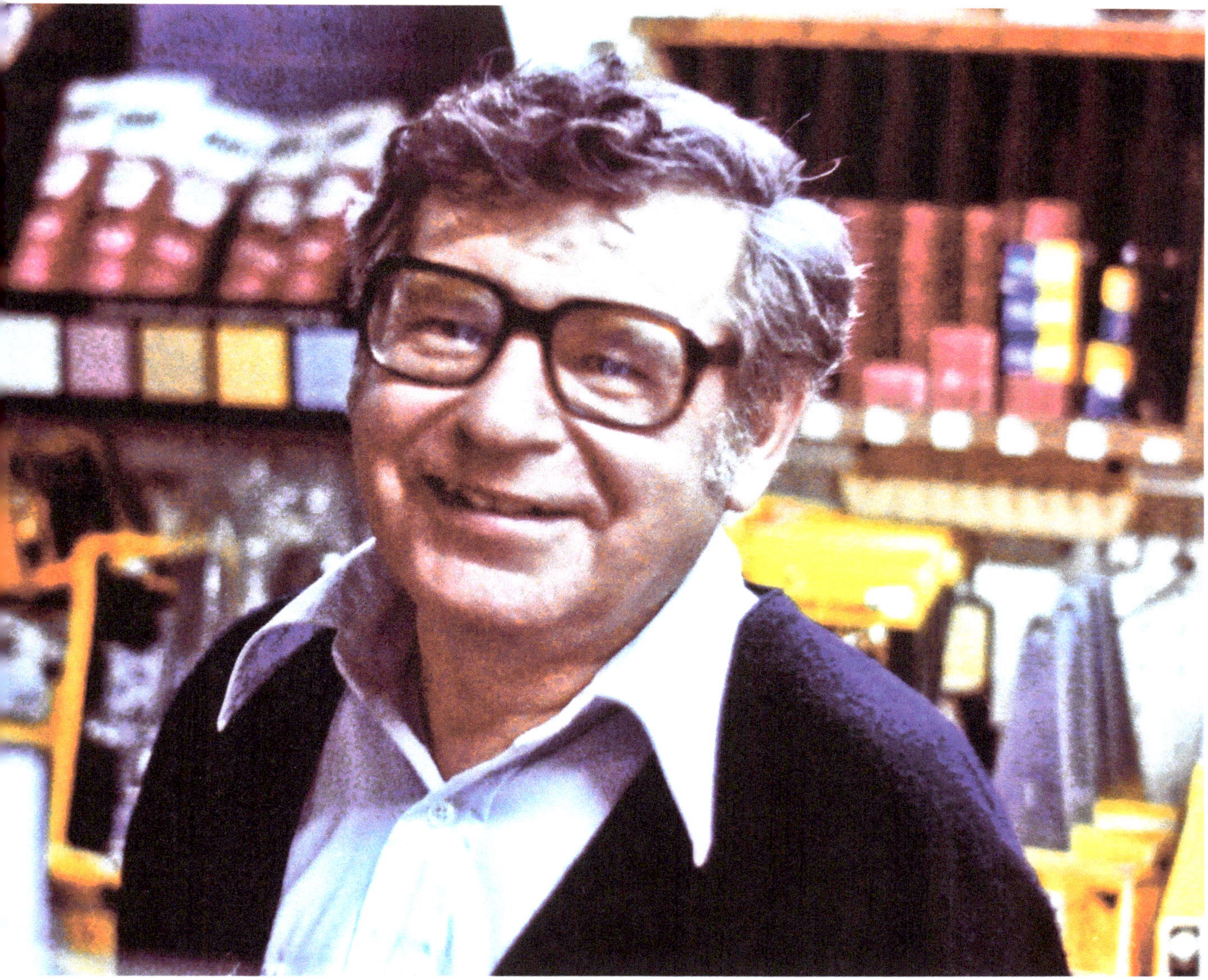

Top Right: My father, Samuel Katz: Arriving in America after WWII with less than nothing, his parents, brother, sister, and one-year-old niece murdered at Auschwitz. He came to America and got a job in our family-owned lumber business in Berkley, Michigan. Working for relatives was not for Dad. After 18 years and many trips to the hospital with ulcers, it was goodbye Michigan suburbs, hello sunny California on Route 66, where immigrant dreams and California opportunity was still possible. His ambition was to open his own hardware store, a dream he achieved. 1977.

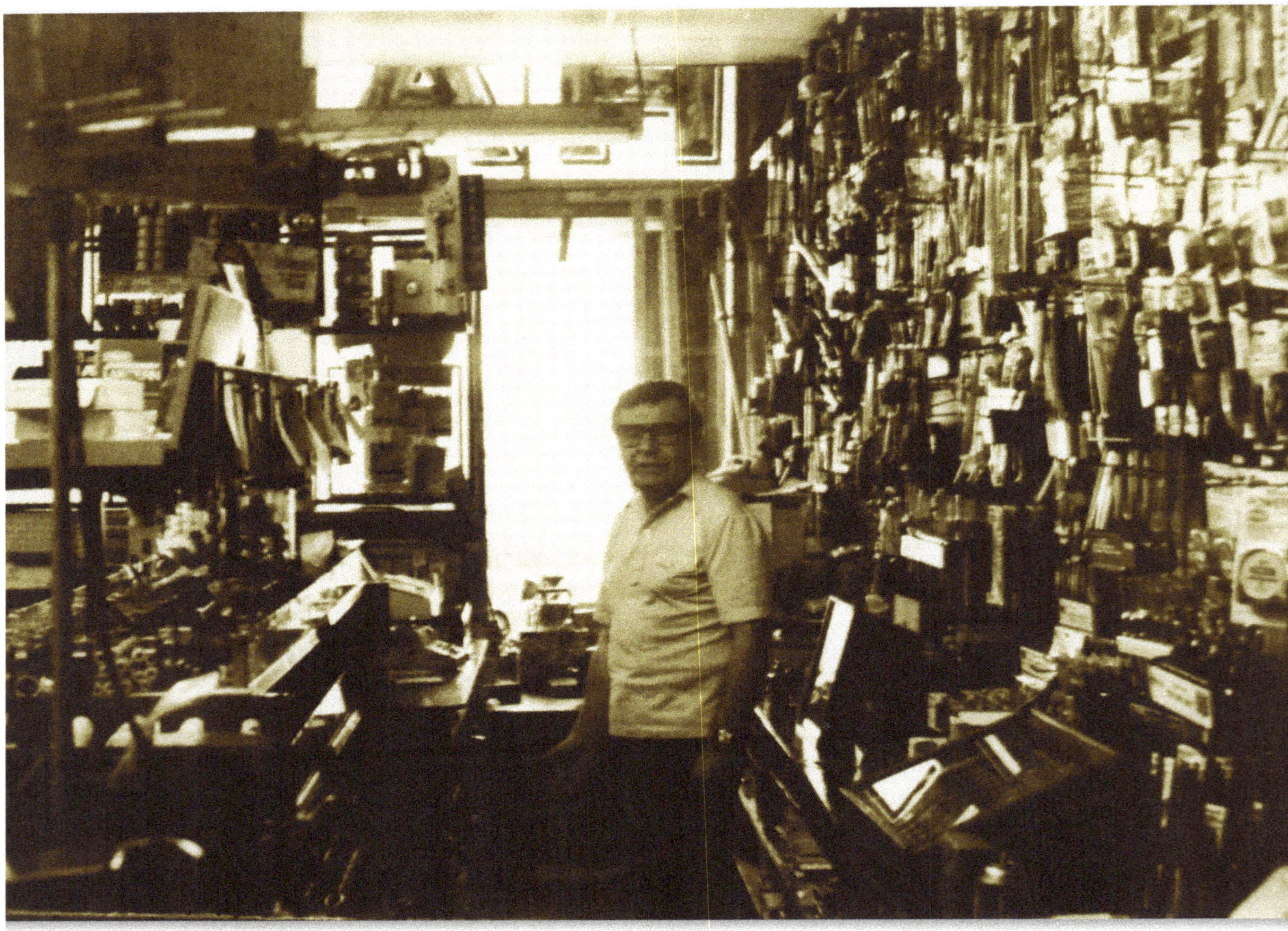

Left: This photo was not in the portfolio. Dad was saying "Stop screwing around and get to work." 1977.
Right: We sold American-made Revere Ware pots and pans and old-fashioned hotplates. You could even put them on layaway! 1977.

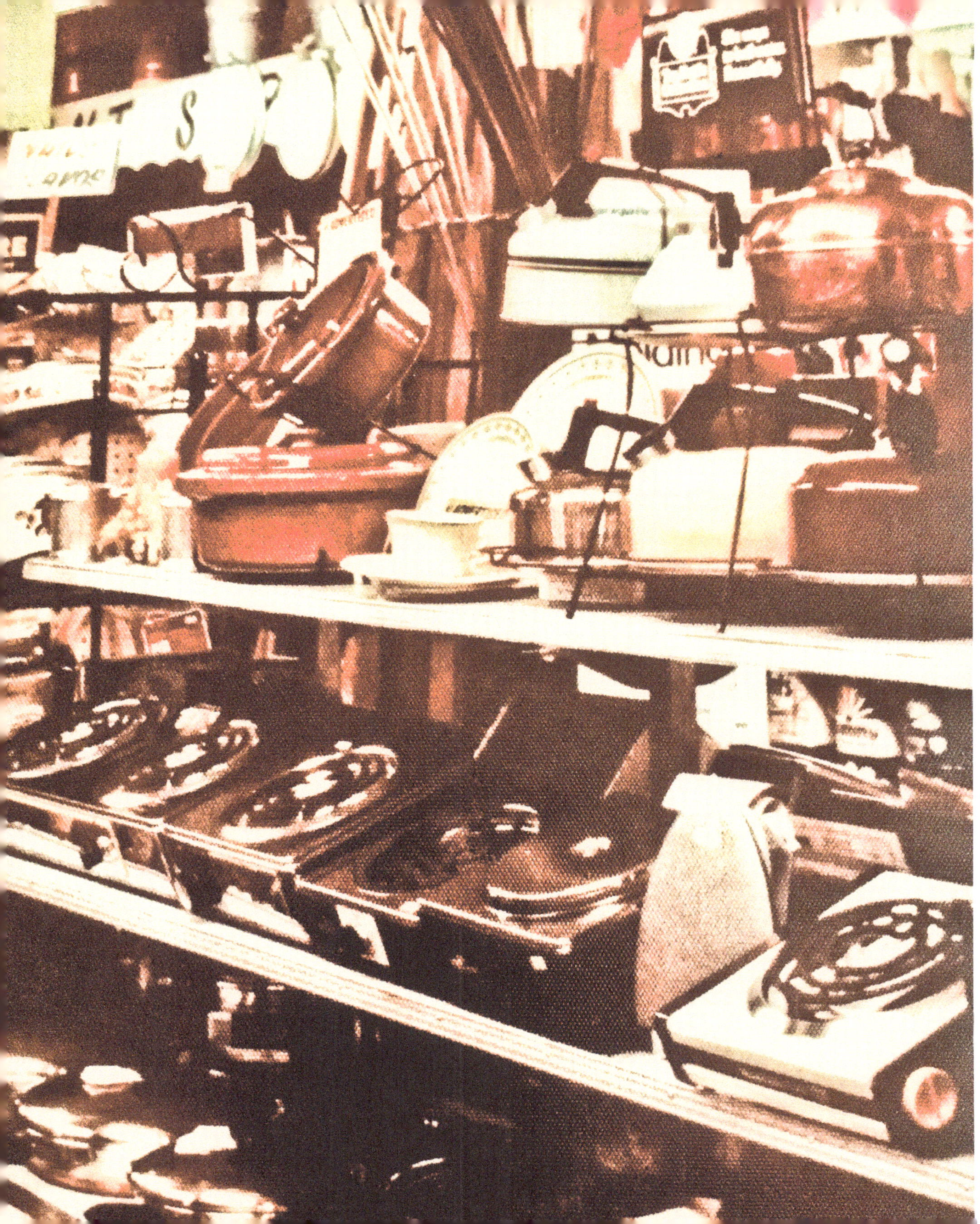

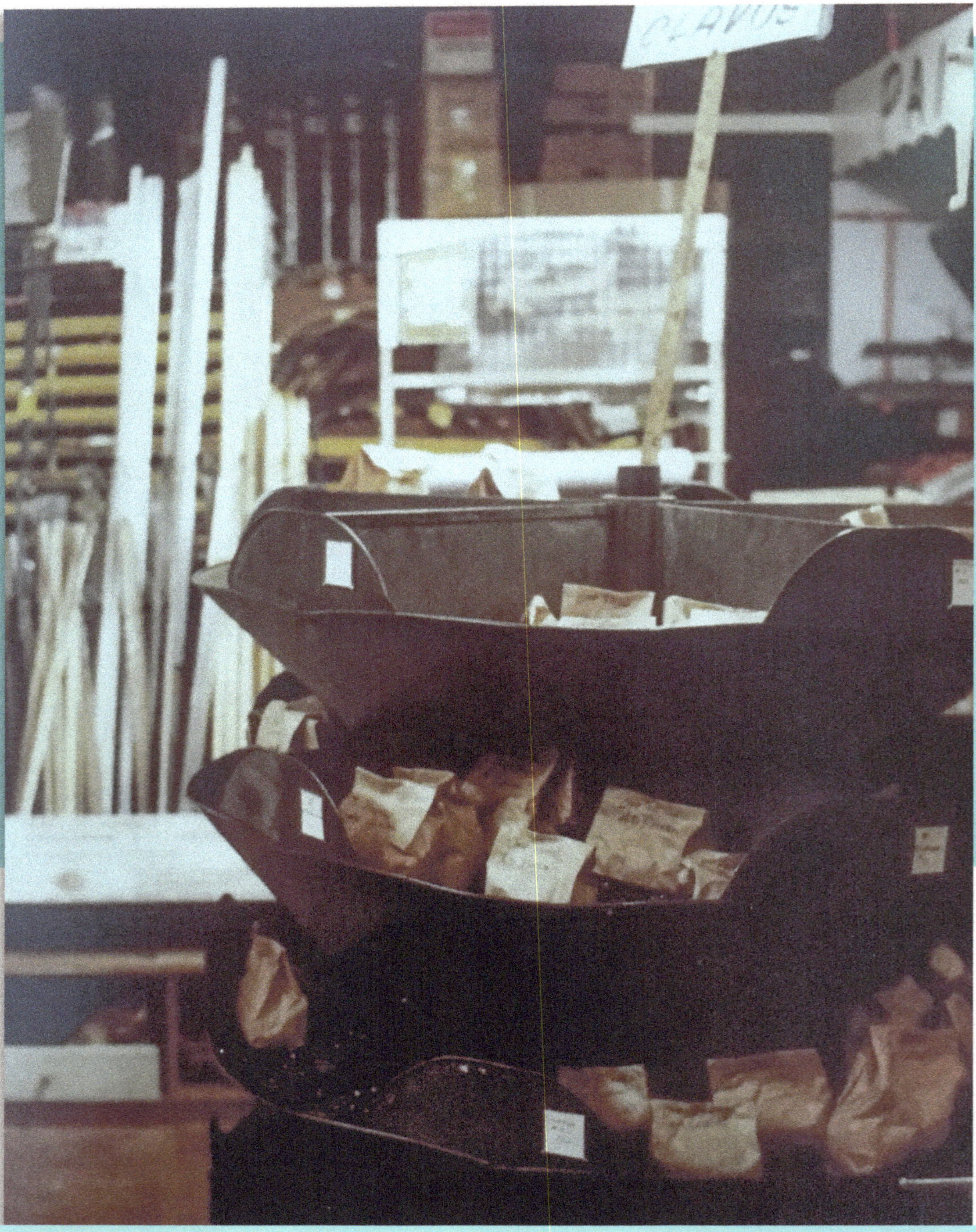

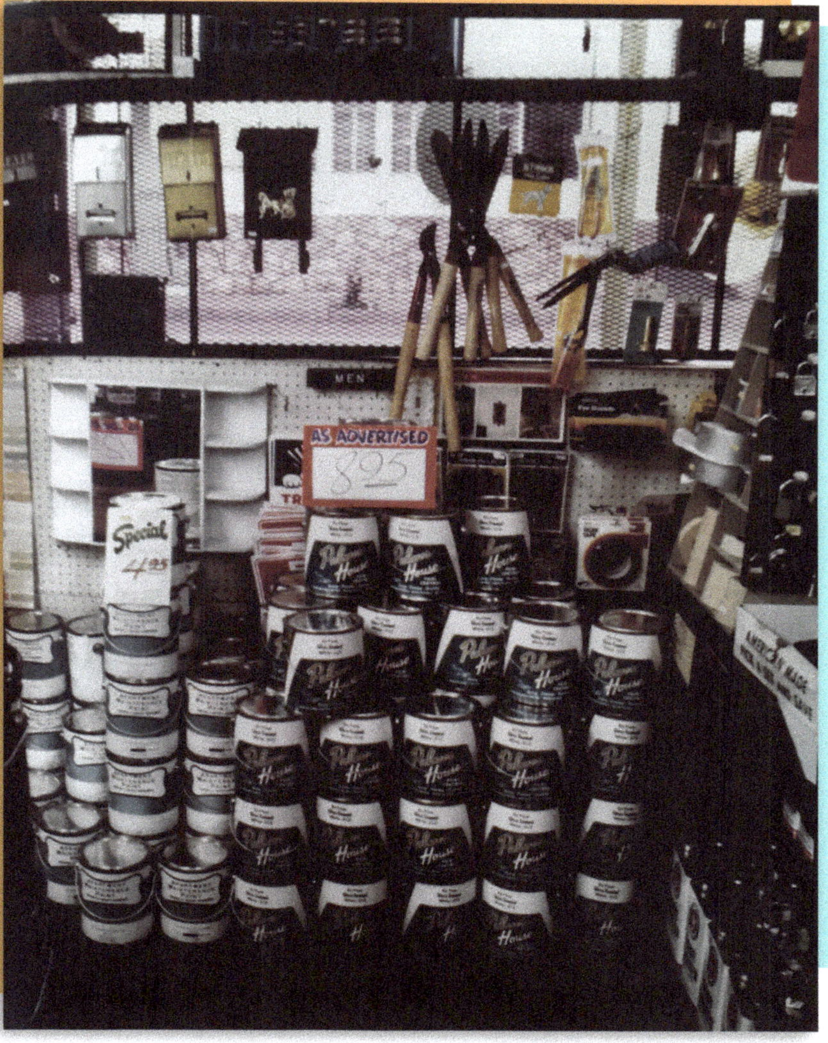

Left: Our old-fashioned hardware store had 1930s-style metal revolving nail bins, similar to those I found in Busy Bee Hardware in Santa Monica before they closed. I used to put nails in paper bags weighing one and two pounds, and customers would grab the bags; we sold way more nails that way. The homemade yardstick sign says "*clavos*" or "nails" in Spanish. 1977. **Right:** The front of the store we loaded with paint. We sold a lot of paint. Hundreds of gallons a month. We were a neighborhood hardware store, but we also developed a large business selling to some of the biggest factories in the area, like Kaiser Hospital, Farmer John (home of the Dodger Dogs), and many others. 1977.

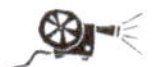

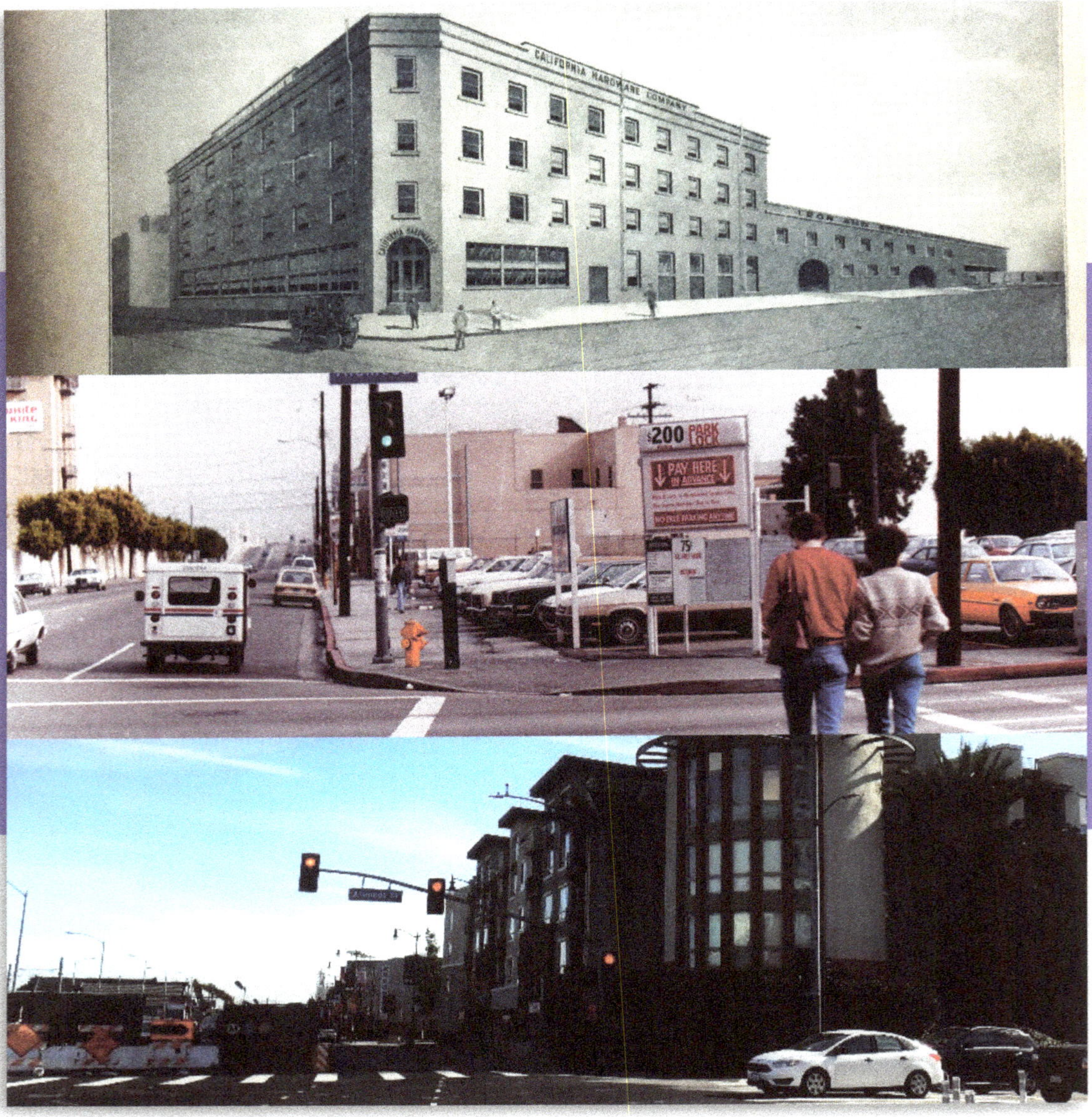

Top: Our main supplier for merchandise was California Hardware Company, on the corner of First Street & Alameda in Downtown L.A. The old brick building was built in 1892. I spent a lot of time there, picking up merchandise, getting to know the streets of downtown Los Angeles as a teenager. Looking back at that corner over time, the original California Hardware Building closed in the late '70s, the middle photo I took in 1984, and the bottom photo in 2018, showing the gentrification of The City of the Angels. **Right:** My father in his very cramped, tiny office. 1977.

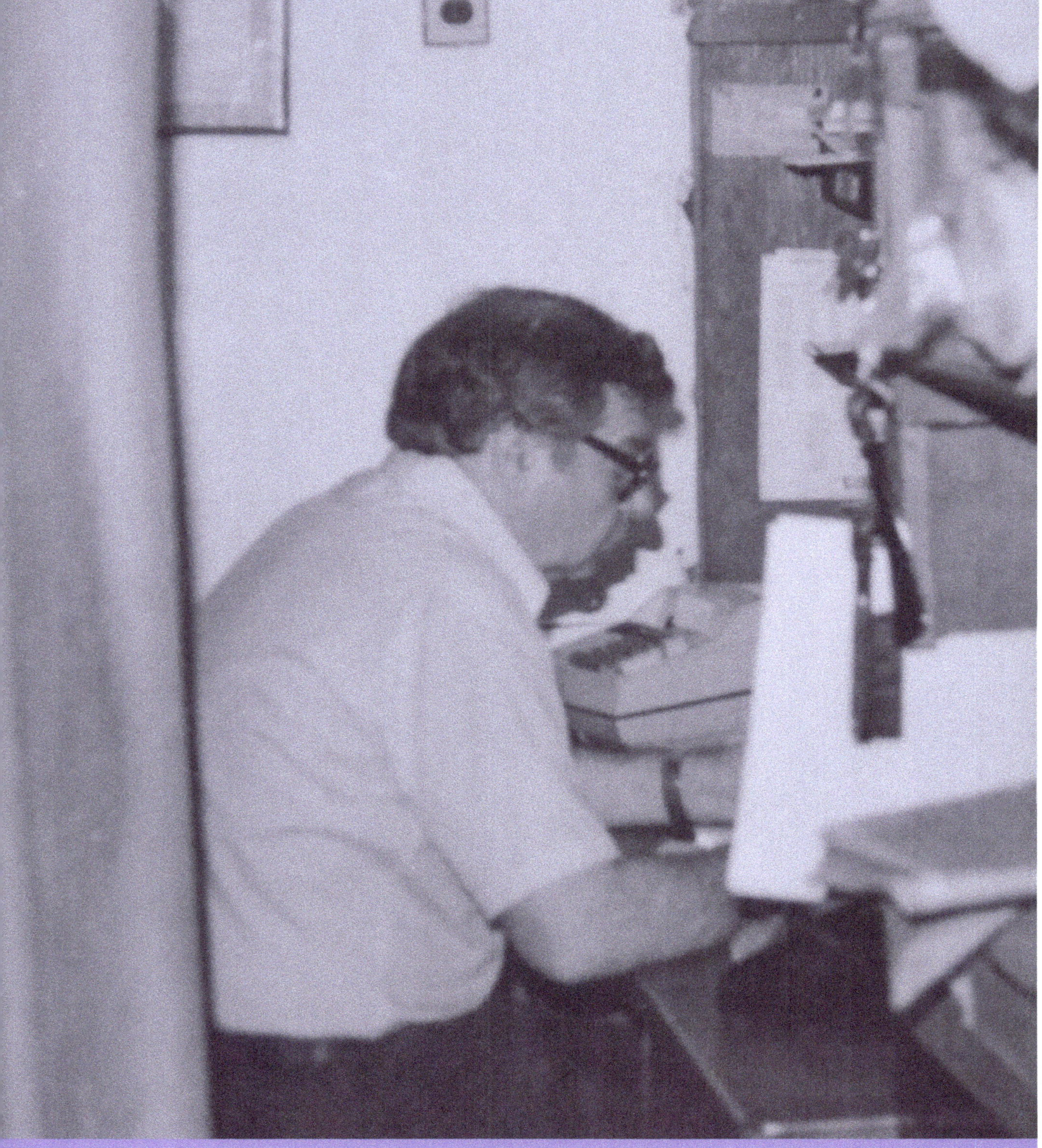

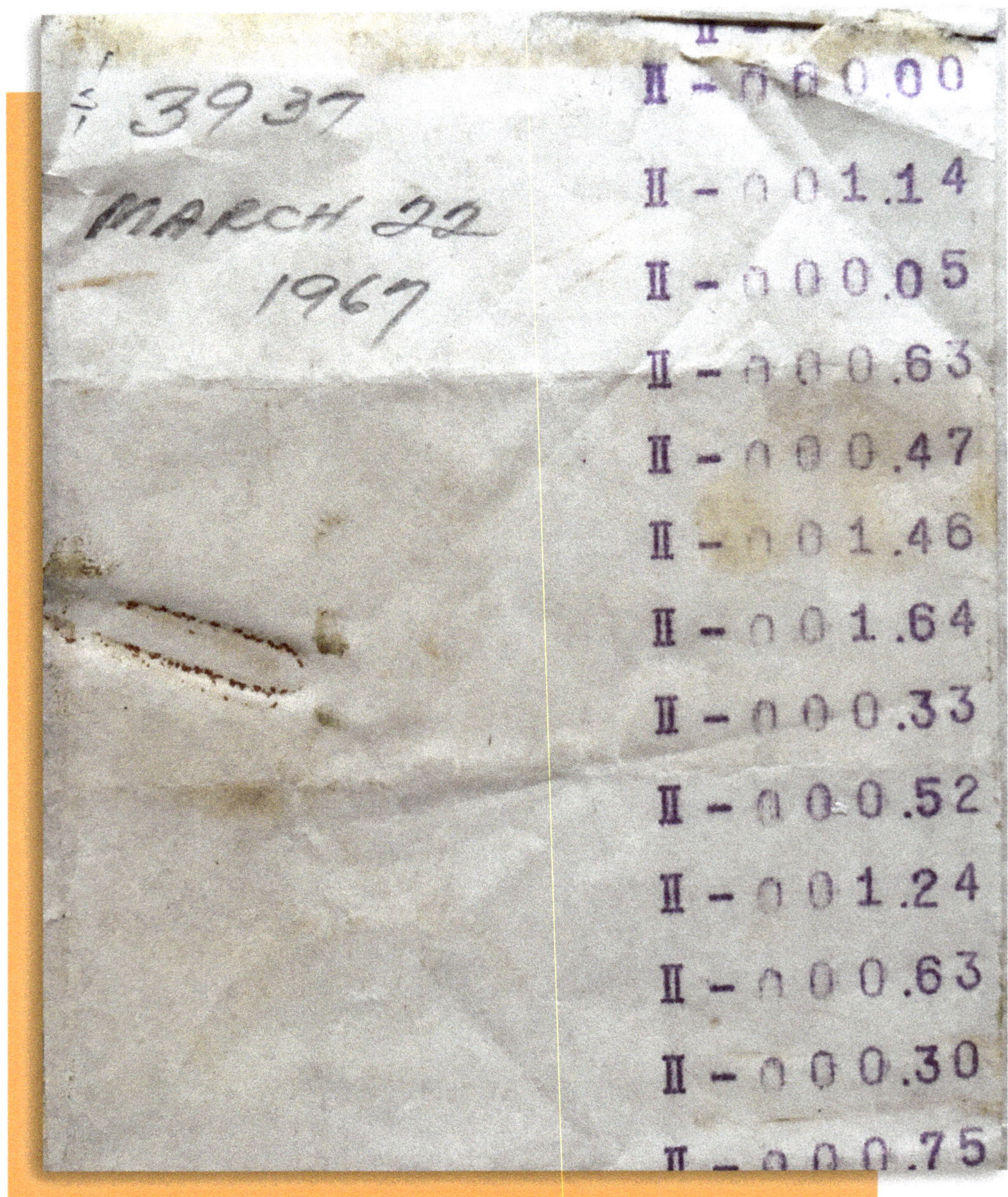

Top: The first day in business, sales were $39.37! Even in 1967 that was not going to feed a family of four. Toughness and perseverance were the characteristics of many Holocaust Survivors, traits Samuel Katz had an abundance of. When he sold the store 16 years later, we were averaging almost $1000 a day in sales.

SANTA MONICA FAMILY TIME

Santa Monica in the '60s & '70s was the beach to go to for families on the Westside. 12 miles west on Santa Monica Boulevard from West Hollywood, the Santa Monica Pier is the end of the 2400-mile road on Route 66. We got our kicks sitting in Dad's 1965 Oldsmobile. Dad drove 500 miles a day the length of Route 66 as we made our way from the suburbs of Detroit to the Golden State in 1966, sandwiched in time between the Watts and Detroit riots.

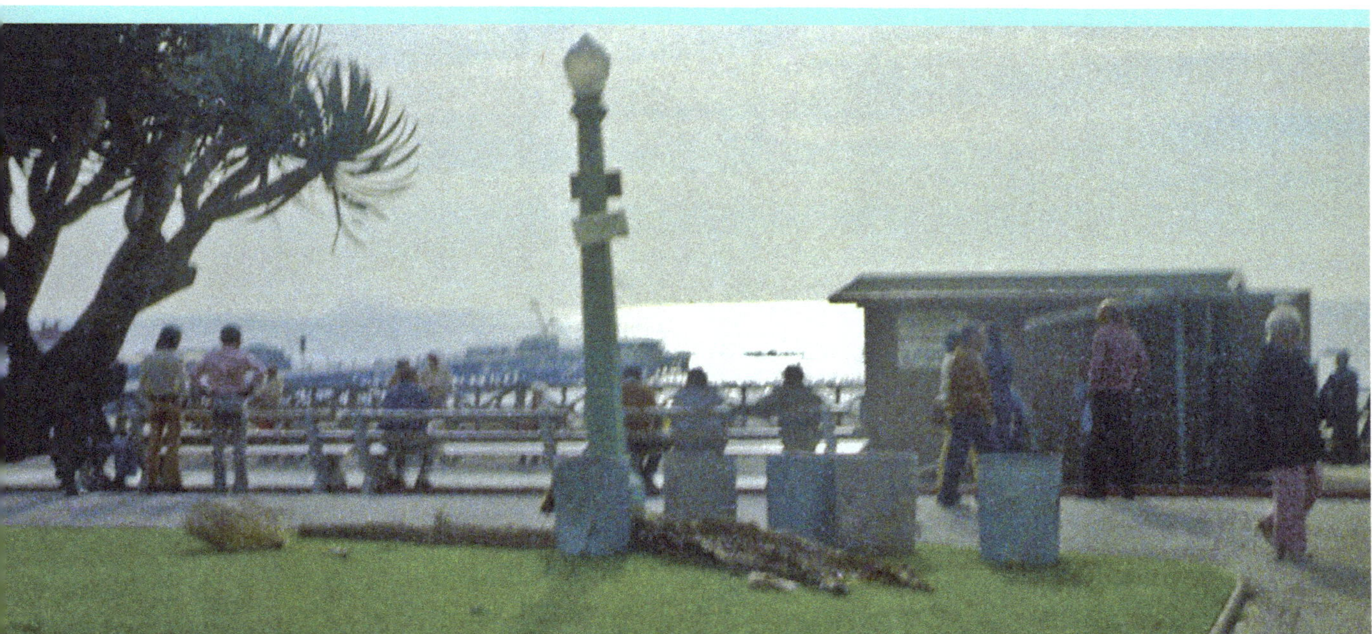

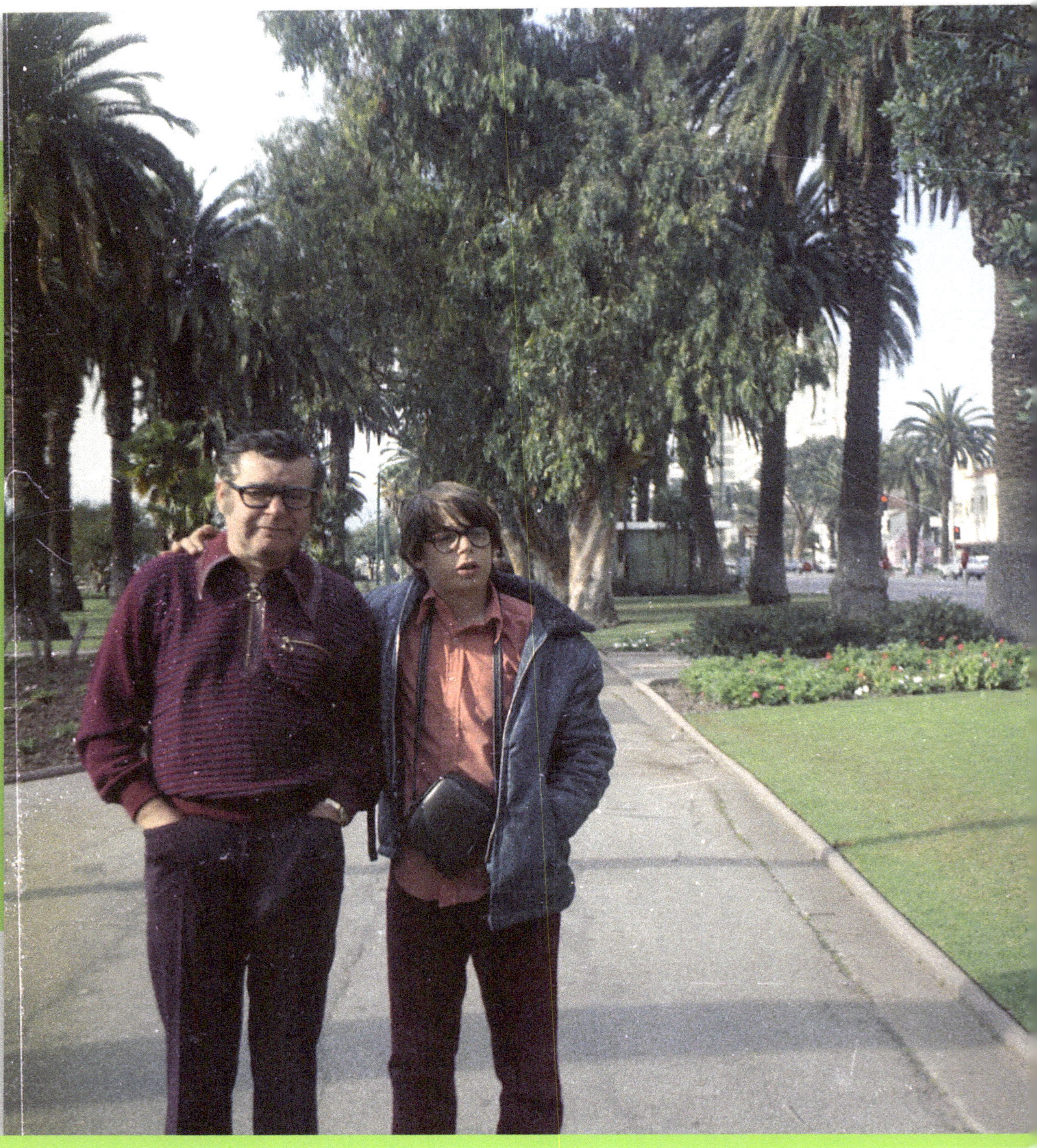

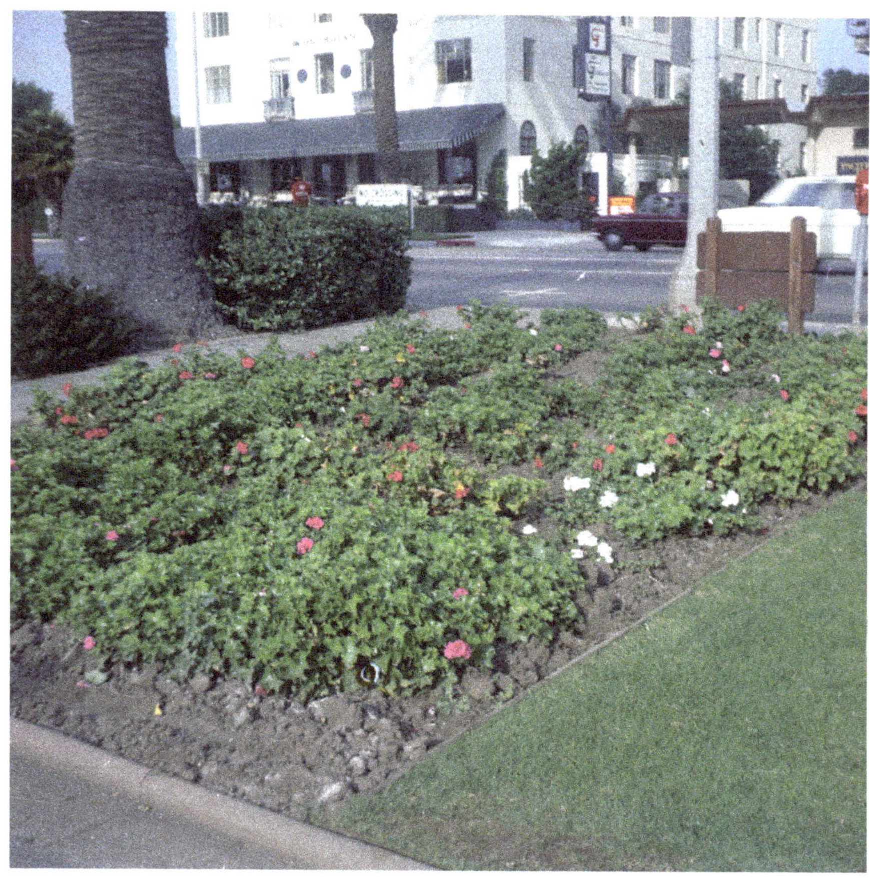

I remember Santa Monica as a small town in those days, a place for retirees and middle-class apartment dwellers—not the gentrified, crowded, expensive city with the massive homeless population it has become. The Santa Monica Pier was old and run down at the time, in contrast to the millions of people who now visit each year. It's a strange feeling to look at photos of my parents, who were younger than I am today but somehow look older. Both my parents were serious people, like their son.

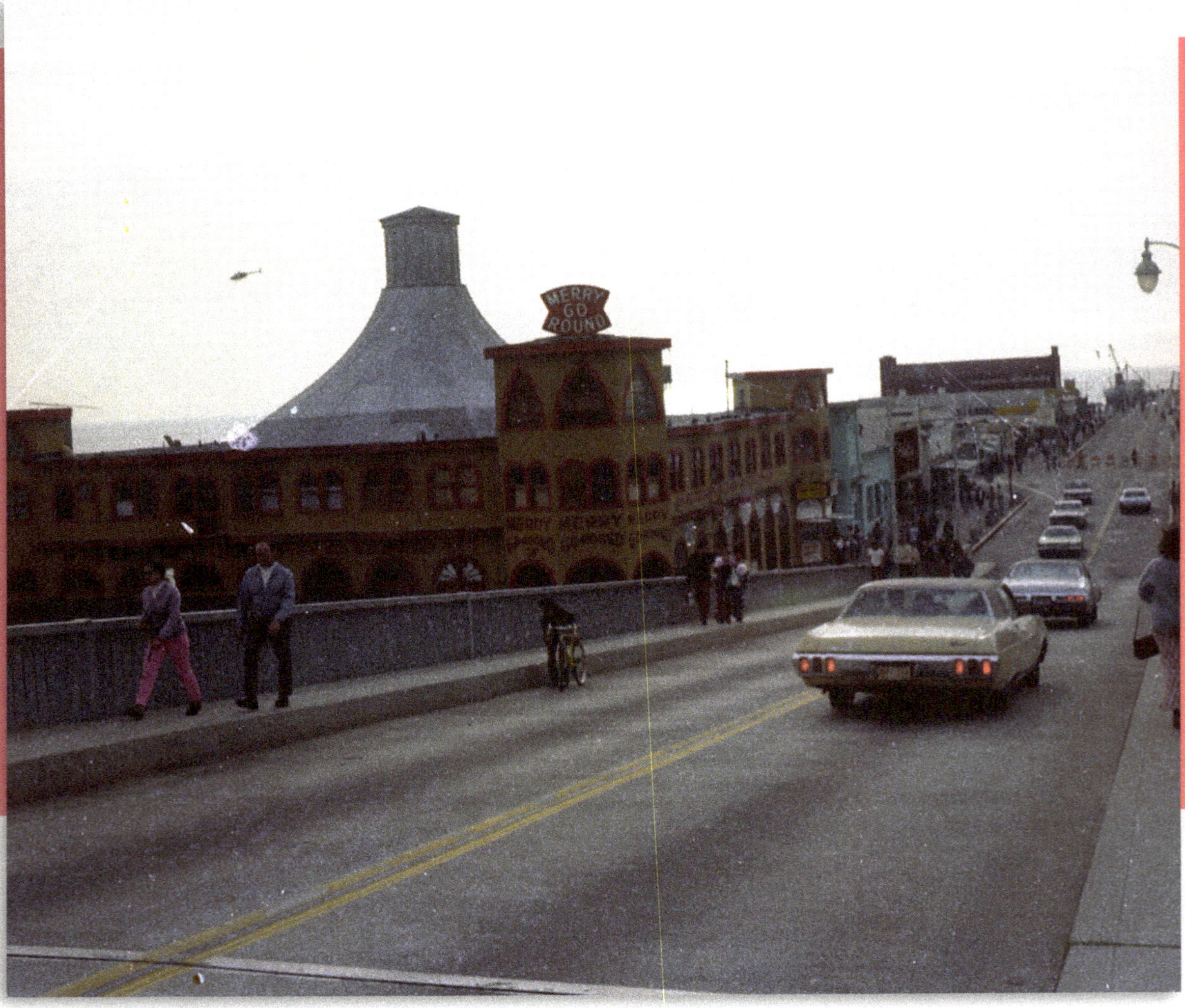

The photos in this short chapter were simple family photos and local scenes, taken with the most basic Kodak Instamatic 126 camera in the winter of 1973, when I was 14 years old. I especially like the man-on-the-bench photo. Whatever happened to him? The Pier, old and tired looking, on a memorable grey winter day.

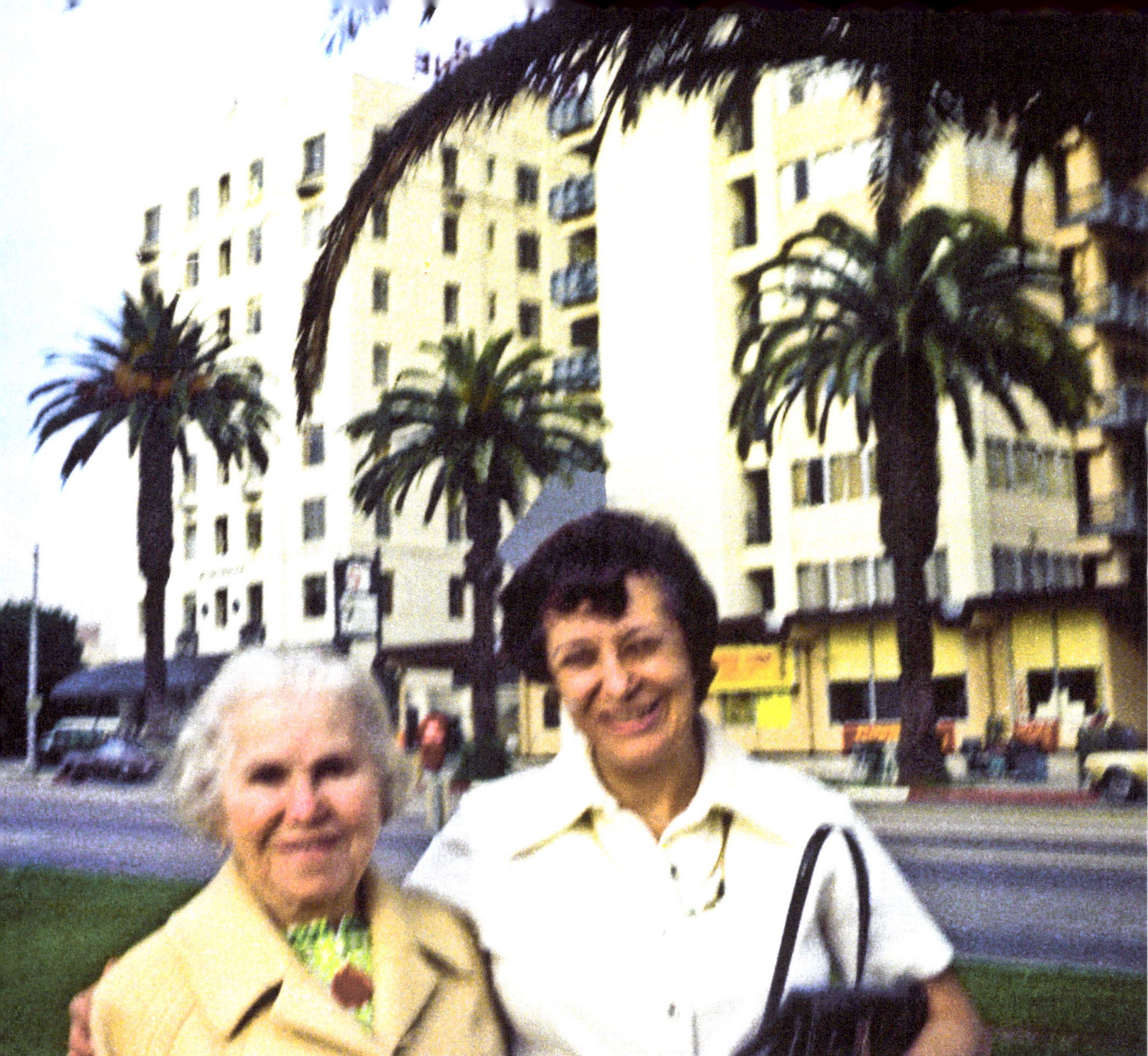

Left: Beginning in Chicago, Route 66 ends 2400 miles later, here at the Santa Monica Pier. Love the old cars and uncrowded pier. The bumper cars were my favorite ride. 1973. **Right:** Blurry photo of Mom and Grandma, the Georgian Hotel in the background, now painted blue. Grandma was forty when she arrived in America from Hungary with her four children, my mom being the oldest child, 12 years old as the Friedmans made the long journey from Europe to America on the HMS *Aquitania*. They arrived at Ellis Island, New York, on September 1, 1939, the very same day that World War II began in Europe. 50 million people lost their lives between 1939 and 1945. They got out of Europe just in time. 1973.

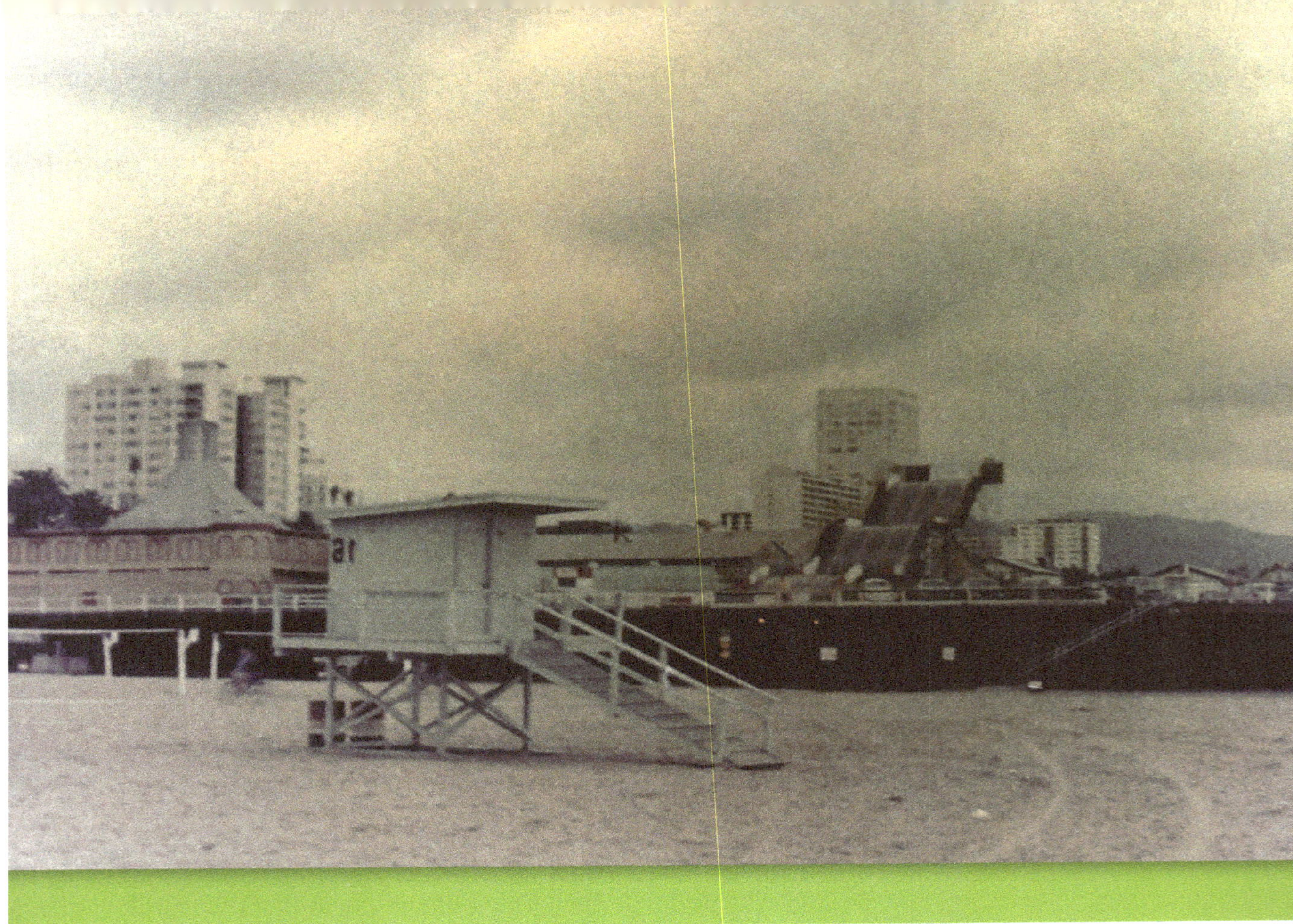

Top: Except for a lone cyclist, the beach on that gloomy day in December 1973 was deserted. **Right:** This is one of my personal favorites. Cold winter day. Ordinary scene. Man reading a paper, as a woman with a head-scarf walks past. I always wanted to dig a little deeper. Whatever happened to them? How did they come to be at the same place and time? I was only 14 when I snapped this photo, an early effort in composition. 1973.

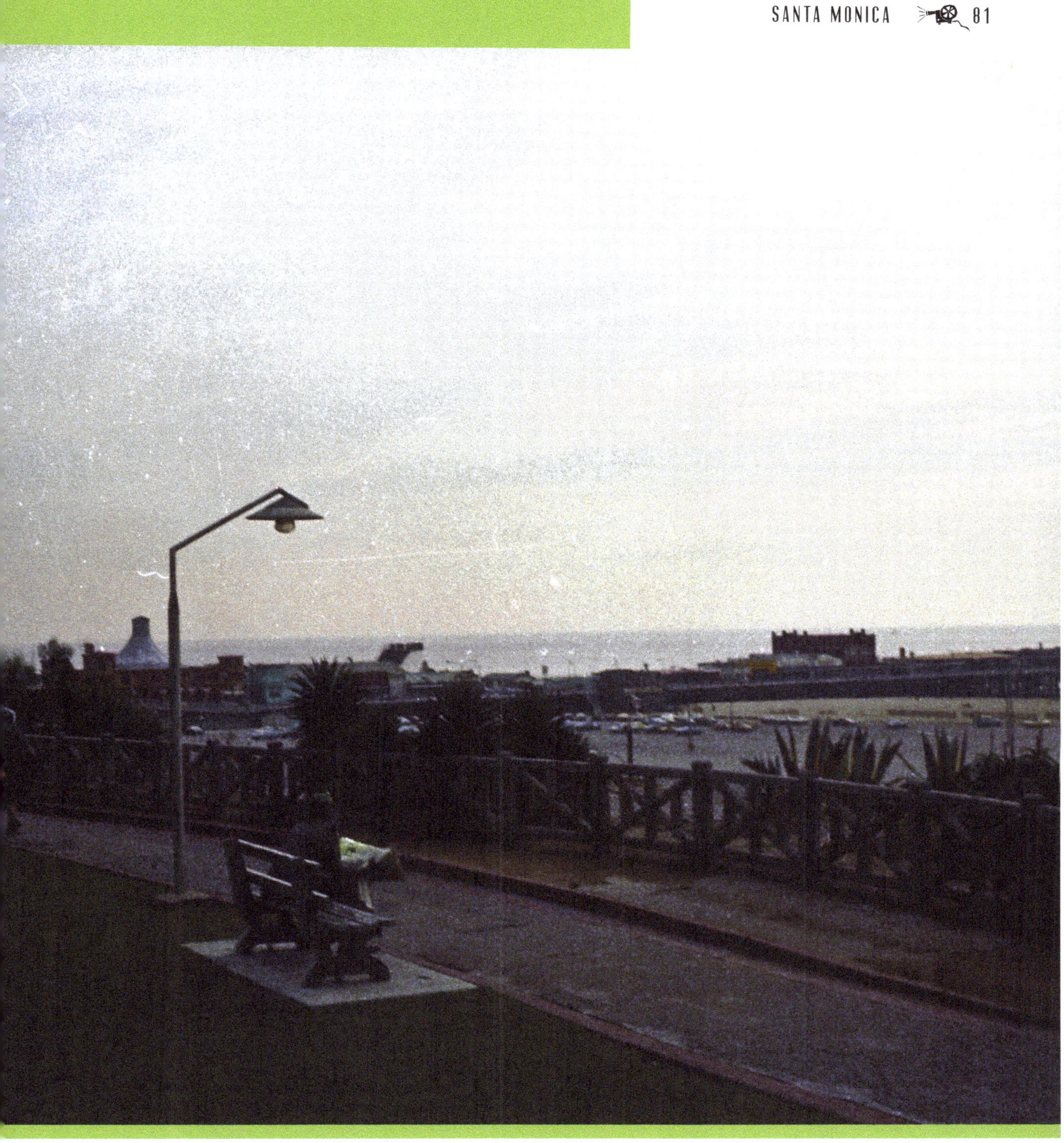

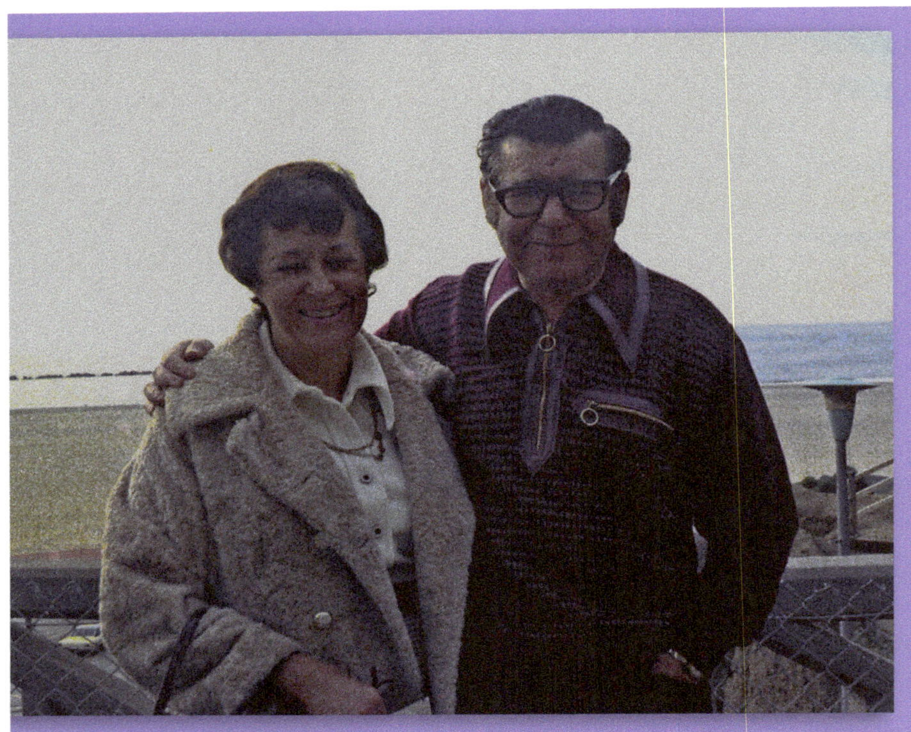

Top: Elizabeth & Sam. My mom would always take off her glasses and then squint because then she couldn't see. Mom never drove and used to walk to Alpha-Beta Market and the Kosher Butcher on Fairfax pulling her metal folding cart. I miss my parents. 1973
Right: Did I look like that? No wonder I got picked on at Bancroft Junior High in Hollywood. 1973.

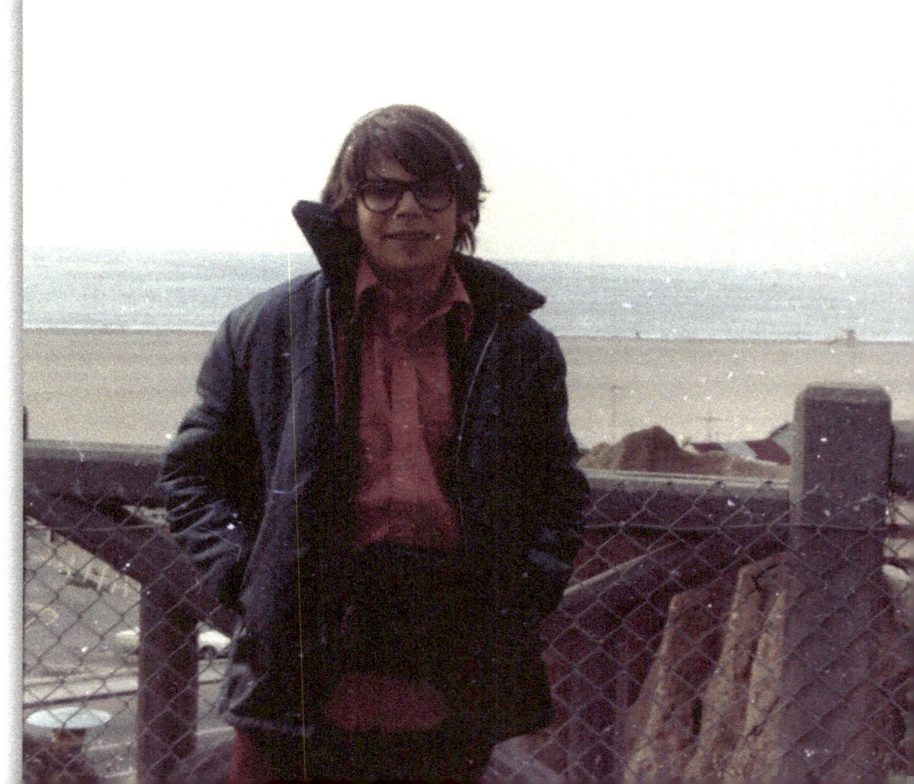

1984 SUMMER OLYMPICS, LOS ANGELES
THE PINNACLE

The glorious history of sport in Los Angeles reached its pinnacle between July 28 and August 12, 1984, with the Games of the XXIII Olympiad. Thousands of hotel rooms were built on the assumption that millions of people from around the world would flood southern California. Predictions of traffic Armageddon and a disastrous crime wave; the boycott of the Soviet-bloc

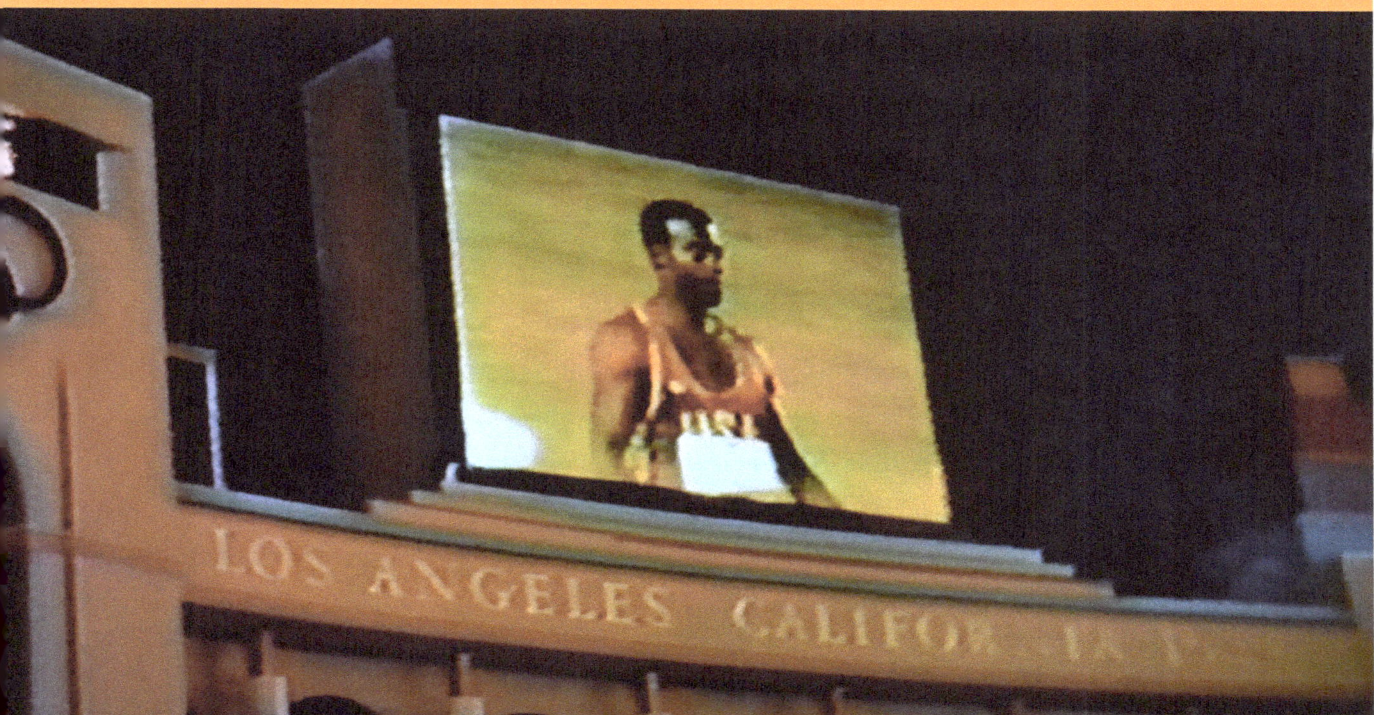

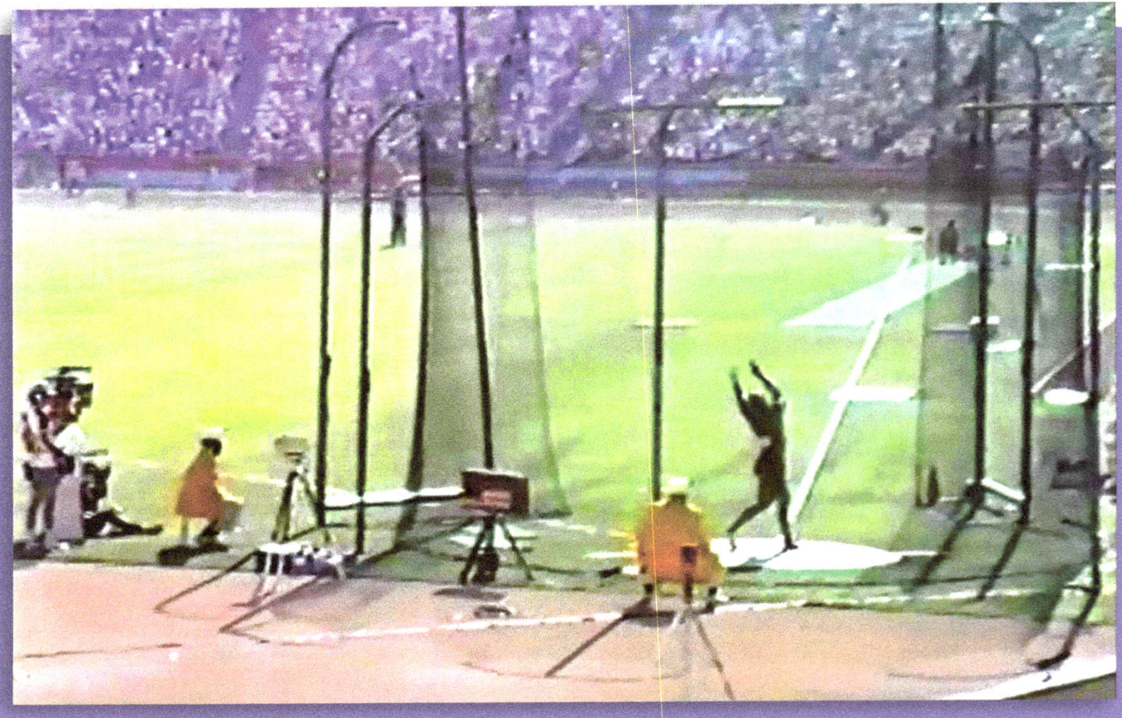

teams implied weak competition, not a "perfect" Olympic Games where all the countries of the world compete against the best. Los Angeles would be ruined financially, like many other Olympic cities.

Not only didn't that happen, but also the dream of freeways that move freely came through. People heeded the warnings of chaos to use the RTD to get to the venues and stay off the roads. Crime dropped, and many said it stopped. Peace and love were in the air, everybody got along, and the Games made a $225 million profit, the only Olympics then, and now, to make money for the host city. The money made was reinvested into the community in youth sports and other noble causes. The Tree People planted more than one million trees in a long-term effort to reduce smog and clean the air. The competition was Olympic in every sense of the word. Most who were in L.A. at the time would say it was a

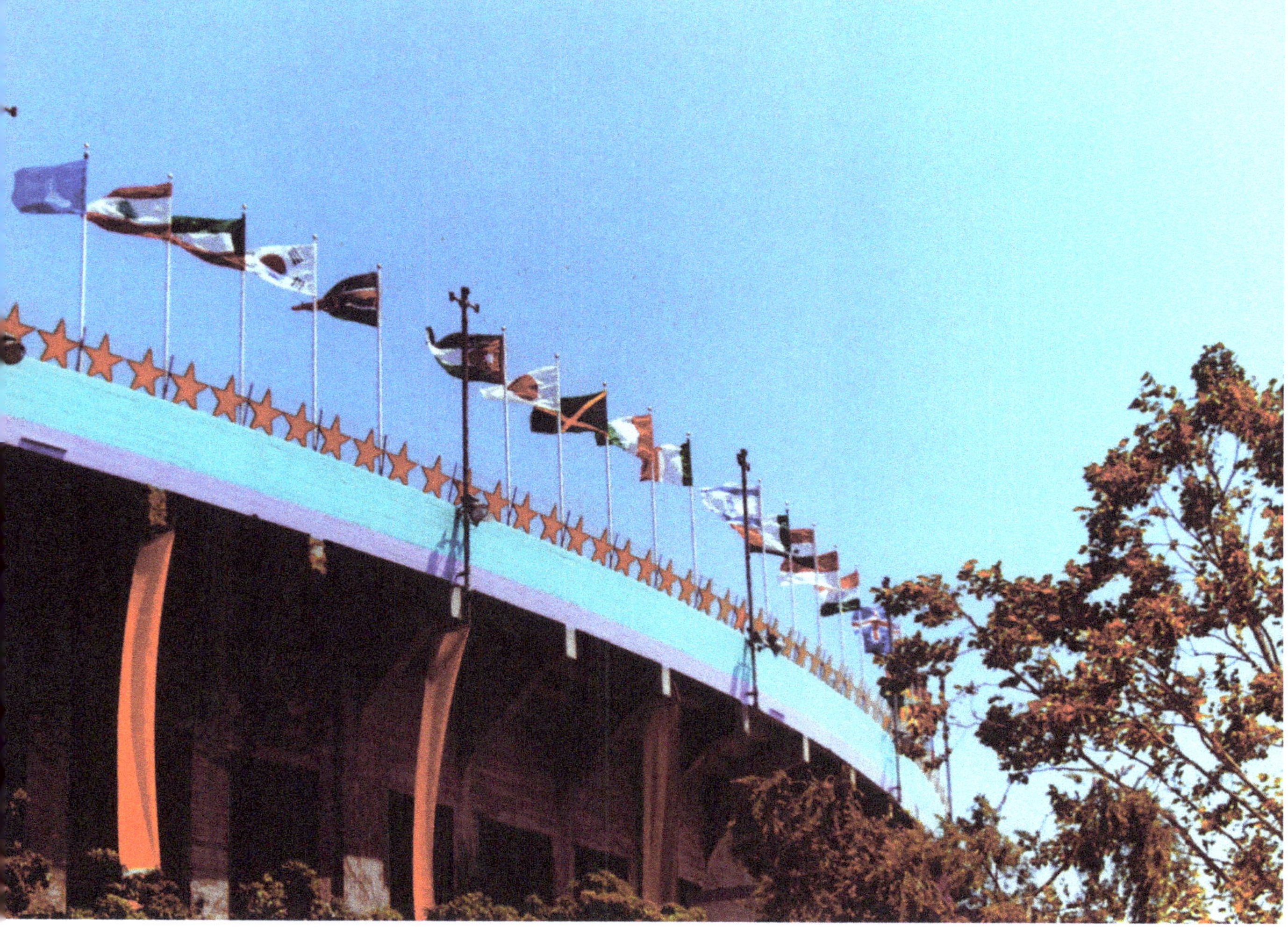

Top: Ed Burke of the USA lets it fly in the hammer throw from this screenshot. I schlepped an ancient and very heavy camcorder and battery pack to record the memory. Burke finished 18th but had the greatest honor of all: Burke led the American team and carried the flag in the Opening Ceremonies, at age 44, the oldest athlete in the American delegation. **Right:** Flags from 140 nations ringed the Los Angeles Memorial Coliseum in 1984. **Previous Page:** Witness to history: The great Carl Lewis jumping for gold in the long jump. The Los Angeles Olympics was the first of four straight Olympic long jump gold medals for Lewis, one of only two Olympic track and field athletes in history to win gold in the same event in four consecutive Olympics.

Top: The five colors in the Olympic flag representing at least one color of every flag in the world. In 2028 the Olympic flag will once again fly in the Coliseum, making Los Angeles, London, and Paris the only cities in the world to host three Olympic Games.

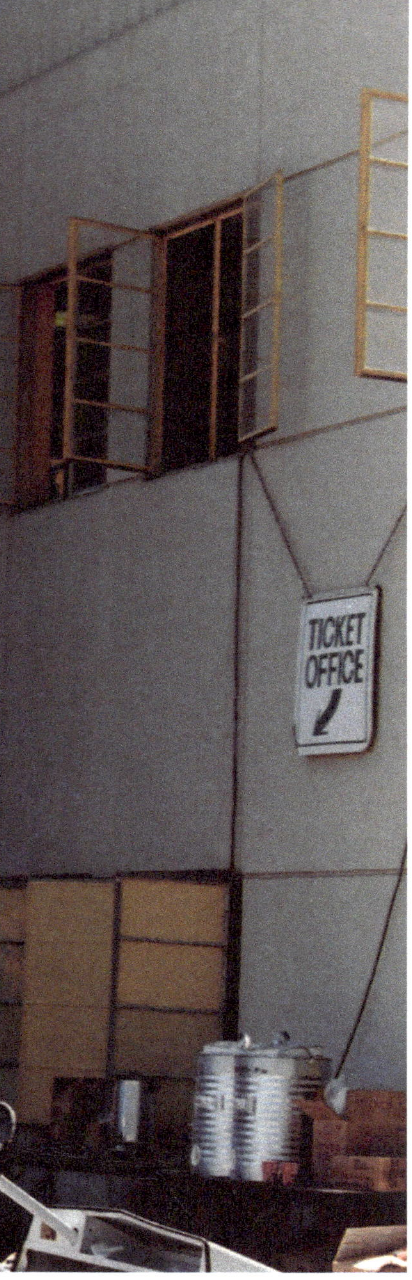

once-in-a-lifetime experience, a social contract where everyone got along for the greater good.

I knew the Olympic experience was history-making, and I wanted to be a part of that. In those pre-internet days, tickets were sold through a lottery-based system. The luck of the draw: I wanted to see track & field, basketball, boxing, swimming, and the opening and closing ceremonies. I was fortunate to have attended the Gold Medal Basketball final game, featuring the great Michael Jordan, then a senior at the University of North Carolina. I took photos at the swimming competition and schlepped an ancient video camcorder and battery pack to record the track and field competition.

Come 2028, Los Angeles will have the honor of being only the third city in the world, along with Paris and London, to have hosted three Olympic Games, forty-four years after I took these photos. I hope to be around to take some more pictures and write another chapter.

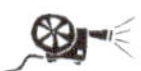

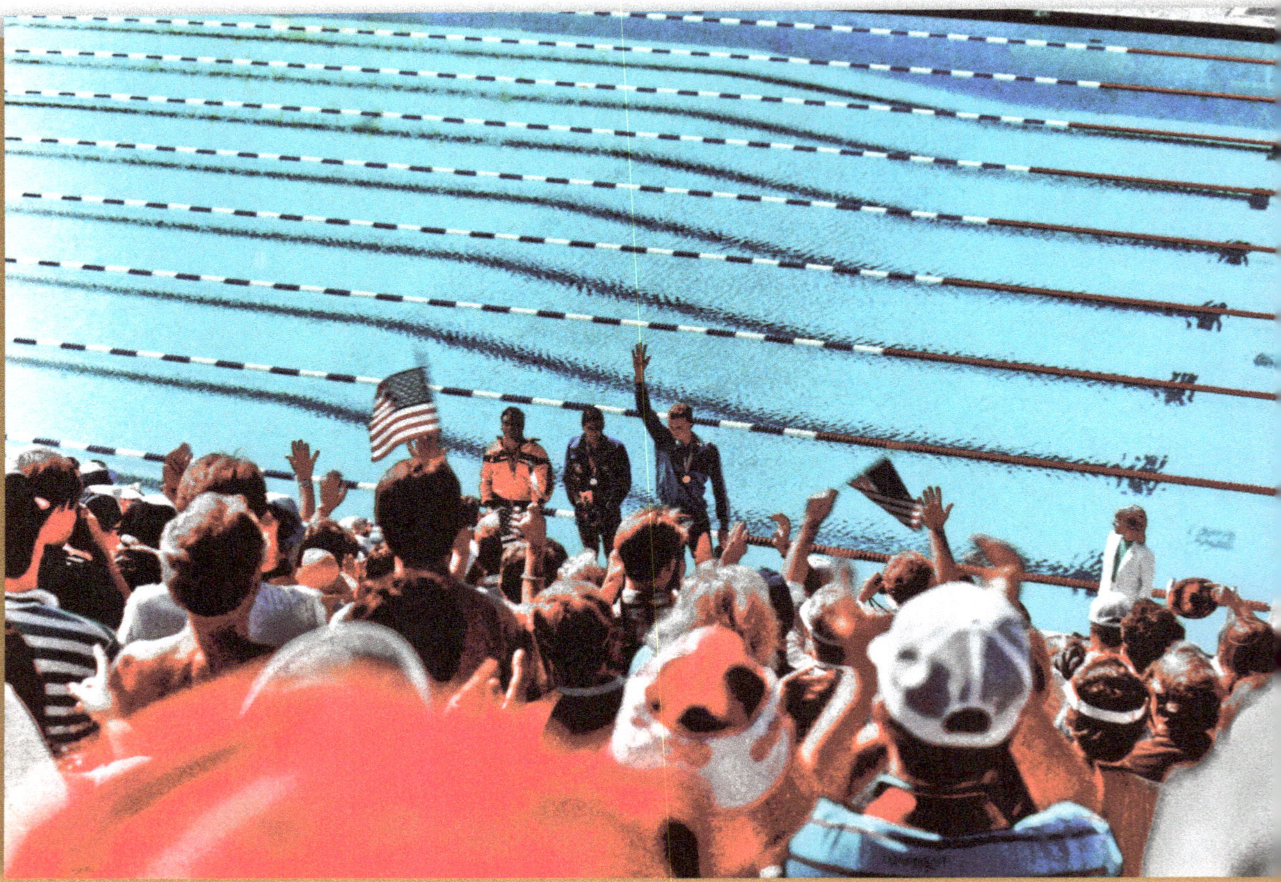

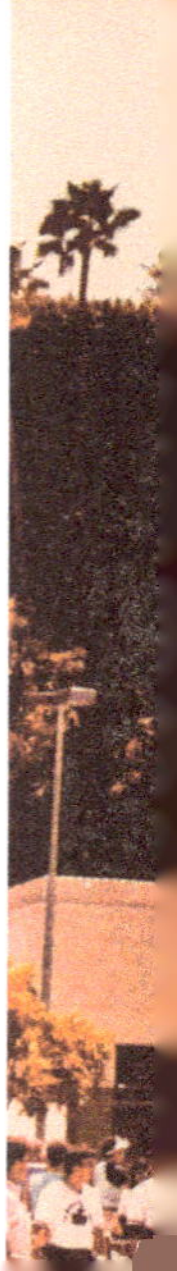

Top: Six-foot-seven-inch Michael Gross, "the Albatross" from West Germany, sets a world record and wins the gold in the 100-meter butterfly. Pablo Morales, USA, silver, Glenn Buchanan, Australia, bronze. **Top Right:** Sam the Eagle, the Olympic Mascot, meet Sam Katz. By this time we were living in Orange County, and four days prior to the Opening Ceremonies, the torch arrived in Fullerton, nearing the final leg of its journey to the Coliseum. **Bottom Right:** At the time Los Angles presented itself as a city where citizens from all 140 Olympic nations resided, and the music of languages could be heard walking around the stadium on August 6, 1984.

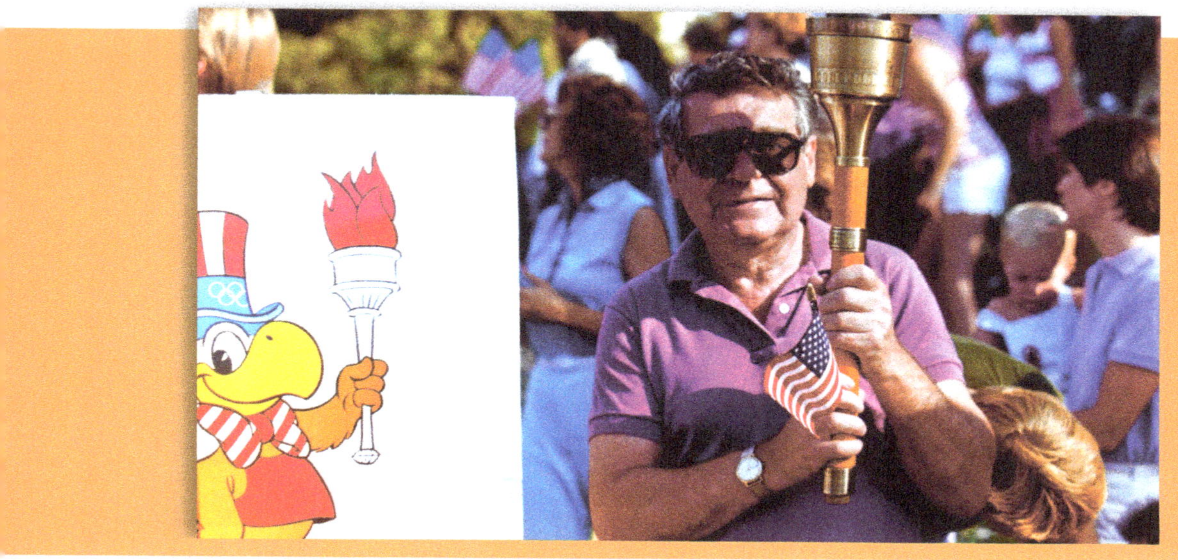

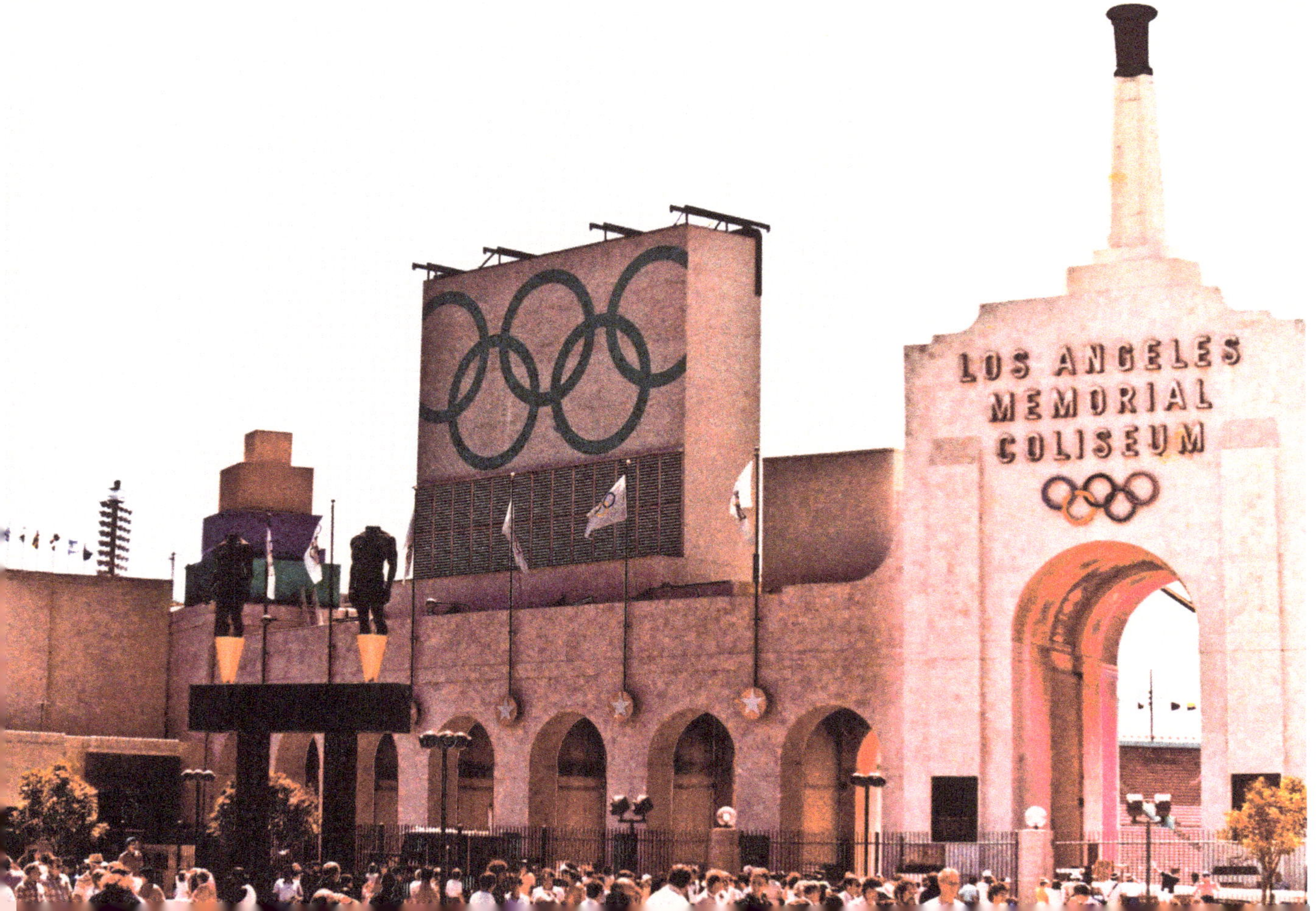

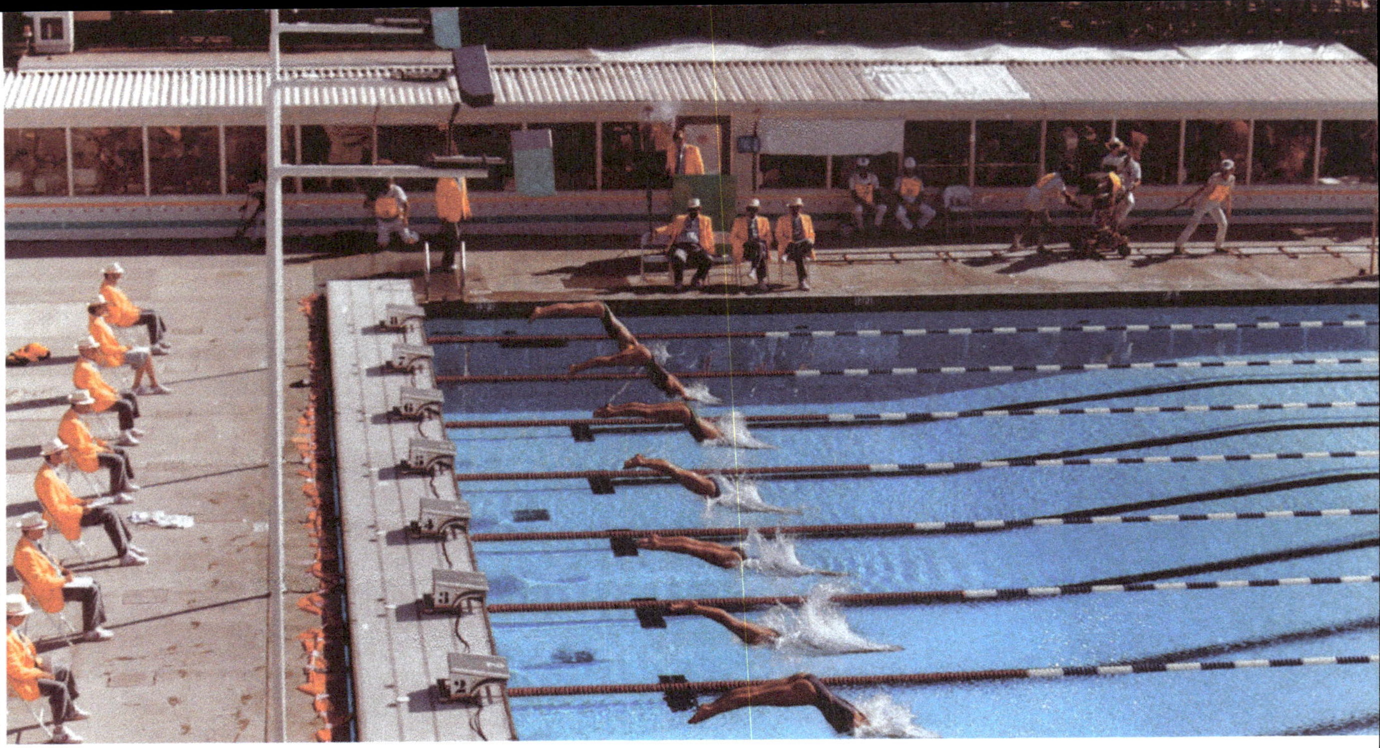

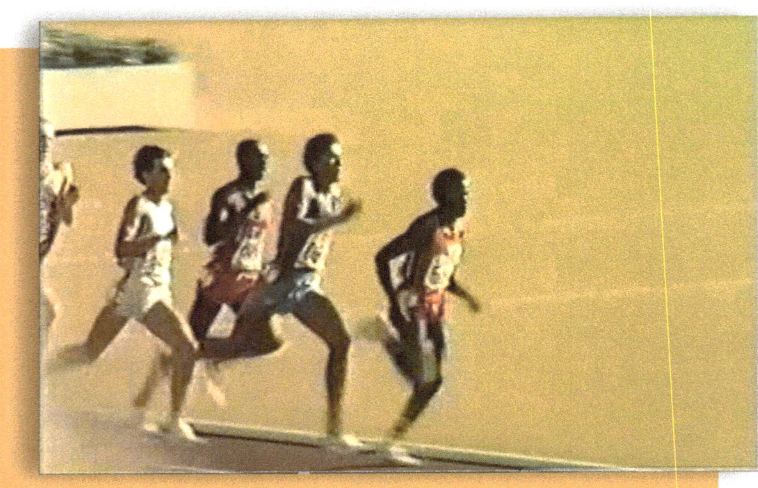

Top: Off the blocks. Symmetry and synchronicity going for the gold. Purposely built on the USC campus for the Olympics, privately funded, jampacked with 16,000 fans. The Los Angeles Summer Olympics was the first Games in 24 years to hold the swimming competition outdoors. Hard to imagine swimming in L.A. being held indoors! **Left:** Screenshot Olympic 800 Meter final. One of the most anticipated track events; the athletes were a blur as they went past my vantage point on the peristyle end of the Coliseum. The tall runner 2nd from left, Joachim Cruz from Brazil, wins gold, world-record holder Sebastian Coe, white uniform, Great Britain, silver, Johnny Gray between them in red, USA, bronze. **Right:** Ready, set, go. Anticipation, then off the blocks. Olympic 4x200 freestyle relay. The USA wins gold and sets a new world record!

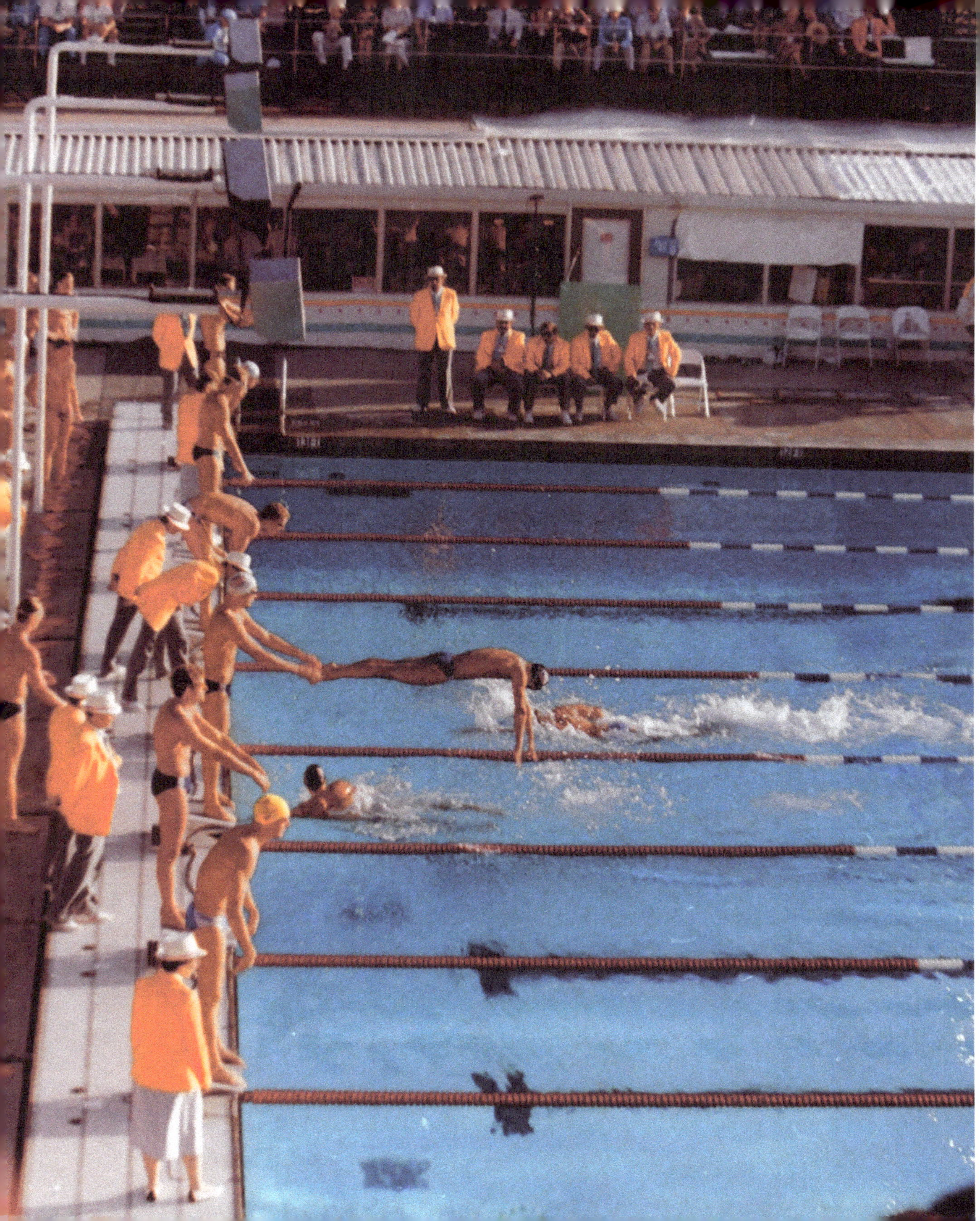

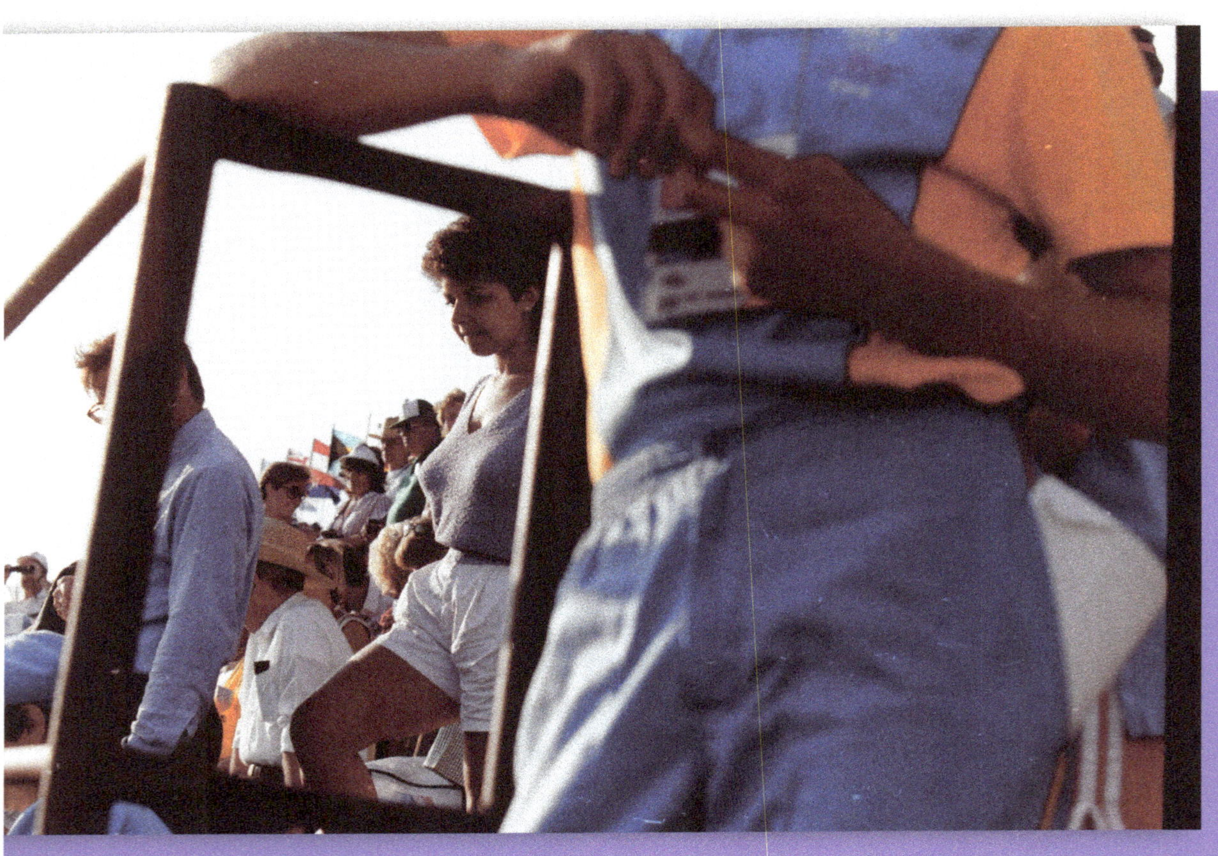

Top Left: Beautiful women! Yes, there were a lot of short shorts during the L.A. summer of 1984, and the new-wave colors were at their stylish zenith! **Top Right:** Chasing it. 16,000 screaming sun-baked fans watching the world's best. The swimming competition was not as impacted as other sports by the Soviet boycott. The 1984 Olympics marked the return of China since 1952 to the Modern Olympics. **Right:** Bikers. The '80s style was alive and well in this photo. I love the biker in front with the tie and behind him, another biker with the classic KMET 94.7 t-shirt. THE rock 'n roll radio station in L.A. at the time and of ALL TIME!

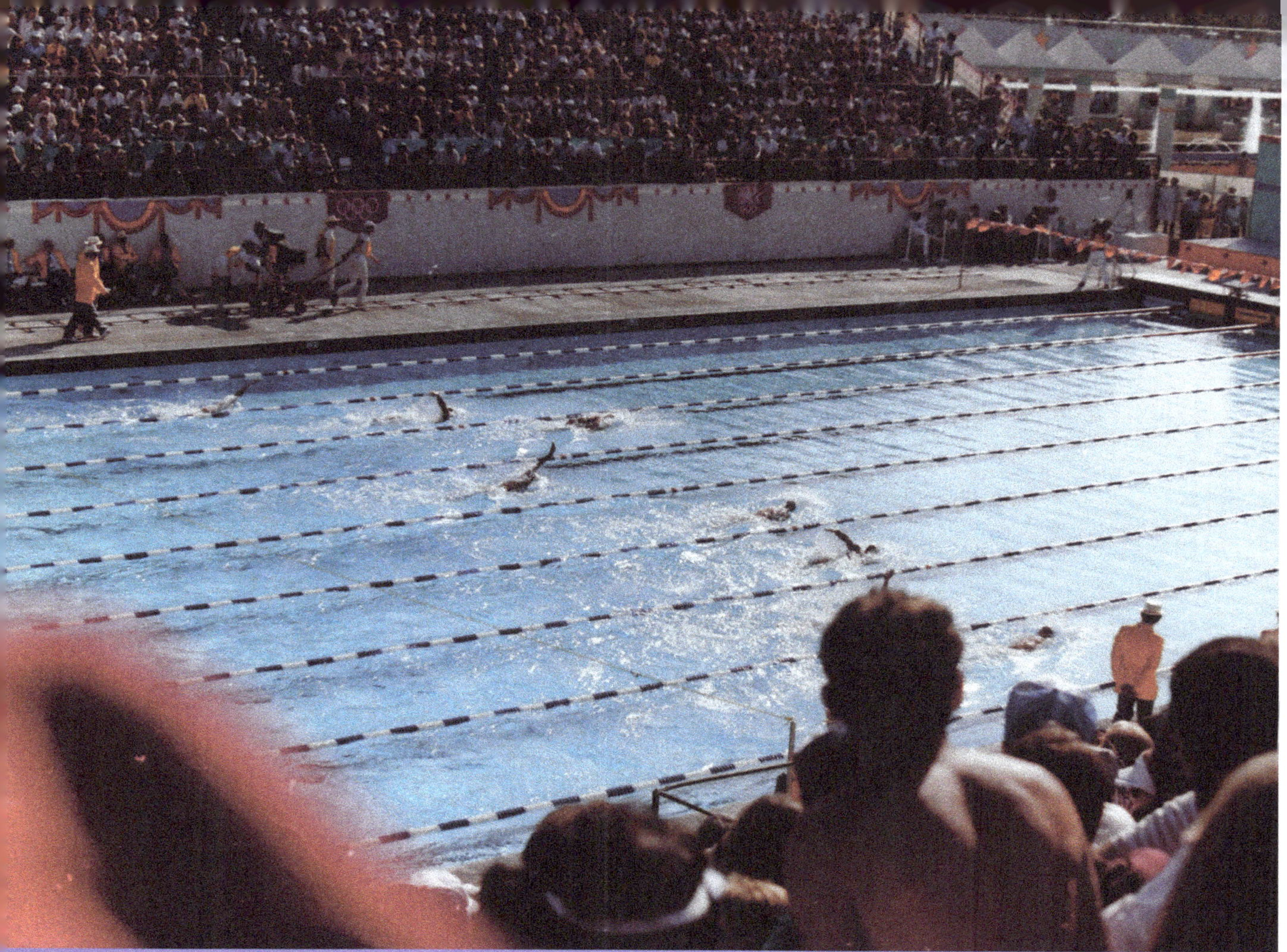

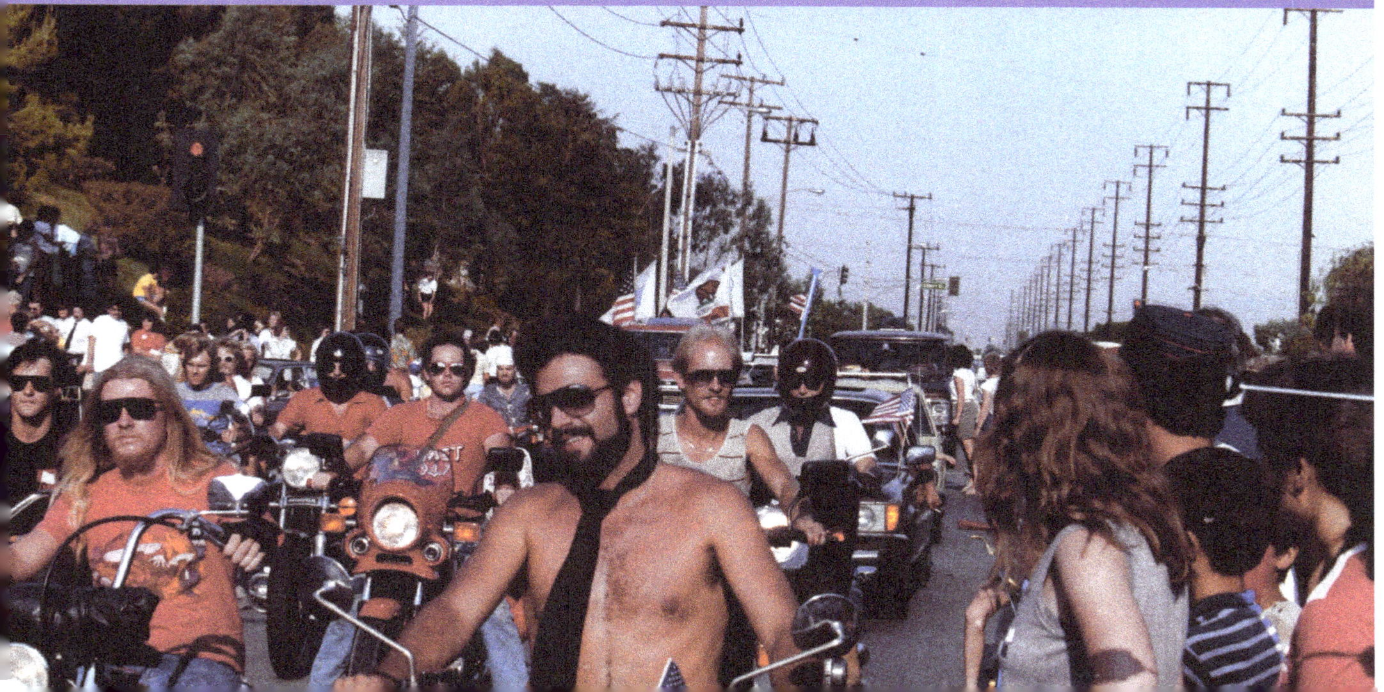

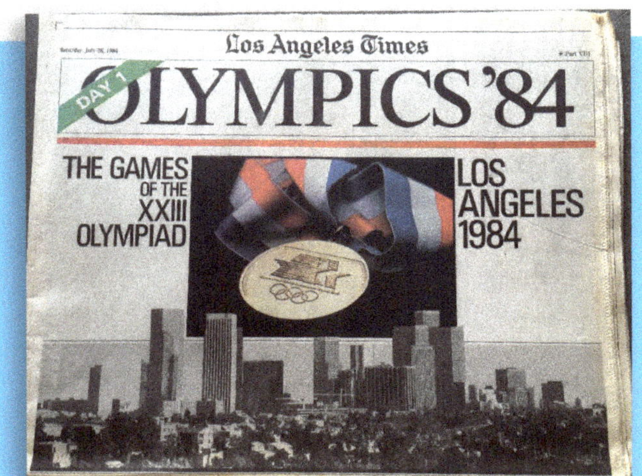

Top Left: Classic opening day edition of the *Los Angeles Times*. Downtown Los Angeles is almost unrecognizable today. I remember those two weeks fondly as a utopian moment of peace and love and respect. It was a successful Olympics in every sense of the word. It was a financially viable and profitable Olympics that took advantage of mostly already-built facilities. One million trees planted by The Tree People and the $225 million profit the Games produced are still benefiting the community 35 years later. A success? YES! See you in 2028! **Bottom:** The Olympic Gateway. The 25' tall headless bronze statues were designed by L.A. sculptor the late Robert Graham. It was very controversial at the time, anatomically correct statues. The *L.A. Times* reported at the time that the male model, Terry Schroeder, Captain of the US water polo team, took 60 hours of modeling.

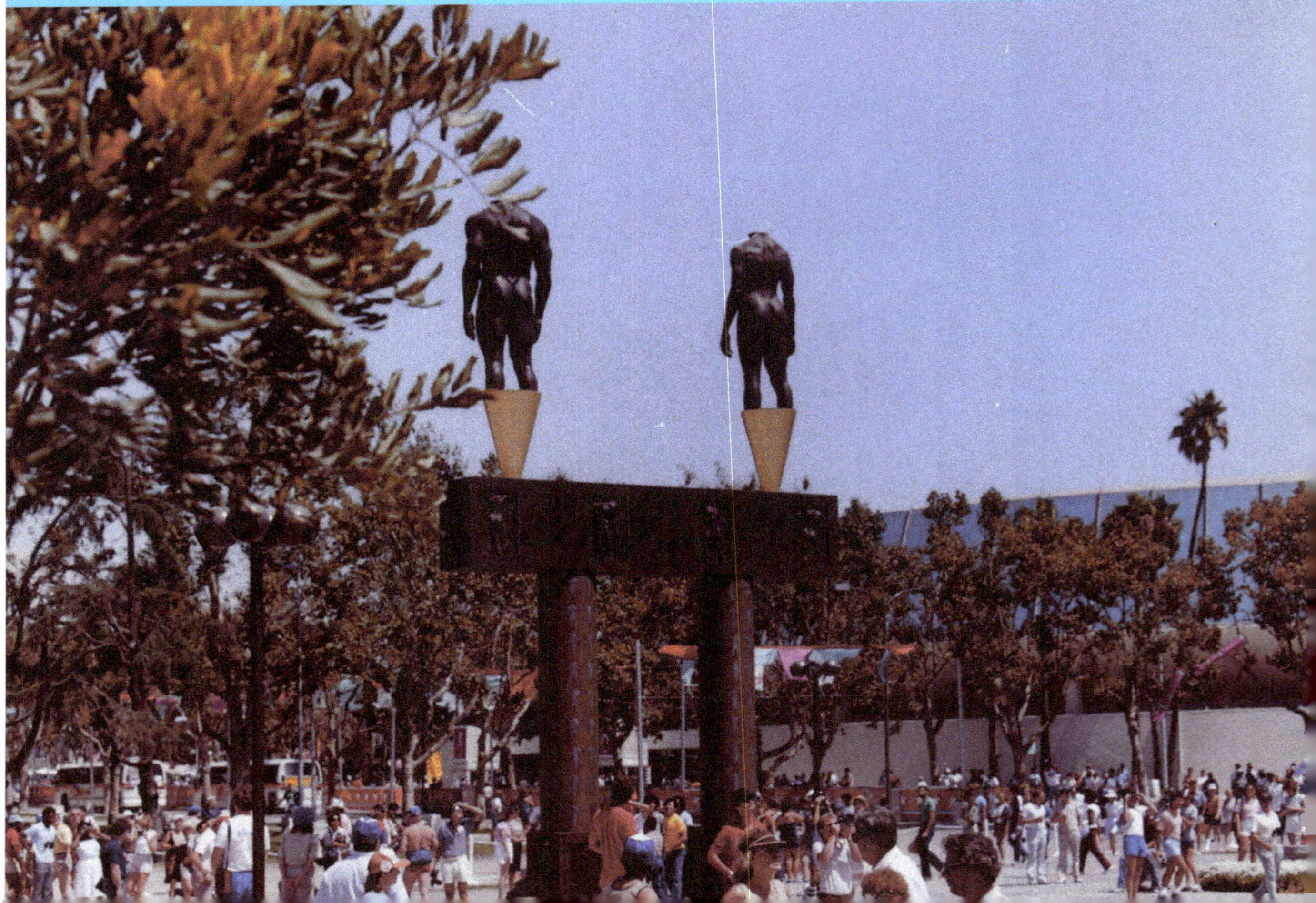

ABOUT THE AUTHOR

In the 1970s, I grew up in West Hollywood, California and worked in our family business in East Los Angeles, getting my education in the Street.

Many people look back on the '70s as the Glory Days of the Sunset Strip, and it was a fun place for an adventurous teenager. The Hyatt House and Tower Records were THE places to hang out on the Strip. The sounds of Joni Mitchell, and The Eagles, and Crosby, Stills & Nash were heard from the Hollywood Hills in 1974.

The photographs capture personal moments in L.A. history from 1970 to 1984. Ordinary photos look interesting decades later when the hand-painted billboards on the Sunset Strip didn't get lost in the shadow of tall buildings and construction cranes.

Growing up in L.A. in the '70s gave me a lifetime of interesting stories, and taking the way-back machine four decades gives me an appreciation for growing up during a period of time that I took for granted as a teenager. Thank you for sharing the journey.

Jeff is married, the father of twin daughters and currently resides in the Bay Area. He is open to speaking engagements. E-mail: jeff@ladetroit59.com

www.ingramcontent.com/pod-product-compliance
Lightning Source LLC
Chambersburg PA
CBHW041033050726
47599CB00018B/1950